'"The books that mean the most to me are the books that teach us subversion, subversion in the face of the world as it is, books that suggest the honour of an alternative." So said John Berger, one of the greatest public intellectuals of his generation. Much needed in increasingly troubled times, this book not only suggests the honour of an alternative education, but grounds its possibility in the contexts of local, national and international realities.'

**Michael Fielding, Emeritus Professor of Education,
UCL Institute of Education**

'The insights offered by the alternative education approaches described in Mills and McCluskey's stimulating collection are not only invaluable to researchers, policymakers and practitioners committed to improving this growing education sector, but will also benefit mainstream schools around the globe.'

**Professor Kitty te Riele, Deputy Director (Research),
Peter Underwood Centre, University of Tasmania**

'This fascinating book highlights the global complexity and diversity of alternative educational approaches and provision. A strong focus on social justice directs the reader to better understandings of education that help rather than hinder equity and well-being.'

Helen Lees, York St John University

'As we look to the future and realize the urgent need to reform schooling to create parity of participation, this is a most needed and timely book. This collection will provoke the pedagogical imagination of what is possible when we reframe schooling through a social justice lens and consider the rich alternative schooling frameworks that enable educational transformation.'

**Penny Jane Burke, Global Innovation Chair of Equity,
University of Newcastle, Australi**

International Perspectives on
Alternative Education

International Perspectives on Alternative Education

Policy and Practice

Edited by Martin Mills and Gillean McCluskey

is an imprint of

First published in 2018 by the UCL Institute of Education Press, University College London, 20 Bedford Way, London WC1H 0AL

www.ucl-ioe-press.com

British Library Cataloguing in Publication Data:
A catalogue record for this publication is available from the British Library

ISBNs
978-1-85856-782-2 paperback
978-1-85856-881-2 PDF eBook
978-1-85856-882-9 epub eBook
978-1-85856-883-6 Kindle eBook

Typeset by Quadrant Infotech (India) Pvt Ltd
Printed by CPI Group (UK) Ltd, Croydon, CR0 4YY

Cover image: © Image Source/Alamy Stock Photo

Contents

PART 1 APPROACHES TO ALTERNATIVE EDUCATION

PART 2 ALTERNATIVE EDUCATION IN INTERNATIONAL CONTEXT

PART 3 ALTERNATIVE EDUCATION AND THE MAINSTREAM

Life of figures

About the contributors

Myungsook Cho is Vice-principal of a South Korean alternative school for young people from North Korean refugee backgrounds. She has many years' experience as an educator, adviser and activist for North Korean refugee youth.

Terri Dwyer was an English teacher, then a Principal Teacher (Pupil Support) in a residential school for pupils with social, emotional and behavioural needs (SEBN), before moving to work as a depute head teacher in another school. Terri has also worked for the Positive Behaviour Team within the Scottish Government, training teachers across Scotland in Restorative Practice and other behaviour management techniques. Terri was then appointed as head teacher in an SEBN school where she has been for ten, amazing, years.

Thilde Graulund has been a teacher at Den fri Hesthaveskole for six years. Maths, art and interior design are Thilde's passion. Thilde worked in architecture before finding her true calling in education. Aesthetics is a priority for Thilde.

Vibeke Helms has been a headteacher at Den fri Hesthaveskole for the past 12 years. Co-ownership with students, co-workers and parents to develop *Bildung* are the key threads in Vibeke's work.

Leanne Hepburn is originally from Edinburgh and has worked within mainstream and special school settings across the city for almost 25 years. She believes in creating positive school environments that focus on resilience, self-regulation and social and emotional development in order to help young people engage better with their learning. Leanne is currently head teacher of a large primary school and feels privileged to work with such amazing children every day.

Jungwon Kim was formerly Project Co-ordinator at the Dropout Prevention and Alternative Education Support Center, Seoul, South Korea. She is currently undertaking doctoral study at the Graduate School of Education and Information Studies at the University of California, Los Angeles. She is interested in youth development, educational equality, the relationship between education policy/practice and broader sociocultural contexts including welfare states.

Britta Klopsch is Research Associate in educational sciences at Heidelberg University, Germany. Her research focus is on the development of school and instruction in real-life situations and professional teacher development.

Gillean McCluskey is Senior Lecturer at Moray House School of Education, University of Edinburgh. Her research focuses on issues of marginalization and inequality in education with a particular interest in school exclusion and restorative approaches. She has worked in mainstream schools and alternative settings in the past, and maintains a close interest in the lived experiences of schooling, and the importance of listening to young people.

Glenda McGregor is Senior Lecturer and Deputy Head of School (Academic) in the School of Education and Professional Studies at Griffith University, Australia. Her research interests include alternative and flexible schooling, pedagogy and curriculum, and teachers' work.

Trine Martens has been a teacher at Den fri Hesthaveskole for 15 years. She is an expert photographer and keen entrepreneur. Her many projects aim to heighten students' knowledge and understanding of the arts. Trine teaches English, Danish and cultural subjects.

Martin Mills is Director of the Teachers and Teaching Research Centre at the Institute of Education, University College London. His research interests include those related to social justice issues in education, teachers' work, pedagogy and school exclusion.

Dale Murray is Director of the Edmund Rice Education Australia Youth+ Institute (EREA Youth+) and has worked for 30 years in the area of flexible education. He has a deep commitment to working with communities, government, families and young people in developing learning environments that offer those disenfranchised a socially inclusive educational pathway.

Jodie Pennacchia is a researcher in the policy-sociology of education. She began her career working in learner support roles in mainstream and alternative schools. She has published work in the field of alternative education and is currently writing papers from her doctoral thesis, which explores the production of academy status in the context of an 'underperforming' school. She is a researcher at the Learning and Work Institute, where her work evaluates the inclusivity of a range of education and training programmes. She tweets @JPennacchia

Carol Reid is a sociologist of education in the Centre for Educational Research at Western Sydney University. Carol's research explores processes of globalization and mobilities on youth, ethnicity and race, and the intersections of these social identities with the changing nature of teachers' work.

Rikke Rasmussen and Niels Nielsen are two school students who accepted the special task of describing their school in Chapter 15. They have now completed their schooling at Den fri Hesthaveskole with excellent results. Rikke is currently an exchange student in South America, and Niels has started at high school.

Ila Rosmilawati is Lecturer in the Department of Non-formal Education, Faculty of Teacher Training and Education, University of Sultan Ageng Tirtayasa, Indonesia. Her research interests include the non-formal education sector, alternative education, transformative learning and critical pedagogy. She teaches in the fields of sociology of education, non-formal basic education and lifelong education.

Wulf Saggau studied theatre and Waldorf education in Dornach, Switzerland from 1987 to 1992. Since 1993 he has worked as a teacher and instructor at the Waldorf School, Frankfurt am Main. Since 2000 he has also worked as an instructor for Waldorf teachers in Frankfurt am Main and Jena, Germany as well as in Seoul, South Korea.

Maren Skotte is Head of communications for the Danish Free School Association, a member organization for free schools in Denmark. Her responsibilities include policy, legislation and communication. Maren has a first degree in communications and is currently completing a Masters in Leadership and Innovation in Complex Systems.

Marnee Shay is an Aboriginal education educator and researcher at The University of Queensland. Marnee teaches and researches in the fields of Indigenous Studies, Aboriginal education, flexi-schooling and Indigenous research methodologies. Marnee is passionate about undertaking ethical, participant-driven research with young people and Indigenous communities in addressing critical social justice issues.

Anne Sliwka is Professor of Education at the University of Heidelberg. Her research focuses on school and school system development, adolescent engagement in learning and teacher professionalism.

Lars Erik Storgaard is Vice-principal of Bernadotteskolen, an international private school in Copenhagen, and was formerly education adviser at the Danish Ministry of Education, where he had responsibility for supervision of private independent schools.

Pat Thomson is Professor of Education at the University of Nottingham. She once set up and ran an alternative school. All of her research is geared in one way or another to understanding and building alternatives to institutional practices that exclude and marginalize; much of her current research focuses on the arts and school and community change. She tweets as @ThomsonPat, blogs at patthomson.net and writes a lot.

Gavin Tierney is a researcher with OpenSTEM Research at the University of Washington, Bothell. His research focuses on youth identity development and engagement, with an emphasis on alternative education and historically underserved and marginalized youth.

Richard Waters recently completed PhD studies at The University of Queensland on 'The effects of alternative schooling practices on student learning, community engagement and equity'. He had a long career of teaching and leadership in alternative education, and is now an educational consultant and works in Southern Cross University's Masters of Educational Leadership programme.

David Wright is Senior Lecturer in the School of Education, Western Sydney University. His research interests include the alternative education sector, ecological understanding, systems theory and the 'perspective of the participant'. He teaches in fields of transformative education and social ecology and has a background in creative expression, principally drama and fiction.

Chulkyung Yoon has served as a senior researcher at the National Youth Policy Institute (NYPI) in South Korea for more than two decades. She is also Director of the Dropout Prevention and Alternative Education Support Center funded by the Ministry of Education, Korea. Her research interests include education supporting at-risk youth, youth policy, school reform and alternative education.

Sujin Yoon is a doctoral researcher at the Moray House School of Education, University of Edinburgh, UK. Her research examines North Korean young refugees' perceptions and experiences of alternative schooling in South Korea.

Annegrete Zobbe has been a teacher since 1979. She worked for 14 years in a school with 1,000+ pupils. The urge to try an alternative school brought her to Den fri Hesthaveskole, where she has been key to developing the school. Her focus has been on Danish and English and she is passionate about teaching children with special needs.

Acknowledgements

We would like to thank the South Korean National Youth Policy Institute (NYPI) and Ministry of Education, through its Dropout Prevention and Alternative Education Support Center, for invitations to present at their 2014 Forum on Alternative Education. It was through these invitations that we met many of the other contributors to this book. We also acknowledge the support that we received through our respective institutions (for Martin The University of Queensland and University College London and Gillean the University of Edinburgh) while carrying out this work. Martin would particularly like to acknowledge the hospitality he received while a visiting scholar at the Moray House School of Education, University of Edinburgh, where the foundations for this book were laid. Martin's contributions were also facilitated through an Australian Research Council Future Fellowship (FT110100203). We would also like to thank those we have worked with closely at Trentham Books and UCL IOE Press, and Gillian Klein in particular, for their patience and support while putting this book together.

Chapter 1

International perspectives on alternative education: Policy and practice

Gillean McCluskey and Martin Mills

Introduction

This book has its origins in an invited two-day conference hosted and funded by the South Korean Ministry of Education and its National Youth Policy Institute. Many of the contributors to this book were, like us, presenters at this conference. Other key researchers and practitioners in the field were invited to contribute to the book. The South Korean Ministry commissioned the conference because, in the words of the Director of the National Youth Policy Institute, 'public education is not fully accommodating the various demands from young students who live in a rapidly changing world'. To meet these demands, an alternative education sector has developed in South Korea that has, in the words of the Ministerial opening speech at the conference, 'helped accommodate young students without discrimination and while acknowledging their differences'. Similar developments have been happening elsewhere. The book aims to bring together diverse voices from multiple locations to explore the field of alternative education.

'Alternative education' encompasses a diversity of schooling types and organizations, but there do seem to us to be commonalities. Value is often given to personalized learning, small classes and small school rolls, student choice, voice and agency, active engagement in learning, informal relationships between teacher and student, and flexible, local systems of governance. However, the term is also used to describe other very different forms of schooling. Alternative education can refer to private fee-paying schools that include those sometimes referred to as democratic (in the mould of Summerhill), or those that have a particular philosophical underpinning (e.g. Steiner Waldorf). As these are fee-paying schools, their students tend to be from middle-class backgrounds, although they may well have had conflicts with previous schools. Alternative education can also refer to schools that have been designed to support young people who have been rejected by or who have rejected mainstream schooling. Such schools can be publicly owned, or places in privately owned schools may be funded through government money, so that students do not have to pay fees. Students at such schools primarily come from marginalized backgrounds. In many locations, as public schooling is affected by differentiation and marketization, opportunities to create alternatives within the public sector have also been opened up, such as free schools in Denmark (as distinct from those in Sweden) and co-operative schools in England.

This book seeks to explore a diversity of alternatives from the position of academics, policy workers and those working (and studying) in such schools. It draws on contributions from Australia, Indonesia, Korea, Denmark, England, Germany, Scotland and the USA. We were keen that the authors represent something of the array and complexity of the current alternative education landscape. The book therefore includes accounts of first-hand experience working and leading in alternative schools and also from those working at the policy level in national contexts. These accounts, which are often highly descriptive and quite personal, bring alive the dilemmas and challenges of working in alternative education and complement the academic contributions, which examine over-arching questions about social justice and the meanings of achievement, success, choice and purpose across education. As editors, while we neither challenge nor endorse these personal accounts, we are particularly grateful to the teachers, school principals and their students who took time to write and reflect on their day-to-day experiences. They have often done this in their own time, and with no expectation of recompense.

Including their accounts raised questions for us as we were editing the book. As academics we tend to write in a particular kind of way, using established, often tacit norms about, for example, style, authorship and referencing. We wanted this book to show how vital it is to have the two groups talking to each other in their own voices and this often gave us pause for thought about when to edit and when to leave alone, particularly when our contributors were writing in English for the first time for an international audience. We have tried to ensure these accounts from practitioners are intact and deliver the messages as intended. We hope we have done them justice but it is important that we acknowledge our own position as White academics in elite institutions.

We also need to acknowledge what we have left out in this book. We would have liked to cover a range of other schools that might be considered alternative. For example, we would have liked to have chapters for schools that are members of the European Democratic Education Community (EUDEC). (As Tierney says in his chapter, there are many types of alternative school.) Short of putting together an encyclopaedia on alternative schools, this collection has by necessity been unable to cover all forms.

However, what we aim to do with this book is to present some of the many interpretations of alternative education and to stimulate discussion about the multiple purposes of these interpretations. We were interested in how, despite some very clear differences across alternative education, there seems to be at its heart a rationale associated with frustration at current forms of conventional education and failure to engage and support young people and to enable them to flourish. We see this edited book therefore as an opportunity to learn more about the possibilities more broadly for socially just forms of schooling.

The book is organized in two main parts, which are followed by our discussion of emerging and long-standing issues for alternative education and implications for future directions in both alternative and mainstream schooling.

Part 1 includes contributions from different international contexts: the USA, South Korea, England, Australia, Indonesia and Denmark. These chapters reveal how these different contexts have helped to shape a range of approaches to matters such as school organization and decision-making, curriculum and pedagogy, student voice, values and philosophies, which all bring both challenges and opportunities.

Part 2 provides accounts of individual schools or sets of schools. In particular, it is concerned with types of schools, issues in relation to their operation, motivations behind their creation and their distinctive characteristics. The chapters include papers from academics and from those working in schools or with a particular set of schools. However, the academics writing in this section (Marnee Shay, Sujin Yoon with Myungsook Cho who works in a school, and Waters) have had extensive experience working in the alternative sector. They therefore have deep insights into the operation of such schools. The accounts here also provide an indication of what draws people to work with these schools.

The chapters in Part 2 focus on schools that deal with highly marginalized young people, others that are (albeit low) fee-paying and hence attract more privileged students, and one that exemplifies the space that alternative forms of schools can carve out within the mainstream government sector, given particular sets of circumstances (in this case Denmark which does allow free schools to charge some fees).

In Chapter 2 Gavin Tierney, an American academic, explores the current landscape of alternative schooling in the context of USA at both elementary/primary and secondary/high school levels. Within his account of the history and range of alternative provision, he raises important questions about definition, noting that the term 'alternative' can be applied to 'a juvenile detention centre, to an online school, to a wilderness focused leadership school'. It can also be applied to function, in which neoliberal ideas of competition and efficiency in USA drive educational priorities. He discusses the challenges and the tensions inherent in alternative schooling: the ways in which such settings can 'provide innovative and supportive opportunities that are different from mainstream schooling', but also act as mechanisms for labelling, sorting and sifting young people in order to portray them as '*deficient* in a *fair* system'. He argues that we need to shift the focus away from a need to change the students, and concentrate instead on changing the schools themselves and fostering a better understanding of the young people they serve and broader definitions of success.

In Chapter 3, Chulkyung Yoon and Jungwon Kim, who work in the policy space, outline current contexts in South Korea. High stakes competition has produced one of the most educationally successful countries in global terms, but has also given rise to serious concerns about dropout and emotional well-being, particularly in light of a rapidly increasing youth suicide rate. As noted above, it was our invitation to the Forum on Alternative Education organized by the Korean Ministry of Education in 2014 that provided a focused opportunity to examine the notion of 'alternative education' and which led on to this book. Yoon and Kim describe how, in the South Korean context, alternative schooling has developed different forms but overall is seen by its advocates as offering a response to the issues of dropout and a more democratic and humane approach to education, based on co-operation and collaboration. Like Tierney in Chapter 2, they argue that mainstream schools now need to learn from the philosophy of alternative education. This is a theme that re-emerges across a number of chapters in this book and to which we return in the final discussion.

In Chapter 4, Jodie Pennacchia and Pat Thomson examine alternative provision in England and offer some comparison with its immediate neighbour, Scotland. In the English context, alternative education is defined and circumscribed by national policy so that it refers primarily to provision such as pupil referral units for children and young people who have been excluded/suspended from school or who are at imminent risk of exclusion. They draw on the work of Bacchi (2012, 2009) to scrutinize 'taken for granted truths'; urging a 'shift from viewing policy proposals as neutral problem statements, representations and solutions, to viewing them as acts of interpretation that are shaped by judgement and values'. This entails revisiting the everyday vocabulary of such provision and its use of terms such as 'risk', 'right course of action' and 'vulnerability'. Like Yoon and Kim in Chapter 3, their concern arises out of the 'pressure cooker' of conventional competitive education and the encroachment of concerns about 'quality' and 'accountability' into alternative provision. They call for a parity of esteem across different kinds of educational provision. Like Tierney, they argue for a move away from efforts to change or 'fix' the child, and towards addressing the structural reasons some (mainly already disadvantaged or marginalized) young people are more at risk of exclusion than others. Pennacchia and Thomson conclude with a discussion of the contrasting approach in Scotland, noting the absence of pupil referral units and the relatively small size of the alternative education sector which, unlike in England, is largely overseen by local authorities as part of the overall public education provision. This is helpful in opening up the possibility of thinking otherwise and of a different kind of future for learners on the margins.

Chapter 5, by Martin Mills and Glenda McGregor, explores policy and practice in Australia in relation to flexi-schools in that country. They indicate that in Australia policy in relation to alternative education is a work in progress. However, there is significant interest from the policy sector as well as from students and schools in alternative schooling for those young people who have been rejected by or who reject the mainstream. They indicate, as do others in the book, that the competitive pressures on schools and students have led to some students becoming unwanted by mainstream schools because of the damage they do to a school's reputation, either by performing poorly in exams or by their behaviour. At the same time as these pressures have been at play, there has been an increasing pressure from government to raise school retention levels. In Australia this is represented by the 'learning or earning' agenda whereby young people need to be in education until they are 17 unless they are employed. Alternative schools have therefore become an increasingly attractive option for those who are not engaged by mainstream schooling. This has led in turn to increased funding for these schools and a concomitant interest in working out how to measure value for money. The chapter draws on data collected from two flexi-schools to illustrate some of the ways in which young people are engaged in these schools. The chapter raises the central question regarding the ways in which these schools might promote or hinder social justice for highly marginalized young people.

In Chapter 6, Ila Rosmilawati, Carol Reid and David Wright offer an account of Indonesia's Equivalency Programmes (EPs), a formal education system separate from the mainstream. Indonesia faces significant issues of poverty and unequal access to education, with 10 per cent of children not continuing to senior secondary school. Rosimilawati *et al.* make clear that for many marginalized young people 'the choice is often not between an alternative or mainstream school, but between an alternative school or no school', in the same way as 'second chance' schools in Australia often represent a 'first chance' in reality, as discussed by Mills and McGregor, and also Shay. They note that many students are sceptical about the value of the learning in this kind of alternative education, an issue noted by many of the other contributors in the book. However, they also draw our attention to the idea of 'ambivalent tolerance' (Illeris, 2007); the ways in which the EPs facilitate 'an understanding that students arrive at by themselves ... they face contradictions yet develop agency'. This model of education has a flexibility about, for example, pedagogy, class size, learning hours, the languages used in teaching and learning, and time of day for teaching. Crucially and perhaps uniquely among the different systems described in this book, the EP school system 'is designed to go to the students', so 'school' can be located near a bus station where children may be working as street sellers, or in middle-class areas where they may be working as cleaners and house servants. Interestingly, there is an explicit focus on transformative learning. It 'requires that the EP students recognize their marginalization ... and their limitations (such as poverty) and conventional educational opportunities' (Rosmilawati *et al.* in this volume) to raise levels of critical consciousness and hence be able to critique, in Freire's terms, the different values assigned to mainstream and alternative education, helping to challenge the deficit views of disadvantaged young people. This resonates with concerns raised by Pennacchia and Thomson about the negative consequences of the narrowing of the curriculum in English alternative provision for disadvantaged youth and the loss of opportunity to engage with social studies and humanities subjects, 'the very areas which might enable young people to develop a better understanding of the structural issues that contributed to their difficult time in school and/or other areas of their life'.

The final chapter in this part is from Maren Skotte and Lars Erik Storgaard, whose experience covers school level and national leadership in education policy. They provide insight into the history, structures and systems of the free schools (*friskole*) in Denmark, and also why we might find it useful to think about education rather than schooling. In Denmark free schools are not-for-profit organizations that receive state funding (generally 75 per cent of the per capita funding given to state schools). They are based on tenets of freedom – ideological, pedagogical, financial – and a strong commitment to the 'rights and responsibilities of parents to decide how their children are to be brought up and educated'. The children who attend free schools benefit from small classes, and an emphasis on personal and social growth through collaboration rather than competition and exams (at least in the early years). However, Storgaard and Skotte also draw our attention to issues now facing the free schools. They note that the students who attend free schools are less likely to be the disadvantaged young people who concern Pennacchia and Thomson, Rosimilawati, Reid and Wright or Mills and McGregor, and for whom the need for family to provide transport to school and to make financial and time contributions to the school would be significant obstacles. They note that the schools have 'complete autonomy with regards to decisions to enrol or expel pupils', which raises the interesting question of whether the greater freedoms and personalized support helps sustain (or otherwise) the education of students who might be at risk of exclusion in a more regulated or marketized and competitive education system. However, they conclude the chapter by describing a challenge facing much of the alternative education provision internationally: the growing demand from governments for similarity with mainstream aims and structures and educational outcomes, which is leading to more systems of testing and 'quality control'.

In Part 2 we look at specific types of alternative schools, and draw heavily on the experiences of those working on or with these schools. We first deal with those types of school that have been variously named as 'flexi-schools', 'second chance schools' (Baker, 2016; Gallagher, 2011; Mills and McGregor, 2010). We then consider 'special schools', those schools that cater to students deemed to have 'special needs', and follow this up with a set of chapters looking at fee-paying alternative schools. The first set of schools considered here are similar to those that are the focus of the earlier chapters by Thomson and Pennacchia and Mills and McGregor. Features of these schools are the support they provide to students in order to 'clear the path for learning' (McGregor *et al.*, 2017) (i.e. through counselling, transport, crèches and accommodation referrals), their flexibility around matters such as uniforms, and attempts to ensure that the students do not miss out on the benefits of completing school. Contributors to this part of the book include Murray, a key figure in the Australian alternative education sector who has been responsible for setting up schools within the Youth+ network across Australia; Shay, an academic, who has worked within that system and has completed substantial research on the impact these schools have had on Indigenous students in them; and Yoon and Cho, who look at the ways in which an alternative school in South Korea is supporting North Korean refugee students.

Dale Murray is Director of Edmund Rice Education Australia Youth+, the most significant provider of flexi-schools outside the government sector in Australia. These schools provide an education to some of the most marginalized students in Australia. In Chapter 8, Murray provides an overview of the Youth+ Flexible model, its underpinning philosophy and some current challenges faced by the Youth+ 'system'. There are some very important concepts raised in this chapter related to social justice. For example, the students at these schools are not referred to as 'disengaged' but 'disenfranchised'. This works to suggest that their exclusion from the mainstream has been an act of oppression rather than the students' own doing. In an era dominated by market forces, Murray refers to a study being conducted through James Cook University in Queensland that has partnered with Youth+, which talks of the 'social return on investment' as a means of considering the benefits of supporting the students who attend Youth+ schools. However, the chapter does much more than provide an account of the model and a justification for its existence; it also gives an insight into the drivers behind his approach to alternative education. The commitment to social justice and seeing these schools not as 'dumping grounds' but as institutions offering transformational opportunities is one found across many of the schools like those associated with Youth+. It also raises issues related to the challenges that many of these schools face.

Marnee Shay is an education academic at The University of Queensland. She is an Aboriginal woman who has worked in flexi-schools and now undertakes research with them. Using critical race theory and Indigenous standpoint theory, in Chapter 9 she explores the ways in which leaders in flexi-schools have supported the learning of Indigenous (Aboriginal and Torres Strait Islander) peoples. In Australia, Indigenous people are over-represented in flexi-schools, as are marginalized minorities in other locations, and under-represented in the teaching profession (and more so in school leadership positions). Given the commitment to social justice articulated by many within the flexi-learning centres in Australia, and exemplified in Dale Murray's chapter, Shay's chapter disrupts any form of complacency that workers in these settings might have in relation to race. Central to her chapter is the disjuncture between the school leaders' commitment to self-learning about Indigenous cultures and ways of learning, and their superficial understandings of culture and Indigenous ways of knowing and learning. Her work is evidence of the need to see social justice as an ongoing project in flexible learning spaces in Australia.

Sujin Yoon and Myungsook Cho also provide an account of the ways in which alternative schools in South Korea support a minority group, North Korean refugees. Their focus, in Chapter 10, is on one particular school, the first alternative school for North Korean refugees, *Haedoji* (Sunshine) Alternative School. Yoon is a PhD scholar at the University of Edinburgh, and formerly worked in an NGO with refugees, and Cho is a teacher at the school foregrounded here. Within this chapter there are some resonances with these types of school in other locations, for example, the highly traumatic nature of many of the students' lives, the support that the school provides for non-education matters, such as accommodation and health, and their actions as advocates for the students when engaging with the authorities. They describe their efforts to ensure that the curriculum is meaningful and that it provides more than just academic qualifications, but also their concerns for sustaining such support when pay levels and conditions for teachers do not reflect those in the mainstream sector. They also raise the question that has troubled many working within this space: whether or not these students would benefit more from being integrated into mainstream schools rather than being in these separate schools. This is a debate we think well worth having. However, underpinning this debate are questions about whether or not it is the student who needs to change or the school. This question was raised explicitly in the chapters by Tierney and Pennacchia and Thomson earlier in the book, and we come back to it in the conclusion. Michael Apple (2013) has asked if schools can change society. Yoon and Cho have high hopes that they can; in particular they have the hope that schools such as Haedoji can play a role in preparing for the hoped for re-unification of Korea.

In some locations 'special schools' still exist within the government sector, in which young people deemed to have 'special needs' are enrolled. These special needs can include 'behavioural needs'. Research regularly reminds us that such schools are often populated by young people from marginalized backgrounds. The schools are alternative in the sense that they operate outside the mainstream, although, as we take up in the last chapter in the book, it could be argued that they, like some other alternative schools, facilitate the smooth running of the mainstream by enabling schools to remove those who disrupt 'normal' activity. Nevertheless, these schools operate on the margins of the mainstream and those who work in them are often highly committed to supporting their students' needs. Two such people are Leanne Hepburn and Terri Dwyer, head teachers of two different special schools in Scotland. Their respective chapters provide an opportunity to see how such schools run and provoke questions related to leadership and to what mainstream schools might learn from alternative education approaches.

In Chapter 11 Hepburn describes her experiences as a head teacher of a purpose-built social, emotional and behavioural needs (SEBN) primary school. The students at the school included those who had become chronic absentees from their mainstream school or who were caught up in the youth justice system. In this personal account, she foregrounds the importance of care, or 'a nurturing approach' (strongly supported by Scottish education policy), as a key component of having the students engage in learning. The importance of small classes, of involving young people in decisions that impact upon them, of working with families, of personalised attention are all raised. The pressures of leadership in a time of austerity are also raised. Leanne demonstrates that the lessons about how to support young people who face serious issues related to behavioural and social needs at this school have, as we would suggest with many of the chapters in this book, relevance to the mainstream. She ends her chapter by describing her own move from the SEBN school to take on the headship of a mainstream primary school, taking lessons learnt to help it embark on change to be 'truly inclusive'.

Dwyer has worked in several SEBN secondary schools and is currently head teacher of an Edinburgh SEBN school. Her chapter reveals a very personal reason as to why she is so committed to the young people in her care. She highlights the significance of restorative practice for working with the young people in her current school. Dwyer notes the problem of homogenizing SEBN students, and suggests that the various supports they need will be very different. She also recognizes that change for these students will not happen overnight, hence staff need patience. It is staff that Dwyer sees as the greatest asset for schools working with young people like those in her schools – this includes support staff. While she indicates that class size matters (despite what some who fund schools may say!), as does curriculum, for her it is the relationships that develop between teachers, between students, and between students and teachers that makes the difference for students at the school. This is, for her, where 'nurture' comes in, where she argues that 'the ethos of the school should be that of a nurturing school'. The importance of relationships is a recurring theme across the schools discussed in this book. As others do here, Dwyer articulates a vision for the future where alternative schools, in this case SEBN schools, no longer exist. However, this would require mainstream schools to adopt some of the practices found in SEBN schools like hers for *all* students.

Another form of alternative school is the fee-paying alternative school. These too can be divided into types. They include schools that are part of a system – which often involves some form of accreditation, for example Montessori or Steiner schools – and schools that are completely independent and have developed their own philosophy. In this section of the book, one school representing each of these types is included. However, we acknowledge that they do not speak for all such schools. That these schools charge fees does mean that they do not face many of the same issues confronting the other schools that we have just discussed. In this section there are chapters from a teacher in a Waldorf school (Wulf Saggau), from an academic who was also a principal in an alternative school (Waters) and from students and teachers in a Danish free school.

Saggau, a teacher in a German Waldorf school (also known as Steiner schools in other locations) who has also been involved in teacher education around the 'Waldorf method' in Germany and Korea, writes about the Waldorf system in Chapter 13. This alternative form of schooling has its roots in the aftermath of the war in Europe in the early twentieth century, and the associated human catastrophes, and in response to an escalating authoritarianism in Europe. It seeks to be inclusive of difference, to reject competition in favour of co-operation, and to making learning fun, meaningful and impactful on the world around. There is also a strong spiritual element to the Waldorf philosophy; a nice phrase coming from this spirituality is that the children learn to 'dance their names'. A key organizational feature of Waldorf schools is that they have no principal. Throughout many of the chapters leadership has been a key theme. However, these schools provide a model of teacher leadership where decisions are made as a group. While this contrasts with the vast majority of schools, it does not go as far as some democratic forms of schooling that also involve students in decision-making. Again, we are confronted with the issue of teacher pay. It appears that many of the people who come to work in the alternative sector are prepared to sacrifice pay and conditions that they would receive in the mainstream because of the emotional benefits that come with working within a system with shared values (see McGregor and Mills, 2014; te Riele *et al.*, 2017 for a discussion of teachers in alternative schools). Saggau also raises the issue of 'compromise' that comes with having to provide students with opportunities to receive formal qualifications, for example, in relation to university entry. Elsewhere in the book we consider the ways in which alternative schools can put pressure on the mainstream to change. However, it is also important to consider the ways in which the 'system' exercises a normalizing pressure. Saggau concludes with a pertinent political message related to the importance of educational practices that help young people to address the challenges associated with another era of 'authoritarian populists' taking centre stage in many nations.

In Chapter 14, Richard Waters, an Australian academic, focuses on an independent, low fee-paying school, Holistic Community College, that also has a strong commitment to the 'whole student', to explore how alternative schooling can 'challenge the competitive logics of the mainstream'. Like many of the authors in this book, he reflects on the advantages of the smaller-scale school and smaller class sizes, and the more personal, non-coercive relationships between staff and students that emphasize the social and emotional aspects of learning as well as academic achievement. His concerns about the effects of neoliberal education policy is also one shared by many in the book, either explicitly or implicitly, and his discussion of the breadth of the College's curriculum (for example in relation to the development of a Quietness programme) raises important questions about the larger purposes of education. Waters also writes about the College's commitment to engaging and working closely with parents in practical ways, actively avoiding a 'fee for service' relationship with them. Although he acknowledges the compromises to the mainstream education system that alternative education often makes, he also lays stress on their important role as 'incubators of change' (te Riele, 2008).

The teachers and students from Den fri Hestehaveskole (DfH) in Denmark provide an insight into the possibilities that can arise within the free school system in that country. Within this system, described by Storgaard and Skotte in Chapter 7, unlike the free school movement in England, the schools charge fees to supplement the state grant. This school for students aged 6–16 was opened by parents in a town where the government school had been closed down due to its small size, and there was an expectation that students would travel to a larger school in a nearby town. The closure of the local school enabled the community to consider what type of school they would like to see for their children. There is a commitment within this school to create a positive environment where students are challenged intellectually, and provided with opportunities to interact with the world within a safe environment. The trust that the teachers have in the students is demonstrated during major excursions and field trips to places such as Berlin. The organization of the school is flexible, lessons can be as short or as long as required, and parents are heavily involved in the school. Perhaps the best indication of how the school functions and how students perceive the school can be found in excerpts from speeches made by students within the chapter. Some of the challenges the Danish free schools face are presented, including finance. As the schools become successful they often attract greater numbers of children and, as families change, there can be pressure to become more mainstream. Similarly, changes in education policy, especially around testing, are putting pressure on the alternative practices in this school to become more mainstream, again echoing issues raised by other authors in this book.

In the last section of the book we seek to explore how the best aspects of alternative education can be integrated into the mainstream. We begin with Anne Sliwka and Britta Klopsch's chapter on alternative education in Germany and conclude with our own take on what the chapters in this book, when taken together, offer to a rethinking of mainstream education in relation to social justice.

Chapter 16 by Sliwka and Klopsch details the ways in which practices in alternative settings have developed over time in Germany. However, the authors argue that these practices were largely ignored by the mainstream sector until the advent of PISA. They note that Germany's low achievement on PISA 2000 for students from low socio-economic status (SES) backgrounds prompted discussion about what would work best for the young people. This led to the creation of a prestigious award system for outstanding practice. As a consequence of several alternative schools winning this award there has been significant media attention on what these schools do, which has in turn led to some of these practices being taken up by mainstream schools. Such practices include more emphasis on formative and criterion-based assessment, more engagement with the local community, and project-based learning. Hence, and perhaps ironically, the performative agenda in schools has opened up possibilities for considering other ways of doing school.

In our concluding chapter we highlight a number of tensions that surface throughout the book. These include definitional issues, including the purposes of alternative education, the social justice implications of different types of schools (including whether they are fee-paying or not, their purposes and the level of choice involved in selection), the extent to which a differentiated curriculum can enhance or restrict social justice, and whether or not 'alternative' represents an improvement on the mainstream. We then go on to suggest ways in which the chapters in this book can help us to promote a more socially just form of schooling.

References

Apple, M.W. (2013) *Can Education Change Society?* New York: Routledge.

Bacchi, C. (2009) *Analysing Policy: What's the problem represented to be?* Frenchs Forest, NSW: Pearson Australia.

Bacchi, C. (2012) 'Why study problematizations? Making politics visible'. *Open Journal of Political Science*, 2 (1), 1–8.

Baker, A.M. (2016) 'The process and product: Crafting community portraits with young people in flexible learning settings'. *International Journal of Inclusive Education*, 20 (3), 309–30.

Gallagher, E. (2011) 'The second chance school'. *International Journal of Inclusive Education*, 15 (4), 445–59.

McGregor, G. and Mills, M. (2014) 'Teaching in the "margins": Rekindling a passion for teaching'. *British Journal of Sociology of Education*, 35 (1), 1–18.

McGregor, G., Mills, M., te Riele, K., Baroutsis, A. and Hayes, D. (2017) *Re-imagining Schooling for Education: Socially just alternatives*. London: Palgrave Macmillan.

Mills, M. and McGregor, G. (2010) *Re-engaging Students in Education: Success factors in alternative schools*. Brisbane: Youth Affairs Network Queensland.

Te Riele, K. (2008) 'Are alternative schools the answer?'. *New Transitions: Re-engagement Edition*, April, 1–6.

Te Riele, K., Mills, M., McGregor, G. and Baroutsis, A. (2017) 'Exploring the affective dimension of teachers' work in alternative school settings'. *Teaching Education*, 28 (1), 56–71.

Part One

Approaches to alternative
education

1

Chapter 2

Alternative schools in the United States: Understanding the landscape

Gavin Tierney

Introduction

Alternative schools fall into an interesting space in education by being able to provide innovative and supportive opportunities that are different from mainstream schooling, yet also acting as part of a mechanism for sorting youth on the margins of education (Vadeboncoeur, 2009). This sorting process allows many schools to discard unwanted youth and narrowly defines what success can mean in mainstream high schools. In the USA, the term 'alternative school' is used to describe a wide array of schools, with differing perspectives on youth (Raywid, 1999) and differing relationships with the school districts in which they exist. In many cases, the policy context of alternative schools can be seen through the types of alternative schools that have been created throughout the past 50 years.

This chapter explores public alternative schools in the United States, discussing the modern history of alternative education and the range of definitions of alternative schools that exist in the USA, also looking ahead to how a changing political climate may impact on alternative schools in the United States. (While aspects of this chapter focus on both elementary school and high school, the main focus of the chapter is on public alternative high schools and the tensions that those schools face.) In this chapter, I will discuss the scope of alternative education in the United States and define the various forms of alternative education that exist. In doing so, I also discuss some cultural views of alternative schools and the youth who attend them. This is all done with the goal of better understanding the landscape of alternative schools and the challenges those schools face. Specifically, this chapter seeks to answer the following questions: What is the current landscape of alternative schools in the United States? In what ways have US society and policy influenced alternative schools in the past 50 years? In what ways can current alternative schools in the USA be categorized? What are some of the challenges and risks of narrowly labelling alternative high schools and narrowly defining success?

I begin by looking, very briefly, at the history of modern alternative schools in the United States, including foundational influences on alternative education. I also describe different periods of alternative education over the past 50 years and how they fit into the general climate of education over time, including the ways in which many alternative schools' practices and philosophies of education are in tension with current state and nationally created standardized tests. (The exact tests and how test scores are used vary across US states. Typically, the test data are used to evaluate the schools' performance. Additionally, in some states, but not all, students need to achieve a passing score on the standardized test in order to graduate, despite the fact that attaching high stakes to standardized tests has been shown to increase dropout rates (Taylor and Nolen, 2008).) I then consider different types of alternative schools, focusing specifically on how different alternative schools view youth and definitions of success.

In order to examine the challenges and tensions that exist for alternative schools, I compare the competing definitions of success (McDermott *et al.*, 2006) in public alternative schools and the neoliberal definitions of success embodied in the policies and practices in current education writ large (McGregor and Mills, 2012). I discuss the impact that these competing definitions of success have on alternative schools and the identities and education of youth who attend alternative schools. I explore the ways labels and stereotypes impact on alternative schools and the youth attending them. Within that exploration, I also describe the ways that educational research should consider and push against negative labels of schools and youth simply because the schools and youth exist outside the mainstream of education.

A brief history of alternative schools in the USA

The history of alternative schools and alternative education in the United States is tied directly to conventional education and normative definitions of success in school, where the goal of formal education is defined largely by the country's economic and social needs (Tyack, 1988). Miller (1992) attributed much of alternative education philosophy to Jean-Jacques Rousseau, Johann Heinrich Pestalozzi and Friedrich Froebel. These philosopher-educators advocated for types of schooling that valorised child-focused education, in contrast to education that focused on societal demands. Pestalozzi took Rousseau's philosophies and put them into practice in schools. Froebel, who taught at one of Pestalozzi's schools, continued this work, focusing on the individuality of students' needs and abilities (Miller, 1989, 1992). The ideas of Rousseau, Pestalozzi and Froebel, as well as educators including Ivan Illich, John Dewey, Paolo Freire, A.S. Neill, Maria Montessori and Rudolf Steiner, were the foundation for the alternative school movements of the late 1960s and early 1970s. By the mid-1970s, these schools, often called 'free', 'holistic', 'humanistic', 'open' and 'experiential' schools, began opening at a remarkable rate in both the private and public sector (Kozol, 1982). The proliferation of alternative schools in the late 1960s and the 1970s aligned with the increasing focus within education on equity and the academic success of all students. This was marked by the Elementary and Secondary Education Act of 1965, which was part of President Lyndon B. Johnson's 'War on Poverty' and provided funding for primary and secondary education and focused on equal access to quality education.

The world of alternative education slowly began to shift in the early 1980s as the political climate also shifted in the USA. Since the 1980s, one of the prominent ideologies within education, both in the USA and internationally, has been neoliberalism, which has focused on establishing free-market capitalism within education (McGregor *et al.*, 2015). An underlying belief of neoliberalism is that competition is the defining characteristic of human relations (Monbiot, 2016). A neoliberal perspective within education is that competition and individual accountability of teachers and students will create better results, but unintentionally creates schools where grades and test scores are prioritized over learning and growth (Pope, 2001).

In 1983, *A Nation at Risk* (United States National Commission on Excellence in Education, 1983) was released, emphasizing neoliberal goals within education, specifically social efficiency and economic growth (Miller, 1992; Mills *et al.*, 2013), while also ignoring the large number of dropouts in US education (Fine, 1991). The landscape of education has changed dramatically since 1983, with an increasing focus on public education to help the economy meet its need for human capital (Gaztambide-Fernández, 2012; Hargreaves and Fullan, 2012; Vadeboncoeur, 2009). The neoliberal discourses shaping education have reinforced schooling as competition instead of education as growth and learning. In the past few decades there has been a dual focus on educational standards and educational choice. Much of the argument behind an increased focus on standards and evaluation is that they are a clear way to measure learning and ensure equity (Kantor and Lowe, 2013). Yet, the focus on standards and evaluation has further restricted definitions of success in school, while also constraining alternative schools' time and ability to implement alternative practices, such as experiential trips and interdisciplinary coursework, and still help students be successful on state and district assessments (Tierney, 2016). Additionally, standardized tests do not capture the range of outcomes that many alternative schools focus on (Lehr and Lange, 2003).

Since the late 1980s, another version of 'alternative' school has emerged. These schools tend to be more remedial, focusing on improving areas where youth are struggling (Settles and Orwick, 2003). The areas of improvement typically focus on the academic, but may also include behavioural improvement (Raywid, 1990, 1994). Continuation schools are one prevalent form of this version of alternative schools, with a defining feature of sending youth back to their conventional home school when they are 'back on track' (Kelly, 1993; Rumberger, 2011). While this flavour of alternative schools may share some similarities to progressive alternative schools that started in the 1960s and 1970s (with some progressive alternatives opening since the 1960s and 1970s, but with far less frequency), there is a fundamental difference in how the schools approach students and their visions of education and success in education (Raywid, 1999; te Riele, 2007). In particular, there is a difference in where the onus of change is placed. Similar to the neoliberal perspective on education, 'back on track' schools often value individual accountability and a prioritization of measures, such as grades and test scores, that help perpetuate competition and a specific definition of success. This is in contrast with more progressive alternative schools that more fully recognize the structural qualities within the education system that contribute to students' lack of success. I will discuss these differences in greater depth later in the chapter.

Running alongside the proliferation of standardized assessments and, more recently, adaptation of common educational standards (Common Core State Standards Initiative, 2018), another strong focus since the early 1980s has been on educational choice, often connected to the expanding charter school movement (NCES, 2015). Though on the surface a focus on educational choice aligns with the ideas of alternative education, much of the choice movement is based on ideas of a market economy supporting competition, individual accountability, improvement and success (McGregor and Mills, 2012; McGregor *et al.*, 2015; Vadeboncoeur and Portes, 2002). The charter school movement has become another force influencing alternatives in the United States in the past two and a half decades (Center for Education Reform, 2015; NCES, 2015). While charter school law differs state by state, in general charter schools are individual schools that use public education funds to contract with private companies or groups to provide educational opportunities different from traditional public schools (Kantor and Lowe, 2013). Charter schools remain controversial for many reasons, but largely because they promote a market-oriented approach to education, allowing private businesses to flourish (Kantor and Lowe, 2013). One result of the proliferation of charter schools is that the number of alternative schools has dramatically increased, including both individual schools and school networks, such as Big Picture Schools (Littky and Grabelle, 2004). However, alternative schools and charter schools are not synonymous. The 'alternative school' label designates that the schools are outside of normative schooling, while a 'charter school' label designates the state law that allows the school to exist, but does not define the form and function of the school. Many alternative schools are not charter schools and many charter schools are not alternative schools. Charter schools have simply created the opportunity for more public alternative schools to exist.

With the recent shift in political power in the United States, it is likely that the number of charter schools will only continue to grow and that federal funds will help support this effort (Richmond, 2017). However, it is unclear how alternative schools will be supported, what types of alternative schools will prosper, and how alternative schools will be affected by a shifting climate in education. Since the Elementary and Secondary Education Act of 1965, education in the United States has focused specifically on the goal of all students being successful in school. Though many of the national education initiatives, such as No Child Left Behind or Race to the Top (United States Department of Education, 2017, 2016), have been controversial, there has been a focus on the achievement of all students (Kantor and Lowe, 2013). It is unclear if this focus will shift in the Trump administration. If it does, then there may be a situation where there may be more money to open alternative schools as charters, yet, at the same time there will likely be a deprioritisation of educational equity in favour of promoting an educational market (Rotherham, 2017), resulting in less money for public education, as funds are diverted to private schools through a voucher system (BBC News, 2017). This is uncertain, but what is clear is that the landscape of alternative education in the United States is in a period of fluctuation.

Judging success in alternative schools
The number of alternative schools in the USA

Approximately 3 per cent of high school students in the United States attended alternative schools in 2010, with that number at over 5 per cent in Arkansas, California, Idaho, Minnesota, Mississippi, Utah and Washington State. In 2007–8, alternative schools in the United States represented

6 per cent of the public k–12 schools, i.e. approximately 5,929 of 98,817 schools (Rumberger, 2011). While the percentage of alternative schools is in the single digits, they still represent a significant number of youth, considering that, in 2015, an estimated 14.9 million youth were enrolled in Grades 9–12 (NCES, 2016a). That means that, at 3 per cent, 447,000 youth attended alternative high schools. Additionally, in California in 2005–6, the number of alternative high schools outnumbered the number of comprehensive high schools 1,154 to 1,037 (Rumberger, 2011).

Alternative school closures in the USA

While the numbers above provide a picture of how alternative schools fit within the general landscape of education in the USA, what this picture does not convey is how these numbers have shifted in the past decade. Due in part to how school districts have responded to alternative schools in the era of testing and standards, many alternative schools have been restructured, shut down and consolidated. Therefore, while charter schools have increased in numbers, schools labelled as 'alternative' have closed. Between 2000 and 2012, public alternative schools have represented 13–35 per cent annually of the public schools that have been closed (NCES, 2016b), though they only represent approximately 6 per cent of public schools (Rumberger, 2011). This number is even higher when focusing specifically on high schools, where, between 2000 and 2012, public alternative high schools have represented 23–46 per cent annually of high schools that have been closed. Additionally, for only two of these years did alternative high schools represent less than 32 per cent of high school closures (NCES, 2016b). The reasons for these closures include, but are not limited to, budget cuts, test performances, student enrolment and retention, and graduation rates. In addition, larger comprehensive high schools may be simply too big to be allowed to fail, while smaller alternative programmes are easier to shut down or restructure. While many of the changes to alternative schools may very well be justified, they often appear to be made with partial data, without considering all the factors, and defining 'success' in specific terms.

Graduation rates as a measure of success

One key element of public high schools, and public alternative high schools as a subcategory, is graduation credits. (The credits needed to graduate high school include specific requirements in various subject areas. So, students may only be credit deficient in one or two subject areas, such as Maths and English, but not others, such as Science, Social Studies and Elective credits. The exact nature of credit deficiency is a case-by-case basis.) For public alternative high schools and the youth attending them, credits are an ever-present pressure, impacting on the courses and opportunities that are offered and on the academic trajectories of youth. I mention this to recognize that while alternative schools may offer programmes that are vastly different from conventional schools, there are still shared currencies, credits being one of the most significant. While by no means the predominant reason, some youth choose to attend alternative schools or are guided to alternative schools as a way to earn credits they are missing.

While each student's progress towards graduation is individual, graduation rates as aggregate data are a consistent measure of school success. However, though graduation rates can be an important feature in judging school success, there is also variation in the ways in which it is defined. Specifically, it is important to consider whether rates are based on on-time graduation or if they also factor in youth who graduate in their fifth, sixth or seventh year. Often graduation rates do not include these youth, lowering alternative schools' percentages (Rumberger, 2011). Doing so imposes a norm on what a high school timeline should be, even if some alternative schools may not focus on this timeline, instead encouraging youth to pursue paths and timeframes that fit their needs and interests. (The notion of choosing to stay an additional year in high school is so unfamiliar to US society that it is typically assumed that the reason youth would not graduate in four years is universally because of credit deficiency. Yet, there are youth who are on-track to graduate and pause in order to stay an additional year at their school (Tierney, 2014).) Defining graduation rates as four-year completion ignores the fact that alternative schools may be made up of a higher population of students on non-traditional graduation timelines, including youth who enter these alternative schools already a year or two behind, thereby making four-year graduation an impossible goal.

Alternative schools as dumping grounds

Though it is problematic to narrowly define alternative schools and youth attending them, there is a portion of alternative schools that focus on youth who have been less successful (measured by earning credits) in school. Alternative schools often receive students at the moment in which they are already 'credit deficient', a term used for youth who have fallen behind in earning the credits needed to graduate high school on time. An alternative school can help youth be successful, yet because of their credits when they began at the school, the students may still not be able to graduate on time. However, in public education, four-year graduation rates are a consistent measure of school performance. So, even if a student transfers to the alternative school in their senior year, whether or not they graduate on time is a reflection on the alternative school. It is similar with student scores on standardized tests, where poor standardized tests reflect on the alternative schools, even when the youth have only attended the alternative school for a brief period of time. Michelle Fine (1991) presented the ways that conventional high schools define success and guide youth who do not fit that definition into pathways that lead to dropping out. The process in which mainstream schools push out problematic students treats these youth as a bad commodity that, if kept, will negatively impact on the school's success. Alternative schools often welcome these youth, yet because of the neoliberal sorting mechanism of education, alternative schools may also become a dumping ground for 'unwanted youth' (Vadeboncoeur, 2009).

Quantitative measures of success

A final way in which the current educational system has defined success and, in turn, alternative schools, is that, by prioritizing quantitative measures, such as test scores and four-year graduation rates, other measures of success are often ignored. The safety youth feel, the feelings of connection they have with the school, and their successful identification with school are all aspects that can be more difficult to measure. Academic work may also become more interwoven with young people's personal and social lives (Tierney, 2014). In alternative schools, academic success may look different and be less siloed than what is measured on a test. Instead of representing learning, test scores may simply represent an incongruent form of assessment. Additionally, test scores may under-represent the rich identity-building experiences that alternative schools support.

Definitions of alternative schools

As I mentioned before, there are fundamental differences between alternative schools in the United States. When saying 'alternative school', one could mean everything from a juvenile detention centre, to an online school, to a wilderness focused leadership school. The educational landscape over the past 50 years has also influenced the landscape of alternative schools. Part of the challenge of defining alternative schools is the wide variety of schools that can be called alternative, as any school that is outside the normative form of conventional schools is, by definition, an alternative.

There are a number of ways to categorize alternative schools, each way providing a different and valuable look at the schools. Raywid (1999) and te Riele (2007) delineated the categories of alternative schools by their approach to youth, specifically how much onus (for success, engagement, involvement, etc.) falls on the youth and how much falls upon the schools.

Put simply, do the schools have an approach that youth need to be changed in order to be successful, or that the school environments need to be changed? Schools that focus on changing youth are those, like many 'Last-Chance' and 'Remedial Focus' programmes (Raywid, 1990, 1994), that view a student's lack of success or disaffiliation as an issue with the student (Vadeboncoeur and Portes, 2002). These schools take what te Riele calls a 'Youth At-Risk' perspective. In part, schools with a 'Youth At-Risk' perspective, while they may be alternative in structure or the youth they serve, perpetuate the neoliberal views of education, mentioned earlier in the chapter. This is in contrast to schools that focus on changing the school and that take a 'Learning Choice' perspective. Schools that focus on changing the school are often innovative schools (Raywid, 1990, 1994) that take the view that: (1) some students need different learning environments; and/or (2) mainstream education is flawed and that unsuccessful students are unsuccessful largely because of the structures of mainstream schools (Raywid, 1990, 1994).

As is often the case, most schools do not reside in a single category. For example, a school may philosophically take a 'Learning Choice' perspective, but elements of the school structure or course offerings may also include a 'Youth At-Risk' perspective. Still, one benefit of using the definitions of alternative schools from Raywid (1999) and te Riele (2007) is, while acknowledging the structural features that help categorize alternative schools, this framework helps focus on how schools view youth and whether the onus for change is placed on the youth or on the schools and the education system.

While recognizing the value of Raywid (1999) and te Riele's (2007) framework, alternative schools in the United States are more often defined in their school districts and communities by other features of their programme. For example, one way alternative schools are often categorized is by the students they serve. Within most states there are alternative schools that serve youth labelled gifted and talented, others serving incarcerated youth, or potential dropouts, or youth who are re-enrolled dropouts, or youth who simply feel alienated, marginalized, or out of place in normative schools. The list goes on and some alternative schools serve youth from more than one of these categories.

Another way alternative schools are categorized is by the contexts in which they were created. Some alternatives were created by community groups made up of teachers, students and parents. Many of these schools were created in the 1960s and 1970s, some of which still exist today. Others have been created as initiatives from school districts to focus on specific populations of students in the district. These types of schools became prevalent in the 1980s and 1990s and often specifically serve students designated 'at-risk' of dropping out of high school. In a third category are charter schools, which may be created by a community group or may be an expansion of a charter school network. There are, of course, schools that exist across these categories and each school has its own unique origin.

Still another way alternative schools are categorized in the USA is by the form and structure that the schools take on. Some examples of these are school size, with the small school movement being a prevalent type of alternative school. Alternative schools can also be categorized by whether the schools are stand-alone, schools within schools or satellite programmes of other schools. The length of the school programmes and age range of those enrolled are another way to categorize alternative schools, with some continuation schools only seeking short-term enrolment and then having youth transfer back to their home school, and other programmes seeking to enrol students until graduation.

Many alternative schools are further categorized by the programmatic focus that the schools have, with some alternative programmes having a particular emphasis, such as Big Picture Schools that seek internships for their students (Littky and Grabelle, 2004), while others have a more general educational focus, but are alternative because of the attention on school community and relationship building.

As with all of forms of categorization, these lines can blur; some alternative schools may be alternative because of size and relationships, but also, because of those things, can offer unique educational opportunities, such as experiential trips. However, within each of these forms of categorization it is important to examine what makes the schools alternative and what roles and opportunities there are for youth in the schools. I would argue that these two things should be directly linked. A school should not be labelled alternative simply because it caters to youth on the margins, but because of the opportunities it offers youth to re-imagine their education. Underlying Raywid's (1999) idea of a 'Learning Choice' perspective is an assumption that the structure and relationships of learning environments have a profound influence on the learning and identity of youth. Framed this way, the structural and relational features of alternative schools are important not as static definitions or branding of the school, but as active opportunities for youth to learn and develop.

Alternative schools as dropout prevention

Describing alternative schools as a form of dropout prevention is tricky, not because it is necessarily incorrect, since many alternative schools were created specifically as a form of dropout prevention. However, doing so without explanation does not recognize the complexity of many youths' reasons for attending alternative schools. Additionally, defining an alternative school simply in terms of dropout prevention reifies certain ideas about alternative schools and the youth attending them. Yet, public alternative schools are one of the current interventions aimed at dropout prevention.

Though there has been a recent decrease in dropout rates in the USA (NCES, 2017), prior studies recorded that up to one-third of students in the USA fail to graduate from high school (Bridgeland *et al.*, 2006). (Note that there is a difference between the number of dropouts and the number of students who fail to graduate. The former counts students who actively dropped out of school, while the latter includes youth who may never have gone through the process of dropping out, but never graduated high school (Rumberger, 2011).) Rumberger (2011) described dropping out in three ways: a label (being a dropout), an event (the moment of dropping out) and a process (the process of disengaging and eventually leaving school.) By considering dropping out to be a process, students, over time, develop identities where they can see themselves as dropouts. Similarly, there is a process as youth who have been marginalized and disenfranchised enter into alternative schools and find success, renegotiating their identities in school.

On one level, dropout prevention at the high school level is about helping students earn the credits and other requirements they need in order to graduate. However, it is also about helping youth re-engage in their education so they will go through the steps and earn the credits needed to graduate. This process of renegotiating one's identity is often in conflict with adolescents' past educational experiences and, possibly, their out-of-school lives. The complexity of dropout prevention requires that educators not only better understand both how factors, such as socio-economic status, gender and ethnicity shape outcomes, but also explore the ways that youth experience school, particularly looking qualitatively at how youth negotiate contradictions in their lives and come to develop visions of themselves as people who are academically successful. Examining the process that youth experience as they wrestle with the multiple tensions involved in developing their identities in alternative schools can help us better understand the interaction, over time, of different factors in the youths' lives that contribute or detract from academic success, graduation and youth identity development.

Labelling schools

While categorizing alternative schools in terms of the schools taking a 'Learning Choice' or 'Youth At-Risk' perspective (Raywid, 1999; te Riele, 2007) may be a useful tool, to the general public the term 'alternative school' carries other baggage. Without personal experience, the term can often become a negative stereotype. In the USA, the label 'alternative' carries enough baggage that many schools have moved away from the label, focusing instead on, for example, Option School, Choice School and Innovative School. Despite the rebranding away from the alternative label, the Option, Choice or Innovative labels still fail to capture the full complexity that is needed to understand these non-conventional programmes. Additionally, many of these schools and the students who attend them continue to suffer from the stereotypes that exist about the school. Whether a school is labelled alternative, option or innovative, negative perceptions of the schools are pervasive and, at times, the students are all viewed as drug users, misfits, losers or poor at school (Eckert, 1989; Eckert and McConnell-Ginet, 1995; Vadeboncoeur and Portes, 2002).

While many programmes have rebranded away from the term 'alternative', the 'alternative' label provides an important positioning that the other labels do not, focusing squarely on the normative nature of most schools. When researchers and teachers look at youth experiences in school, be it success, failure, disengagement or marginalization, all of these constructs exist as interactions between the youth and their school context (McDermott *et al.*, 2006; Nolen *et al.*, 2011; Tierney, 2016). When youth are disengaged, disenfranchised, unsuccessful or marginalized, and then enter into an alternative school, the fact that the school is an alternative to their previous school is an essential feature. Alternative schools are always an alternative to mainstream schooling, and that is part of their power to help youth redefine their identities in school (Tierney, 2014). However, public alternative schools also always exist in the context of public schooling.

Labelling youth

For the past 50 years in the USA, and particularly since the 1980s, alternative schools have been primarily developed as an intervention or option for youth who have been unsuccessful and/or unhappy in conventional school (Rumberger, 2011). However, it is important not to ascribe negative narratives to these youth, but instead to reflect on the factors that make students unsuccessful and unhappy in school. Often alternative schools cater to youth who may exhibit characteristics (such as truancy, failing grades, disengagement, anxiety, and drug and alcohol use) that can designate them as at-risk of dropping out of school. Yet this is not always the case and, when it is, it is never a simple story. In tackling major challenges, such as disengagement, marginalization, disaffiliation in school, or reducing the high numbers of high school dropouts, it can be tempting to lean on certain narratives of youth. However, doing so can neglect the complexity of these issues and often ascribes unfair narratives onto students, labelling them as at-risk, unmotivated or just needing a different type of learning environment. Fine (1991: 5) reflected on the process in which dropouts were positioned:

> Who is served by this seamless rhetoric of dropouts as losers? What is obscured by a portrayal of dropouts as *deficient* in a *fair* system? If youths who drop out are portrayed as unreasonable or academically inferior, then the structures, ideologies, and practices that exile them systematically are rendered invisible, and the critique they voice is institutionally silenced.

While Fine focused specifically on youth who dropped out of school, her description of dropouts can seemingly apply to all youth who leave the walls of conventional schools, those who are labelled potential dropouts and those who feel alienated or disengaged. In part, Fine calls for schools to more closely examine the structures and practices that both contribute to students' success and failure. Similar to labelling dropouts as losers, labelling alternative schools and the youth attending them as academically inferior, 'druggie' schools or schools for kids who don't fit in, obscures the structures, ideologies and practices of both the schools that the youth have left behind and the alternative schools they have joined.

Looking ahead

In this chapter, I explored the landscape of alternative education in the United States, looking at the history of alternative schools, some current tensions and struggles that exist for public alternative schools, and, in the second half of the chapter, the challenges of defining and labelling alternative schools and youth who attend alternative schools. As happens at any time of change of political power, the educational landscape in the United States is currently in flux. It is unclear the exact course that education will take and how national and state-level policy decisions will impact on alternative schools. However, it is important to take stock of the history, climate and challenges that alternative schools have faced. Doing so may provide a useful perspective as alternative schools enter into what could potentially be a new phase of existence in the United States. Looking historically, we can see how alternative schools have been created as a result of, and in response to, national policy, but also the needs of local communities and school districts.

In recent decades, public alternative schools have existed in a space where there have been more opportunities for alternative schools in the United States, provided through charter school law and an overarching focus in public education on equity and increasing graduation rates. Yet, at the same time, definitions of success, and thus evaluations of schools and students, have become increasingly narrowed and focused on performance on standardized tests. Put briefly, there has been increased opportunity for alternative schools to exist, but decreased opportunity for alternative schools to create programmes that are radically alternative to mainstream education.

In the future, as alternative schools are created, rebranded or repurposed, it may be useful to explore the historical context in which the schools exist and what policies and values the schools are responding to. One specific way to do this would be to examine the definitions of risk and success that exist in public education. Examining the history of alternative schools and the tensions they have faced is also an examination of how success and risk have been defined in the United States and perspectives of how best to respond to those definitions. In the United States, alternative schools will most probably always exist and be a response to normative education. By examining the historical and policy contexts that exist and have existed in the past, alternative schools can more purposefully fulfil their role as providing a counter balance to many of the prevalent ideas and practices in public education.

However, to do so, alternative schools must face the challenge of how to define themselves and how to define styles of education that exist outside of normative schooling. This challenge of defining alternative schools and alternative education is complicated by the often unfair labels that get placed on alternative schools and youth who attend alternative schools. Defining alternative education in the USA requires schools to recognize the realities of the youth they serve, thus helping youth find success in school, yet, at the same time push against the narrow and negative labels that can be placed on schools and youth. In this chapter I propose that alternative schools examine the ways in which they view youth and the ways they define success. A 'Learning Choice' (Raywid, 1999) perspective includes a more expansive view of youth in alternative schools, focusing on how educational contexts shape students' learning and academic identities. This perspective challenges notions that it is youth alone that need fixing, instead examining the ways all schools, mainstream and alternative, impact youths' identities and learning.

I began this chapter by recognizing the tension alternative schools face as they act both as a sorting mechanism in public education and a unique, supportive and innovative learning environment for youth (Vadeboncoeur, 2009). Looking ahead, I believe it is just this tension that can allow alternative schools not only to provide opportunities for youth on the margins of education, but also to closely examine and advocate for broadening definitions of success in public education in the United States.

References

BBC News (2017) 'Why is Betsy DeVos, Trump's pick for education secretary, so unpopular?'. *BBC News*, 7 February. Online. www.bbc.com/news/world-us-canada-38875924 (accessed 23 February 2018).

Bridgeland, J.M., DiIulio, J.J. and Morison, K.B. (2006) *The Silent Epidemic: Perspectives of high school dropouts.* Washington, DC: Civic Enterprises.

Center for Education Reform (2015) *Charter School Law Rankings and Scorecard: 2015.* Washington, DC: Center for Education Reform. Online. www.edreform.com/wp-content/uploads/2015/03/CER-CharterLawsChart20151.pdf (accessed 29 April 2018).

Common Core State Standards Initiative (2018) 'Standards in your state'. Online. www.corestandards.org/standards-in-your-state/ (accessed 29 April 2018).

Eckert, P. (1989) *Jocks and Burnouts: Social categories and identity in the high school.* New York: Teachers College Press.

Eckert, P. and McConnell-Ginet, S. (1995) 'Constructing meaning, constructing selves: Snapshots of language, gender, and class from Belten High'. In Hall, K. and Bucholtz, M. (eds) *Gender Articulated: Language and the socially constructed self.* New York: Routledge, 469–507.

Fine, M. (1991) *Framing Dropouts: Notes on the politics of an urban public high school.* Albany: State University of New York Press.

Gaztambide-Fernández, R.A. (2012) 'Decolonization and the pedagogy of solidarity'. *Decolonization: Indigeneity, Education and Society*, 1 (1), 41–67.

Hargreaves, A. and Fullan, M. (2012) *Professional Capital: Transforming teaching in every school.* New York: Teachers College Press.

Kantor, H. and Lowe, R. (2013) 'Educationalizing the welfare state and privatizing education: The evolution of social policy since the New Deal'. In Carter, P.L. and Welner, K.G. (eds) *Closing the Opportunity Gap: What America must do to give every child an even chance.* Oxford: Oxford University Press, 25–39.

Kelly, D.M. (1993) *Last Chance High: How girls and boys drop in and out of alternative schools.* New Haven, CT: Yale University Press.

Kozol, J. (1982) *Alternative Schools: A guide for educators and parents.* New York: Continuum.

Lehr, C.A. and Lange, C.M. (2003) 'Alternative schools serving students with and without disabilities: What are the current issues and challenges?'. *Preventing School Failure: Alternative Education for Children and Youth*, 47 (2), 59–65.

Littky, D. and Grabelle, S. (2004) *The Big Picture: Education is everyone's business*. Alexandria, VA: Association for Supervision and Curriculum Development.

McDermott, R., Goldman, S. and Varenne, H. (2006) 'The cultural work of learning disabilities'. *Educational Researcher*, 35 (6), 12–17.

McGregor, G. and Mills, M. (2012) 'Alternative education sites and marginalised young people: "I wish there were more schools like this one"'. *International Journal of Inclusive Education*, 16 (8), 843–62.

McGregor, G., Mills, M., te Riele, K. and Hayes, D. (2015) 'Excluded from school: Getting a second chance at a "meaningful" education'. *International Journal of Inclusive Education*, 19 (6), 608–25.

Miller, R. (1989) 'The history of alternative education'. *Mothering*, 50, 78–81.

Miller, R. (1992) *What Are Schools For? Holistic education in American culture*. 2nd ed. Brandon, VT: Holistic Education Press.

Mills, M., Renshaw, P. and Zipin, L. (2013) 'Alternative education provision: A dumping ground for "wasted lives" or a challenge to the mainstream?'. *Social Alternatives*, 32 (2), 13–18.

Monbiot, G. (2016) 'Neoliberalism – the ideology at the root of all our problems'. *The Guardian*, 15 April. Online. www.theguardian.com/books/2016/apr/15/neoliberalism-ideology-problem-george-monbiot (accessed 23 February 2018).

NCES (National Center for Education Statistics) (2015) 'Table 216.20 – Number and enrollment of public elementary and secondary schools, by school level, type, and charter and magnet status: Selected years, 1990–91 through 2013–14'. Online. https://nces.ed.gov/programs/digest/d15/tables/dt15_216.20.asp (accessed 29 April 2018).

NCES (National Center for Education Statistics) (2016a) 'Fast facts: Back to school statistics'. Online. http://nces.ed.gov/fastfacts/display.asp?id=372 (accessed 29 April 2018).

NCES (National Center for Education Statistics) (2016b) 'Fast facts: Closed schools'. Online. https://nces.ed.gov/fastfacts/display.asp?id=619 (accessed 29 April 2018).

NCES (National Center for Education Statistics) (2017) 'Fast facts: Dropout rates'. Online. https://nces.ed.gov/fastfacts/display.asp?id=16 (accessed 29 April 2018).

Nolen, S.B., Ward, C.J. and Horn, I.S. (2011) 'Motivation, engagement, and identity: Opening a conversation'. In McInerney, D.M., Walker, R.A. and Liem, G.A.D. (eds) *Sociocultural Theories of Learning and Motivation: Looking back, looking forward*. Charlotte, NC: Information Age Publishing, 109–35.

Pope, D.C. (2001) *'Doing School': How we are creating a generation of stressed out, materialistic, and miseducated students*. New Haven, CT: Yale University Press.

Raywid, M. (1990) 'Alternative education: The definition problem'. *Changing Schools*, 18 (4–5), 25–33.

Raywid, M.A. (1994) 'Alternative schools: The state of the art'. *Educational Leadership*, 52 (1), 26–31.

Raywid, M.A. (1999) 'History and issues of alternative schools'. *Education Digest*, 64 (9), 47–51.

Richmond, E. (2017) 'What is the future of public education? Four agendas beyond school choice the new administration might look to advance'. *The Atlantic*, 10 January. Online. www.theatlantic.com/education/archive/2017/01/what-is-the-future-of-public-education/512651/ (accessed 23 February 2018).

Rotherham, A.J. (2017) 'What does Betsy DeVos believe? 5 questions for Trump's nominee to run the Department of Education'. *US News*, 9 January. Online. www.usnews.com/opinion/knowledge-bank/articles/2017-01-09/what-matters-to-betsy-devos-donald-trumps-pick-for-education-secretary (accessed 23 February 2018).

Rumberger, R.W. (2011) *Dropping Out: Why students drop out of high school and what can be done about it*. Cambridge, MA: Harvard University Press.

Settles, D. and Orwick, B. (2003) *Alternative Education: Past, present and next steps*. Lexington: Kentucky Center for School Safety Clearinghouse. Online. https://kycss.org/clear/pdfs-docs/AltEdLit.pdf (accessed 29 April 2018).

Taylor, C.S. and Nolen, S.B. (2008) *Classroom Assessment: Supporting teaching and learning in real classrooms*. 2nd ed. Harlow: Prentice Hall.

Te Riele, K. (2007) 'Educational alternatives for marginalised youth'. *Australian Educational Researcher*, 34 (3), 53–68.

Tierney, G. (2014) 'Defining success in an alternative high school: Resources for the reframing of education'. In Polman, J.L., Kyza, E.A., O'Neill, D.K., Tabak, I., Penuel, W.R., Jurow, A.S., O'Connor, K., Lee, T. and D'Amico, L. (eds) *Learning and Becoming in Practice: The International Conference of the Learning Sciences (ICLS) 2014: Proceedings* (Vol. 1). Boulder, CO: International Society of the Learning Sciences, 543–50.

Tierney, G. (2016) 'Agency outside the Margins: Identity development of youth attending alternative high schools'. Unpublished PhD thesis, University of Washington.

Tyack, D.B. (1988) 'Ways of seeing: An essay on the history of compulsory schooling'. In Jaeger, R.M. (ed.) *Complementary Methods for Research in Education*. Washington, DC: American Educational Research Association, 24–59.

United States Department of Education (2016) 'Race to the Top Fund'. Online. www2.ed.gov/programs/racetothetop/index.html (accessed 29 April 2018).

United States Department of Education (2017) 'No Child Left Behind: Elementary and Secondary Education Act (ESEA)'. Online. www2.ed.gov/nclb/landing.jhtml (accessed 29 April 2018).

United States National Commission on Excellence in Education (1983) *A Nation at Risk: The imperative for educational reform: A report to the Nation and the Secretary of Education, United States Department of Education*. Washington, DC: Department of Education.

Vadeboncoeur, J.A. (2009) 'Spaces of difference: The contradictions of alternative educational programs'. *Educational Studies*, 45 (3), 280–99.

Vadeboncoeur, J.A. and Portes, P.R. (2002) 'Students "at risk": Exploring identity from a sociocultural perspective'. In McInerney, D.M. and Van Etten, S. (eds) *Sociocultural Influences on Motivation and Learning: An historical perspective* (Research on Sociocultural Influences on Motivation and Learning 2). Greenwich, CT: Information Age Publishing, 89–128.

Chapter 3

Alternative education in the South Korean policy context

Chulkyung Yoon and Jungwon Kim

Background

In this chapter we explain the background to the emergence of alternative education in Korea. We then go on to describe the different forms of alternative education in Korea and the different groups it serves before discussing the policy context for this development and the role of legislation and policy. Finally we reflect on some of the questions that alternative education raises and suggest that mainstream schools have much to learn from alternative approaches if we are to address the very high youth suicide rates in Korea and find an improved balance between academic success and personal health and well-being.

As with many other countries, the emergence of mass schooling in Korea[1] has been closely related to the goal of nation development (Meyer *et al.*, 1992; Ramirez and Boli, 1987). In the mid-twentieth century there was great political upheaval in Korea, with the ending of Japanese control, the beginning of the Cold War and then the Korean War (1950–3), which led to the nation being divided into North and South Korea. During the period of Japanese control, educational opportunities were very limited but following the end of the Korean War and with a centralized education system, families embraced elementary school enrolment with great enthusiasm. This led rapidly to the expansion of secondary schools using private resources (Kim, 2002). For the state, the main aim was to meet the newly decolonized society's need for a qualified workforce to help modernize and rebuild the nation. In their efforts, the state was supported by economic arguments showing a strong correlation between school enrolment and economic development (Kim, 2002; T. Kim, 2006). This approach to mass schooling has been effective in establishing strong national wealth, but has not been without adverse consequences. In the sections that follow we discuss the development of Korea's highly successful education system, some of these negative consequences and how the values of alternative education may help change this.

From the early 1950s to the 1980s Korea was led by a military dictatorship, which initiated a form of compressed economic development, known as 'The Miracle on the Han River'. This was implemented strategically through a series of five-year economic development plans (1962–86), with schools, the workplace and society in general adopting a one-for-all approach that promoted civic values of conformity, adherence, anti-communism and patriotic loyalty (Sorensen, 1994). During this time, democratic values had little place in schools and the social/civic purpose of education was underdeveloped.

At the same time, many Korean parents, keen for their children to share in the rising levels of prosperity, were turning to shadow education: private supplementary schooling, often known informally as cram schools (Yoon, 2014) to give their children an advantage. A recent study by Yang (2013) estimated that 2,041 million Korean Won was spent in 1982 on shadow education, rising to 25 trillion Korean Won in 2007. In this same time period, the difference in spending between the top 20 per cent income group and bottom 20 per cent income group also increased significantly. Following the Asian financial crisis in 1997, private spending abruptly increased, so that it is currently at levels close to national spending on public education (Yang, 2013). This level of spending by families on education leads to enormous stresses and burdens on students and their families amid fierce competition for places at elite colleges. Korean education is often called a 'pressure cooker', with Ripley (2013: 57) noting that 'Korean kids essentially go to school twice every weekday', once to regular schools and the second time to private cram schools in the evening. This means that children have very little or no free time, and this pressure begins as early as kindergarten, continuing through to college entrance exam stage.

The Korean higher education entrance exam is taken on one designated day each year by all applicants. Students know that they have just one opportunity on one day to show the fruits of 12 years of schooling, further intensifying the already severe pressures on students and their families. Seth (2002) described this annual event in *Education Fever*:

A great air of tension hovered through South Korea on 17 November 1999. A special task force had spent months planning for that day. The night before, President Kim Dae Jung had appeared on television to announce that the nation was prepared for the event. All nonessential governmental workers would report to work only later in the morning, as would employees of major firms. Thousands of special duty police were on hand in many cities; thirteen thousand police had been mobilized in Seoul alone. Flights at all the nation's airports had been restricted, and special efforts had been made to halt construction to avoid creating noise or commotion of any kind. It was the day of the national university entrance examinations. (Seth, 2002: 1)

In our view, all this pressure leads to a kind of 'Prisoners' Dilemma'[2] for parents, with a lack of information and trust preventing co-operation to find the best solutions (Park, 2011). Inevitably, the pressures of such a competitive school climate and social expectations affect children and adolescents, and their distress is shown in a variety of ways, such as suicide, school bullying, and deviant behaviour. In Korea, annual rates of youth suicide have drastically increased over time and often peak around the time of the college entrance exams.

As the 1960s drew to a close, some Korean activists began to raise concerns about the effects of this system, calling for a more democratic approach. Their arguments gained ground in the 1980s and culminated in the 1987 Seoul Spring (Lee, 2010). The national teachers' union played a major part in this in the 1980s, voicing strong criticism of state-dominated, ideologically driven educational practice and raising important questions about what they saw as an inhumane and undemocratic schooling system that was failing to tackle educational inequality and lacked a sense of purpose beyond immediate economic imperatives (Cho-Han *et al.*, 2007). Questions about the state-controlled regime's control over its people in terms of schooling, ideology, thoughts and activity (Desjardins, 2013) continued despite the sacking of teachers who had voiced these criticisms (Cho-Han *et al.*, 2007) and concerns about the overall quality of education (Cheng, 1992). This led some small groups and individuals to begin a search for new, more democratic kinds of schooling, with some of the teachers who had lost their jobs as a result of criticizing the government taking up work in alternative schools (Cho-Han *et al.*, 2007).

As the 1980s and 1990s progressed, and at the same time as the success of Korea's education system was drawing increased international interest and plaudits, the state and the general public were also becoming alarmed by the very high levels of youth suicide (Cho-Han *et al.*, 2007; Lee, 2013), so that by the late 1990s there were calls to address what many now saw as a crisis in education (Lee, 2013; Seo, 2003, 2006). Calls for change gained further support from the annual analysis of the Korean child well-being index and its international comparison with other OECD countries, which started in 2009 and still continues. The well-being indexes used in this analysis are based on the UNICEF report, *Comparing child well-being in OECD countries: Concepts and methods* (Bradshaw *et al.*, 2007). Korea is not a participant in the UNICEF comparison study, but the research team uses multi-dimensional indexes and surveys on Korean children and adolescents, and compares the results with other OECD countries (Park *et al.*, 2010). Since 2009 (with the exception of 2015) Korea has consistently scored lower than all the other OECD countries on measures of subjective well-being.

The birth of Korean alternative education and civic society

Around the end of the 1980s and into the early 1990s, alternative education was mainly associated with camps and after-school and weekend programmes (Cho-Han *et al.*, 2007; Lee, 2013), but in February 1995, 47 teachers and scholars from 17 different groups gathered to share concerns about the problems in society and to look for new directions in education. This gathering was known as 'The meeting for people who dream of a new school' (Cho-Han *et al.*, 2007; Song, 2005). In the same year, another group organized 'A workshop searching for alternative education' and in the following year, the first group held another meeting and discussed a plan for building a new school. Some individuals from the latter group also participated in this event, developing ideas for an alternative education community that might not be necessarily associated with the school establishment. In the winter of 1996/7, a third meeting took place, and for the first time the term 'alternative school' was used instead of 'new school', since it was felt that this better described the critical views of public schooling and its monolithic values. The core ideas for this new movement were that education should be humanistic, holistic or ecological, and that the school itself should be small in size, with local community governance (Song, 2005). Since 1995, alternative educators have organized an annual meeting, 'The alternative education *hanmadang* (festival)', to present a variety of practice models and to increase public understanding and awareness of alternative education. It has gradually attracted more and more parents and students, and it is estimated that 260 alternative schools have been established outside the state system since 1995 (Lee, 2013).

Twenty years later, it is still difficult to articulate one precise definition of alternative education and the alternative school in Korea. In part, this is because the pioneering scholars who advocated alternative education movement did not set out to develop a theory. They expected that practice in the long term would lead to theory (Song, 2005). Rather than settling on one particular form or definition, the alternative approach is generally held to contrast with public education and formal schooling (Shin and Nho, 2007).

Types of alternative education

Within a necessarily broad definition of alternative education, then, we find examples such as innovative education, experiential learning, identity development and career choice exploration, whole-person character education and an ecological approach. Sometimes this is combined with communal living; sometimes it has particular driving principles such as commitment to peace education or global citizenship. Often it is characterized by a climate of care for students (Cho-Han *et al.*, 2007).

Cho-Han *et al.* (2007) have classified three common types of alternative school. First, there are schools with a traditional school structure, often mainly financed by parents and civic endowments, which operate in a regular school building and have a large school roll, but are distinguished from public schooling by a distinct ideology and an alternative approach to pedagogy, emphasizing co-operation and coexistence rather than individualistic competition for college entrance. Gandhi Youth School and Ewoo School are two such kinds of alternative school. These are often middle-class schools that educate students who tend to go on to higher education. The second type of alternative school is called 'group homeschooling', where like-minded families gather together to teach their children in an informal setting. An extension of group homeschooling is the group home, which emerged particularly after the Asian financial crisis in 1997, and in which young people, often from families heavily affected by the crisis, live and learn together. It is important to note that homeschooling is not officially sanctioned in Korea, although plans are being developed to address this. The third type of alternative school supports young people traditionally regarded as 'misfits'. These students come from across the socio-economic spectrum. Student profiles are varied and include those with high levels of creativity and motivation who are seeking an innovative environment, but also include those who are demotivated and lethargic. The common solution for them is an individualized approach. Some will argue that this individualized teaching is very expensive, but we suggest that by co-ordinating community resources these costs can be much reduced.

Each of these three types of alternative education, despite their differences, shares a commitment to values that have been largely neglected within the Korean public school system. As with some other alternative education approaches internationally, such as Summerhill in the UK or Waldorf Steiner in Germany or 'back on track' schools in USA, they all have an orientation towards a more holistic education (Shin and Nho, 2007).

Policy intervention for dropout prevention and alternative education

Although the alternative education sector is still very small in Korea, it is possible to track how its emergence has echoed broader social and political changes over time as the country has moved away from military dictatorship and towards democracy. Understanding a particular education policy and its practices requires understanding of the context in any given society. Whether we take a functionalist or critical theorist view, it is always the case that school as an institution is shaped by its society's norms and structures (Paulston, 1994). The history of schools and society are always intertwined; in the case of Korea, attention has traditionally been given to expanding the quantity of education rather than addressing issues of equality of opportunity overall (Cheng, 1992).

Many of its values can be seen to align closely with those of Korean democratic activists, progressive Korean civic society (Seo, 2016) and political change overall. Kim Young-sam, for example, was a popular democratic activist, long-time leader of the opposition and, from 1993 to 1998, the country's first civilian president in over 30 years. During his time in office, the first full-time alternative school was officially established. The two succeeding presidents, Kim Dae-jung and Rho Moo-hyun, were also strong democratic activists and under their watch, public social expenditure increased and social policy was systematized (Choi, 2014). In this climate alternative schools and progressive education were also supported.

As a result of public outcry about the schooling crisis in the 1990s, the government announced a plan for school diversification in 1995. The plan included the introduction of vocationally focused Specialized High Schools (e.g. design, media, cooking) to be benchmarked against US magnet schools (Cho-Han *et al.*, 2007), and included alternative schools in this category. A year later, in 1996, in response to the stark rise in the dropout rate, the government announced a full plan for dropout prevention. While searching for solutions, the Secretary of Education visited an alternative school and acknowledged that it could be an effective model for intervention, and this led to state approval of the alternative-education specialized school and six other schools in this category in 1998 (Cho-Han *et al.*, 2007). The category included Gandhi Youth School and other religious-based schools that mainly support marginalized students. This enabled these alternative schools to be formally recognized for the first time, bringing to an end the threat of legal action for operating an unauthorized school (H. Kim, 2006). These specialized schools are permitted some curriculum flexibility – 30 per cent in middle schools and 70 per cent in high schools – but are still required to teach the national core curriculum (Cho-Han *et al.*, 2007).

However, this level of flexibility does not grant the freedom and autonomy that many alternative schools have sought (Cho-Han *et al.*, 2007) and in reality, the requirement to follow the core curriculum means that the curriculum flexibility is limited only to the specialist subjects (H. Kim, 2006). As of 2016, 38 alternative-education specialized schools had been approved, six of which are public and the rest private (Ministry of Education, 2016). Approximately 70 per cent of these are religious-based and around 50 per cent are located in rural areas, often for ecological purposes but also because of the more affordable land prices in rural areas. According to 2006 statistics, 90 per cent of graduates of these specialized schools go on to college, 2 per cent choose to work, and 8 per cent have a gap year (Cho-Han *et al.*, 2007).

It was not until 2005 that Congress passed legislation to add alternative schools into the category 'other types of schools', so that 'alternative school' was recognized as an official term and those schools could now can seek official authorization as places of education. This legislation defines alternative schools as schools that provide a variety of different kinds of education, such as experience-based education or field education, education for those who have dropped out of school, or for students seeking an individualized education programme. The legislation also exempts alternative schools from certain rules governing regular schools, such as those related to teacher qualifications and training, curriculum, class size, student records, age and stage progression, prescribed textbooks, and management. Alternative schools can now legally offer, for example, a curriculum that integrates elementary, middle, and high school level in one class. The national core curriculum requirement is limited to only two subjects: Korean and social studies (Korea Ministry of Government Legislation, 2016). All in all, these clauses give individual alternative schools much greater space for freedom and autonomy.

Nonetheless, it is estimated that approximately 260 non-authorized alternative education institutions still exist (Lee, 2013) compared with only 25 authorized institutions at elementary and secondary levels, six of which are public and 19 private (Ministry of Education, 2016). These non-authorized alternative education providers recognize the importance of credentials and the benefit of public funding but question whether the recently introduced legal provisions about curriculum, for example, give them the freedom they are looking for (H. Kim, 2006). There are also practical barriers to becoming an authorized alternative education provider. Legally, the bar is set higher for alternative schools than for regular schools in terms of, for example, buildings regulations and financial oversight. In 2014 the government moved to introduce a registration system for alternative education that would have led to the closure of non-authorized institutions over concerns about excessive tuition fees and health and safety issues (Byun, 2015). However, this proposal was controversial and subsequent protests led the government to withdraw its plan (Byun, 2015).

Alongside these independent alternative education providers, the state has also provided alternative education within the public school system since 2001, primarily for dropout prevention (Cho-Han *et al.*, 2007). This takes two forms; commissioned alternative education arranged by regional education offices and more recently, via alternative classrooms within schools (Lee *et al.*, 2014). The former is a transfer programme that enables young people to move to youth centres, lifelong institutions or social welfare organizations while maintaining their student registration in schools for approximately one year. Only a third of the common curriculum is required and the rest of the time is spent on a variety of youth programmes. The system of alternative classrooms within schools provides a separate class within elementary and secondary schools and partially or fully replaces the regular curriculum. The alternative curriculum is devised by teachers and overseen by the school principal, and may include, for example, group counselling, cooking, crafts, career guidance and work experience (Lee *et al.*, 2014).

School choice and the political economy of alternative education in the twenty-first century

During the 1960s and 1970s, under the influence of critical thinkers such as Ivan Illich, A.S. Neill, Hartmut von Hentig, John Holt, Jonathan Kozol, Herbert Kohl, and Paulo Freire there was upsurge of concern about public schooling, its forms and purposes (Sliwka, 2008). These critical ideas found widespread support among students and teachers, leading to popular demonstrations and student strikes as part of a widespread social movement. During this time Korea was pursuing its compressed economic development and it was not until the democratization movement of the 1990s that support for alternative schools and alternative education approaches took hold in Korea, leading to wider support for greater diversification, parental rights and school choice.

The debate over parents' rights in education was often central to the development of alternative education. The majority of Korean cities and regions have adopted an egalitarian approach to education, aimed at ensuring social integration and equality (Jung, 2012). This policy is perhaps best exemplified by its commitment to a randomized school assignment policy, known as the High School Equalization Policy, within which secondary school students are allocated to schools near their homes by a lottery system (Byun, 2010). However, this policy has become increasingly controversial, with some arguing about its effectiveness while others have raised concerns that it is unconstitutional (Jung, 2012) because it does not acknowledge the individual rights of parents over their child's development (Han, 2008).

It is interesting to see how these social concerns have been reframed in the neoliberal era and in light of the prominence of a marketized education system and ideology (Angus, 2015; Hyslop-Margison and Sears, 2006). Global neoliberalism has, in our view, had a negative effect on the original purposes of alternative education, with its commitment to whole-person learning and collaboration rather than competition (Angus, 2015). Some alternative schools established since 2000 now offer curricula aligned to neoliberal values and expect very high levels of time spent on study. Our concern is that by allowing some alternative schools to become educational institutions for the privileged few, the principles and values that led people to first seek an alternative to public education in Korea risk being seriously undermined.

This also raises a question about the relationship between mainstream public education and alternative education. We have noted that the strengths of alternative education, as it developed in Korea, lie, for example, in its recognition of the value of school diversification and the assertion of parental rights. But we also see that once adopted by the state, school choice and parental rights are likely to be gradually expanded and lead to greater social inequality. History shows that diversification often equates with stratification in reality, which legitimates social reproduction of class through schooling (Bourdieu and Passeron, 1977), even in socially democratic countries like Sweden let alone the UK, the USA and Australia, once school choice has been adopted (Angus, 2015). So there is an interesting dilemma here and one that calls for deeper engagement with ideas about the relationship between state and parents in Korean civic society. We suggest that it is important to see parents not simply as consumers in discussions regarding school diversification issues. While it is essential to respect individual values and approaches, education also carries societal/civic values that should be actively encouraged. In the neoliberal context, school diversification based on market principles can limit learners' capacity as citizens and weaken social integration by facilitating social polarization. In our view, therefore, it is vital that the state seeks to mitigate the neoliberal impact of policies by encouraging emphasis on a collaboratively strong civic society.

We believe, therefore, that there should be a strong case for wholescale qualitative reform of Korean public schooling. Korean education is internationally regarded as a highly successful system and the quality of school education has improved in many ways in the last 20 years, in terms of access to education, teacher–student ratios, education expenditure and facilities. However, intense pressure and high stakes testing have often led to neglect of whole-person education and democratic school management (an exception is the innovative public school system supported by Gyeonggi education office, launched and spread in recent years by a progressive superintendent of education). If the alternative education ideals can be shared beyond the very small number of students that benefit – currently 0.2–0.3 per cent of the total student population (Lee, 2013) – then the overall quality of schooling for all children and young people in Korea can be improved.

Finally, it is important to acknowledge that even where there are alternative schools doing excellent work, they do so in the context of a mainstream society, governed by neoliberal ideology, an instrumental idea of education, competitive and inhumane work practices and corporate economic logic. Education is seen to offer the most important path to success in Korean society, but there is a widening gap in student outcomes. For example, entry-level income is likely to be highest for those who have attended a top ten university. The gap, for instance, between 26- to 28-year-old males with equal university qualifications from a top ten and other universities has drastically widened over time: 4 per cent in 1999, 10.8 per cent in 2002 and 23 per cent in 2008 (Ko, 2011). Likewise, the suicide rates give cause for serious concern. A rate of 15.2 per 100,000 in 1996 rose to 21.7 per 100,000 in 1998 and 33.5 per 100,000 in 2010 (OECD Data, 2016).

This narrowly focused and competitive education system may also affect motivations behind the kinds of college major choices and career choices made by individuals – as we have witnessed, a majority of college students now prefer science and engineering to humanities or social sciences. Although research on this particular aspect is limited, we draw here on reflections on a visit we made to Germany to study dropout provision there in 2014. We were struck by the fact that while exemplary dropout prevention practices in Germany were similar to Korean practices (e.g. community-based experiential learning), parental engagement and student participation were much higher. We saw much less of the student resistance to alternative education which is still prevalent in Korea. We noted that vocationally focused schools have their own identity and that students in them take pride in developing their aptitudes and achieving their potential. In this context, young people at risk of dropping out or academically underachieving have a second chance and often make good use of it.

It is a paradox that Korea has one of the lowest dropout rates in the OECD countries, but as we have discussed in this chapter, this arises from the pressures to succeed in a highly competitive society. We have discussed our concerns that the high levels of academic achievement expected of students impact significantly on their quality of life and discourage the development of a variety of talents and aptitudes. We suggest that the values of alternative education and the breadth of learning that alternative schools encourage are necessary for all children and young people and that public education must now learn from alternative education to bring about change for all.

Notes

[1] This chapter focuses on South Korean education and 'Korea' here refers to South Korea; 'Korean' refers to South Korean.

[2] Korean scholars often use the term 'Prisoners' Dilemma', as educational competition is so high that it leads to an undesirable situation for students and parents. The prisoners' dilemma results from multiple parties pursuing self-interest, rather than co-operating for the benefit of all. That is to say, Korean parents spend too much on extra educational experiences even though only a handful of students may succeed in the college admission competition.

References

Angus, L. (2015) 'School choice: Neoliberal education policy and imagined futures'. *British Journal of Sociology of Education*, 36 (3), 395–413.

Bourdieu, P. and Passeron, J.C. (1977) *Reproduction in Education, Society and Culture*. Beverly Hills: Sage.

Bradshaw, J., Hoelscher, P. and Richardson, D. (2007). Comparing Child Well-Being in OECD Countries: Concepts and methods, *Innocenti Working Papers* no. 2006-03: Unicef.

Byun, S. (2010). 'Does policy matter in shadow education spending? Revisiting the effects of the High School Equalization Policy in South Korea'. *Asia Pacific Education Review*, 11 (1), 83–96.

Byun, T. (2015) 교육부, 대안학교 등록제 반년 만에 없던 일로 [The Ministry of Education, please bump that alternative school registration system]. *Korea Times*, January 16. Online. www.hankookilbo.com/v/671e3af3a48d44dd86b45 76abc071983 (accessed 23 February 2018).

Cheng, T.J. (1992). 'Dilemmas and choices in educational policies: The case of South Korea and Taiwan'. *Studies in Comparative International Development*, 27 (4), 54–79.

Cho-Han, H., Kim, J., Lee, E. and Lee, M. (2007) 대안교육백서: 1997–2007 [Alternative education white paper: 1997–2007]. Seoul: Ministry of Education.

Choi, B. (2014) 'The past and future of Korea's social welfare policy'. *Journal of Budget and Policy*, 3 (1), 89–129.

Desjardins, R. (2013) 'Considerations of the impact of neoliberalism and alternative regimes on learning and its outcomes: An empirical example based on the level and distribution of adult learning'. *International Studies in Sociology of Education*, 23 (3), 182–203.

Han, S. (2008) 교육을 받을 권리와 국가교육권한의 한계: 교육평준화 및 학교선택권 제한의 헌법적 한계를 중심으로 [The right to be educated and the limitation of state authority over education right: Focused the constitutional limitation of egalitarian education and school-choice restriction]. *Korean Lawyers Association Journal*, 57 (4), 5–46.

Hyslop-Margison, E.J. and Sears, A.M. (2006) *Neo-Liberalism, Globalization and Human Capital Learning: Reclaiming education for democratic citizenship*. Dordrecht: Springer.

Jung, Y. (2012) 헌법상 교육기본권과 학부모의 학교선택권 [The constitutional analysis on unconstitutionality of current equalitarian schooling: The constitutionalism on the legislature of school evenness]. *Hongik Law Review*, 11 (2), 255–82.

Kim, G.-J. (2002) 'Education policies and reform in South Korea'. In *Secondary Education in Africa: Strategies for renewal* (Africa Region Human Development Working Paper). Washington, DC: World Bank, 29–40.

Kim, H. (2006) 'A discussion on the institutionalization and legal direction of the alternative schools in Korea'. *Journal of Educational Idea*, 19, 1–22.

Kim, T. (2006) 교육열의 경제적 가치 추정을 위한 실증연구 [The empirical research of the economic value estimation of educational enthusiasm]. *Policy Research 2006–05*. Seoul: KDI.

Ko, E. (2011) 'Changes in wage differentials among college graduates in South Korea, 1999–2008'. *Korea Journal of Labor Economics*, 34 (1), 103–38.

Korea Ministry of Government Legislation (2016) 대안교육 특성화고등학교 [Alternative education-specialized high school]. Online. http://oneclick.law. go.kr/CSP/CnpClsMain.laf?csmSeq=745&ccfNo=3&cciNo=4&cnpClsNo=2 (accessed 23 February 2018).

Lee, J. (2013) 대안교육에 대한 소고 [A brief view of alternative education]. *Education Review*, 32, 87–110.

Lee, M. (2010) *The History of the Democratization Movement in Korea*. Seoul: Korea Democracy Foundation. Online. http://en.kdemo.or.kr/book/data/book/ page/3/post/8304 (accessed 23 February 2018).

Lee, S., Park, H. and Kim, S. (2014) 학업중단 예방 법령┌제도 국제비교 및 시사점 도출연구 [Dropout prevention legislation and system international comparison and analysis study]. Sejong: Ministry of Education.

Lee, S.-M., Yu, K. and Lee, S.-H. (2005) 'Helping academic development of low socioeconomic status students: The role of school counselors in Korea'. *Asian Journal of Counselling*, 12 (1–2), 47–77.

Meyer, J.W., Ramirez, F.O. and Soysal, Y.N. (1992) 'World expansion of mass education, 1870–1980'. *Sociology of Education*, 65 (2), 128–49.

Ministry of Education (2016) 2016년 대안학교 및 대안교육 특성화 중고등학교 현황 [2016 the current state of alternative schools and alternative-education specialized middle and high schools]. Online. www.moe.go.kr/boardCnts/view.do?boardID=348&lev=0&statusYN=W&s=moe&m=040103&opType=N&boardSeq=63032 (accessed 23 February 2018).

OECD Data (2016) 'Suicide rates: Total, per 100,000 persons, 1988–2013'. Online. https://data.oecd.org/healthstat/suicide-rates.htm (accessed 8 March 2017).

Park, J. (2011) 'Government as a solution of prisoner's dilemma'. *Korean Journal of Philosophy*, 108, 149–71.

Park, J., Park, C., Seo, H. and Youm, Y. (2010) 'Collection of Korean child well-being index and its international comparison with other OECD countries'. *Korean Journal of Sociology*, 44 (2), 121–54.

Paulston, R.G. (1994) 'Comparative and international education: Paradigms and theories'. In Husén, T. and Postlethwaite, T.N. (eds) *The International Encyclopedia of Education* (Vol. 2). 2nd ed. Oxford: Pergamon, 923–33.

Ramirez, F.O. and Boli, J. (1987) 'The political construction of mass schooling: European origins and worldwide institutionalization'. *Sociology of Education*, 60 (1), 2–17.

Ripley, A. (2013) *The Smartest Kids in the World: And how they got that way*. New York: Simon and Schuster.

Seo, D. (2003) '교실붕괴'기사에 대한 비판적 담론 분석: 조선일보를 중심으로 [A critical discourse analysis on the 'classroom collapse' reports: Focusing on the Chosun Ilbos]. *Anthropology of Education*, 6 (2), 55–89.

Seo, D. (2006) '교실붕괴'이후 신자유주의 교육담론의 형성과 그 저항 [The formation of neo-liberal discourse on education after 'classroom collapse', and resistance to it: A critical discourse analysis on homeschooling reports in South Korea]. *Korean Journal of Sociology of Education*, 16 (1), 77–105.

Seo, Y. (2016) 혁신학교가 만들어가는 민주·대안적 학습생태계 [Innovative school creating democratic and alternative learning ecology]. Online. www.kdemo.or.kr/blog/school/post/1234 (accessed 23 February 2018).

Seth, M.J. (2002) *Education Fever: Society, politics, and the pursuit of schooling in South Korea*. Honolulu: University of Hawai'i Press.

Shin, H. and Nho, C. (2007) 'Comparative study on internalizing and externalizing problems among students at alternative and regular high schools'. *Mental Health and Social Work*, 27, 199–229.

Sliwka, A. (2008) 'The contribution of alternative education'. In Centre for Educational Research and Innovation *Innovating to Learn, Learning to Innovate*. Paris: OECD Publishing, 93–112.

Song, S. (2005) 'The evolution, characteristics, and major issues in "alternative education" in Korea'. *Journal of Holistic Education*, 9 (2), 33–56.

Sorensen, C.W. (1994) 'Success and education in South Korea'. *Comparative Education Review*, 38 (1), 10–35.

Yang, J. (2013) 'Analyzing the trends of private tutoring expenditure from 1982 to 2017'. *Korean Journal of Educational Administration*, 31 (4), 421–48.

Yoon, K. (2014) 'The change and structure of Korean education policy in history'. *Italian Journal of Sociology of Education*, 6 (2), 173–200.

Chapter 4

Alternative provision in England: Problematizing quality and vulnerability

Jodie Pennacchia and Pat Thomson

Introduction

Across the past 25 years English education policy has espoused a commitment to inclusive education, and the ideal of educating all young people together in mainstream schools has been enshrined in law since 1993 (DfES, 2001; DfE and Department of Health, 2015). Despite this, a minority of young people continue to be permanently excluded from school every year. Official figures showed that in 2015/16 there were 6,685 permanent exclusions across all state-funded primary, secondary and special schools (DfE, 2017). During the same academic year there were a further 339,360 fixed period exclusions (DfE, 2017). (These exclude a pupil for a predetermined amount of time, although fixed period exclusions cannot total more than 45 school days for a pupil in a single academic year.) In this context, Alternative Provision (AP) remains an integral part of the educational landscape in England. Its role is to provide a full-time education for young people who have been permanently excluded. The government has also defined AP as a provision for improving behaviour (DfE, 2013). In such cases, AP may become a complementary feature of a young person's educational entitlement where they are felt to be at risk of permanent exclusion (DfE, 2013; Pennacchia and Thomson, 2016). The full extent of AP usage in the English context remains unclear because data showing the number of young people receiving some support from a complementary AP provider are not available (Ogg and Kaill, 2010).

The gradual reduction of permanent exclusions since their peak in the late 1990s obscures important questions about the minority of young people who continue to be excluded from school and who receive the support of AP. Stubborn patterns continue to mark exclusionary practices. Higher rates of exclusion are experienced by older students, boys, those in receipt of free school meals, those with SEND (Special Educational Needs and Disabilities), Black Caribbean pupils, and pupils from Gypsy/Roma and Traveller or Irish heritage ethnic groups (DfE, 2016b). (With regard to free school meals, entitlement beyond Year 2 of compulsory education is linked to receipt of other means-tested state benefits in England. It is widely used as a proxy for poverty in government statistics and education research, although it is a crude measure.) These are not groups who do well on measures of attainment. Data show that 1.3 per cent of young people in AP achieve the dominant performance measure of five or more A*–C GCSE grades including English and Mathematics (DfE, 2015) compared to 59.2 per cent of their peers in all state-funded schools (DfE, 2016b). This bodes poorly for their future opportunities. However, as there is no systematic data on those who have experienced some form of complementary AP but stayed within the mainstream, it is difficult to track outcomes for all young people who access AP. Nonetheless, the lower test and examination results of young people who attend AP rather than mainstream school has been used to justify increased focus on the operations and quality of these provisions (Ofsted, 2016; Taylor, 2012).

In this chapter we explore the discourses that surround AP in contemporary policy texts in England, at a time when there is increased scrutiny of the quality of AP. We aim to understand how AP and the young people who attend it are represented and produced through policy documents that contend with the 'improvement' of AP. We engage critically with these texts through three interlinked analytical phases. First, we draw on the work of Carol Bacchi to position the idea of problematizations as central to current conceptualizations of AP and those who attend it. Second, we refer to findings from a 2014 UK-wide study of quality in AP in order to consider the effects of policy representations on practice. Third, the English case is compared with the Scottish context to illuminate the way choices have been made about how to represent and reform AP, and to challenge the inevitabilities of policy direction. The chapter begins by introducing the policy context for AP in England.

Research and policy context: Improving the quality of AP

The term AP applies to diverse educational offerings in the English context (IOE and NFER, 2013). These vary according to a number of features: the length of placement; the number of hours young people attend; the location of the provision (e.g. in/out of school, further education colleges, work-places, churches and other community buildings); and the curriculum offering (e.g. national curriculum, apprenticeship-style or vocational learning, arts-based curricula) (Thomson and Pennacchia, 2014). There is an array of

AP providers including local authorities (LAs), further education colleges, independent providers, charities, churches and schools with their own in-house provision (Ogg and Kaill, 2010; Taylor, 2012). Keeping track of the number and types of AP provisions is a difficult task. The flexible nature of AP, and the often precarious nature of its funding, means that providers come and go from one academic year to the next (Thomson and Russell, 2009). The latest statistics show that 21,403 students of compulsory school age and above are registered with an alternative provider (including pupil referral units) as their sole or shared main school registration (DfE, 2016c). Grey areas remain in the processes of accounting for the number of young people in AP. For instance, the above figure excludes 10,424 pupils who are dual registered, but where the AP provision is not their main, or joint main, provision (DfE, 2016c). Furthermore, there continue to be unregistered APs and undocumented use of them (Ofsted, 2016). Provisions are inspected if they are registered, which they must be if they provide full-time education to five or more pupils of compulsory schooling age, or one pupil who has a statement of special educational needs (Ofsted, 2016). However, it is unclear whether unregistered provisions are documented in government statistics and reports on AP. It is also unclear whether schools that pay for alternative providers to work inhouse are required to account for this to their various auditors. This means that the full extent of AP usage in England remains ambiguous.

A substantial international literature on AP practices draws attention to the unique and diverse nature of provisions for young people who have been or are at risk of being excluded from school. The best practice literatures on AP reveal remarkable consistency across countries and time (Thomson, 2014). AP is characterized by:

- flexibility
- curriculum specialisms, particularly in relation to vocational options, outdoor learning and the arts
- less hierarchical and more personal teaching and learning relationships
- teachers with pedagogical approaches that cover young people's social and emotional development, as well as their intellectual development, where the young person is 'visible in their full humanity'. (Pirrie *et al.*, 2011: 536)

For a fuller discussion of the best practice features of AP see Thomson, 2014).Where the views of young people accessing AP have been sought, these have emphasized the quality of relationships as particularly important. Less hierarchical relationships, where students felt they were listened to and understood rather than shouted at and too frequently disciplined, have been repeatedly highlighted in research (e.g. Mills *et al.*, 2016; Pennacchia and Thomson, 2016). Students in AP also speak of valuing the greater independence and choice they are given, the smaller class sizes and lower pupil–teacher ratio, and the flexible and relevant nature of the curriculum (Hallam *et al.*, 2007).

Over the past decade, there has been increased policy interest in demarcating the nature and function of AP, on improving its quality, and on governing its 'transformation' (DCSF, 2008: 1). This marks a departure from the historical neglect of AP, which, in England as elsewhere, has been accused of being a 'dumping ground' for 'difficult' students (Mills *et al.*, 2013). The traditional ability of AP to operate outside mainstream accountability frameworks has been key to creating room for the curriculum flexibilities and less hierarchical relationships that characterize these provisions. However, this flexibility and the ambiguous relationship with accountability frameworks has also become the locus of criticisms of AP. A variety of concerns have been raised, including:

- inequitable access to good quality provision
- unsatisfactory pupil outcomes
- lack of curriculum breadth
- unsafe buildings and spaces
- poor safeguarding
- ambiguous registration and inspection procedures
- erratic behaviour management
- negligible tracking of pupils post AP
- inadequacies in commissioning, referral and reintegration processes. (DCSF, 2008; Ofsted, 2011; Pirri *et al.*, 2011; Taylor, 2012; Ofsted, 2016)

The focus on improving AP is important, but is also potentially problematic. Young people accessing AP have existed on the periphery of education. The diversity of AP has been its unique offering, but this is also a site of inequality, where young people have received variable access to their educational entitlement and to a fulfilling education. There has been consistent evidence over time that supports the criticisms raised in policy texts; such studies take a range of different perspectives, and predate the current concentrated policy concern over quality AP (Thomson, 2014). Our own research has documented the continued presence of an 'out of sight, out of mind approach' detrimental to the care and education of some young people (Thomson and Pennacchia, 2014). There are ongoing issues over the consistency of staff training and development in AP, including in particularly concerning areas such as safeguarding children (Ofsted, 2016). The negative impacts of exclusion from school have been carefully documented across a large body of research (Blyth and Milner, 1993; Evans, 2010; Lumby, 2012; McCluskey *et al.*, 2016). Addressing some of these issues, and giving more attention to young people on the periphery of education, is a core and pressing social justice issue.

However, we take Bacchi's (1999) point that policy presentations of a problem and its solution are never neutral statements of the facts of an area of government policy and reform. Instead they are constructions, and a site where choices and judgements are being made. Taking this perspective as our starting point we analyse the current problematizations of AP policy in England, beginning with the 2008 Department for Children, Schools and Families strategy for modernizing AP and ending with the 2016 Ofsted review. We focus on this period of time first because we want to understand the contemporary positioning of AP, and second because of the attention across this period of time to the task of improving the quality of AP, despite changes in government. We begin by outlining Bacchi's approach as a tool for interrogating AP policy, before detailing the texts our analysis has drawn on.

Bacchi's WPR approach

Bacchi's WPR (What's the Problem Represented to be) approach is informed by the Foucaultian tradition of discourse analysis and offers a toolkit for interrogating policy problematizations (Bacchi, 2012). Bacchi's starting point is that policymakers' agendas reveal, either explicitly or implicitly, what they think needs to change, and thus reveals their conceptualization of 'the problem' (Bacchi, 1999). Bacchi's approach entails a shift from viewing policy proposals as neutral problem statements, representations and solutions, to viewing them as acts of interpretation that are shaped by judgements and values (Bacchi, 1999). The 'taken for granted truths' of a policy are understood as constructions, and thus their status as 'inevitable' or 'common-sense' is challenged. It thus becomes important to probe the assumptions that are inherent in policy proposals.

Bacchi's approach encourages us to question what is left unsaid or unproblematic within AP policy proposals, and how different representations of the AP 'problem' might lead to different solutions, and indeed different methods of governance (Bacchi, 1999). Bacchi offers a set of questions as a starting point for the WPR approach. These are presented as an adaptable tool rather than a strict formula for research. We focus here on the following questions about AP policy in the English context:

1. What is the problem of alternative provision represented to be in the policy debates since 2008 in the English context?
2. What presuppositions and assumptions underlie this representation of the problem?
3. What effects are produced by this representation?
4. What is left unproblematic in this problem representation?
5. How would 'responses' differ if the 'problem' were thought about or represented differently? (After Bacchi, 1999: 13)

Our analysis draws on reviews of AP from 2008 to the present. Since New Labour's 2008 report on AP, which 'set out a new strategy for transforming the quality of alternative educational provision' (DCSF, 2008: 1), there has been a series of reports focused on the task of naming the problems with AP and proposing solutions. Successive governments have responded to reports on the quality of AP, and commissioned further research, creating a traceable policy dialogue concerning the 'problems' and 'solutions' of AP. The following reports have been key to this discourse of quality:

*   Department for Children, Schools and Families (DCSF) (2008) *Back on Track: A strategy for modernising alternative provision for young people*
*   White, R., Martin, K. and Jeffes, J. (2012) *The Back on Track Alternative Provision Pilots: Final report* (Research Report RR250), Department for Education
*   Ofsted (2011) *Alternative Provision*
*   Taylor, C. (2012) *Improving Alternative Provision*, Department for Education
*   Department for Education (DfE) (2013). *Alternative Provision: Statutory guidance for local authorities*
*   IOE (Institute of Education) and NFER (2013 interim report) and (2014 final report) *School Exclusion Trial Evaluation*, London: Department for Education
*   Department for Education (DfE), 2010 to 2015 government policy: children outside mainstream education
*   Ofsted (2016) *Alternative Provision: The findings from Ofsted's three-year survey of schools' use of off-site alternative provision.*

We selected these texts because they were produced, commissioned, disseminated, endorsed by and/or engaged with by the government on their AP information pages at GOV.UK (DfE, 2015). The analysis that follows draws on these texts, reading across them to understand points of commonality and to trace the development of the concern with quality. The context for analysis is provided by the wider set of reports on AP and exclusion by other agencies and institutions (inter alia CSJ, 2011; OCC, 2013a and 2013b; Ogg and Kail, 2010; Evans, 2010).

Problematizing quality and/of AP

The overarching narrative thread across the reports we analysed depicts the 'problem' of AP to be one of inconsistent and insufficient quality. This discourse of concern over quality is conveyed through recurring critiques of particular areas of AP practice. Rather than take this emphasis on quality at face value, or as an unequivocally good thing, we argue that 'quality' merits deconstruction. Our task is to ask AP policy what it has 'to say about the problems with which it [is] confronted' and to 'question it about the positions it takes and the reasons it gives for this' (Foucault, 2003: 21). Our reading of the textual emphasis on ambiguous signifiers such as 'quality', 'improvement' and 'effectiveness' suggests that, in contemporary presentations of AP policy, the representation of 'the problem' is fraught and contradictory, and has potentially problematic implications for practice. We focus on two discursive fields that recur across the texts we analysed.

Representations of young people accessing AP

We start from the view that current policy conceptualizations of quality in AP produce particular subject positions. Nested within policy problematizations are particular representations of the young people located in AP. Across the corpus of documents, the contradictory positioning of young people who access AP occurs and re-occurs. The concern with quality in AP is frequently justified through discourses of 'vulnerability'. Young people accessing AP are represented as 'the most vulnerable and disenfranchised in our education system' (Ofsted, 2016: 5; IOE and NFER, 2014). Their vulnerability centres on key characteristics such as:

- having been excluded from school
- having short- or long-term medical issues
- being school phobic
- being pregnant or a parent
- being without a school place after newly arriving in a local authority area.

There is concern for the outcomes of these young people, who are perceived to be more likely to leave school without the qualifications they need to pursue further education or employment (Lumby, 2012). At the time of writing, Ofsted (2016) had noted continued concerns with safeguarding practices in AP, continued weaknesses in English and mathematics outcomes, and a lack of clarity concerning what constitutes good progress in AP settings. The concern over outcomes is underpinned by a view of the young person as a 'becoming' adult, who must contribute to society. This means being employable, if not actually employed. Additionally, to emphasize the particular vulnerability of young people who are excluded from school, links are made between exclusion from school and the likelihood of spending time in prison, a cost to the state and society more generally. We note that Charlie Taylor, the government's chief adviser on behaviour and a reviewer of AP practice, also conducted a review of children in custody (Taylor, 2016).

However, government policy discussions about AP are marked by an ongoing tension between divergent representations of young people, through which the 'vulnerability' of young people is problematized. Across the reports we analysed, young people accessing AP are simultaneously produced as 'vulnerable' and 'risky'. When the policy discourse on AP is positioned alongside wider discourses on exclusion, inclusion and discipline in schools, young people are framed as 'at risk' and 'a risk'. According to Bacchi, these must be seen as policy proposals. Since there are no fixed meanings for 'risk', the terms are used to suggest the 'right' course of action, to legitimize how policymakers and practitioners must proceed. To avoid risk to the young person and to society, government must act on and through AP to ensure that its economic and civic goals are met.

Alongside this concern for the vulnerability of young people accessing AP, behaviour in schools has been increasingly in focus. The history of inclusive policy and rhetoric has been marked by a fear of the young person whose behaviour threatens the achievement of others (Jonathan, 1997). Education is a project in which 'the good of all and the good of each interact (and often conflict) in particularly complex ways with respect to education's benefits' (Jonathan, 1997: 60). The apparent 'vulnerability' of young people accessing AP continues to be tempered by a wariness over their impact on other young people and on wider society. These young people are simultaneously positioned as vulnerable and as a threat to the performance of other children, and to the image and performance of their school. This is a long-standing tension, which has intensified in the 'pressure cooker' context of English education (Perryman *et al.*, 2011).

These fears remain present in current attempts to govern the quality of AP. Young people are increasingly located as a site where it is possible to see the failings of schools, parents and communities. The government's response to the 2011 riots and the 'troubled families' initiatives both highlighted the emphasis on narratives of individual deficit and responsibility (Cameron, 2011; Jones, 2016; Mckenzie, 2015; Crossley, 2016). We suggest that the focus on improving quality in AP is taking place alongside the desire to make young people and their parents more responsible for 'turn(ing) bad behaviour around' (DCSF, 2008: 4).

AP policy is thus marked by a double-edged, and rather contradictory framing of the young person, through variant formulations of 'the problem'. On the one hand, these are young people who deserve better and who are prone to poor educational outcomes and indeed life chances (Pirrie *et al.*, 2011). At the same time, the figure of the 'risky' student remains a shadowy presence through this discourse (Foucault, 1990). AP students are presented as a source of risk in the education sector and wider society. The product of these twin concerns can be seen in recent attempts to mould and shape AP practice and the forms of accountability and governance that have informed it.

Quality and accountability in AP

There is an apparent tension between the notions of quality that have come to dominate AP, and the recognition of what has characteristically been important about AP. Flexibility is generally seen as crucial for AP to fulfil its varied and complex role (IOE and NFER, 2014). There is recognition in government reports that flexibility is the lifeblood of AP: it depends on having 'a range of tailored provision geared to meeting diverse individual needs' (DCSF, 2008: 2), with provision starting 'from what will work best for each young person taking account of his or her different needs' (DCSF, 2008: 5). However, the current problematization of AP flexibility is coupled with a desire for closer, more systematized control and governance. There is increased emphasis on AP being held accountable, and on developing standards for 'robustly' measuring progress, success and failure (Ofsted, 2011: 6). In the current problematization of AP, measuring progress and success are crucial to the development of quality. Further, both the mechanisms for ensuring quality, and notions of what quality is, are understood through the lens of mainstream schooling. This denotes an important shift in how the work of AP is understood and valued.

All state-funded schools in England are subject to a policy agenda that positions benchmark standards and school comparisons as key policy levers for ensuring quality and accountability. These shifting benchmarks have also become the focus for evaluating the worth and quality of a school's work, inseparable from understandings of effective schooling. Practice has increasingly become tailored to the production of the data that matters (Ozga, 2009), with resources directed towards young people deemed most capable of achieving key benchmarks (Gillborn and Youdell, 2000; Ball *et al.*, 2012). The impact of this on inclusive work and exclusionary practices means that young people who 'will not or cannot accommodate the prevailing practice' are 'removed or disempowered, most commonly not through deliberate explicit exclusion but by subtle signals of their perceived outlier nature' (Lumby, 2012: 275). Quality as accountability thus not only leads to but also justifies practices of exclusion.

AP is being aligned with this overarching regime of monitoring and accountability. First, there has been a movement to require full-time, registered APs to meet a universal standards-based approach to accountability. The expectation that APs will cover the national curriculum and enable young people to sit national examinations, as they would in mainstream schools, has become commonplace (Thomson and Pennacchia, 2016).

Second, there are attempts to align with the mainstream through the extension of the academies policy. An AP can now become a stand-alone academy, be part of an AP trust, or become attached to a chain of mainstream academies. There are contradictions here between autonomy and regulation. The academies policy agenda suggests that APs can be higher quality if they have the greater autonomy that academy status brings, but at the same time that autonomy is being challenged through the implementation of standardized forms of accountability. This captures an ongoing tension in the wider education policy context between schools being individual and innovative, whilst conforming to benchmark standards that ensure the national curriculum is followed. In this context, the greater autonomy and flexibility schools are given is drawn on to justify individualized, standards-focused monitoring systems, as autonomy is combined with 'intelligent accountability' (DfE, 2016a). It is particularly interesting that AP, which is characteristically diverse, is now facing these challenges. We return to this point in the final section.

Third, one of the understandings of quality AP presented in policy is that AP is responsive to the needs of schools. Whereas traditionally AP has been valued for its responsiveness to the diverse needs of the students it caters for, it is now seen as an extension of, and a tool for supporting the work of, mainstream schools. This shift is justified on the basis of equity, where AP is presented as part of a continuum of provision that provides all young people with a high-quality education. Given AP's history of being siloed as a separate, lesser educational offering, this approach may be justifiable. However, our concern is that the current process is not designed to create parity of esteem across education provisions. If a principle for reforming APs is to make them more responsive to the needs of schools, given the current high stakes culture of mainstream schools, the role of AP as a tool for facilitating an unchanged mainstream context is being cemented. The increased monitoring of AP provision, in ways which align with schools, serves the dual purpose of schools being able to document their continued interest in, and monitoring of, those students they send off-site, whilst allowing them to make a quicker assessment of whether a student has made sufficient improvement in their behaviour and/or achievement for them to return to the mainstream setting. Thus, whilst the 'out of sight, out of mind' approach to AP has been long-standing, bringing AP into the spotlight for accountability in the current context of high stakes performance adds to this ongoing concern a new set of problems.

Governing quality, accountability and the management of risk

So far, we have argued that the increased focus on governing quality in AP, and the fraught conceptualization of young people accessing AP, maps onto the notions of quality as accountability that are materializing through policy. The notions of quality that are being formed through current policy work on AP seem geared more to the management of risk than they are about the young person's marginalization, or the educational factors that contribute to this. The excluded child continues to be problematized and located as a site for transformation. AP provides the services to do this, and notions of quality attend to the nature and efficiency of these transformations. This has led to particular forms of monitoring in AP, which we describe in the next section.

We suggest that in the current problematizations of quality in AP, the very need for such provisions to exist remains unproblematic. The question of why young people with particular characteristics continue to have damaging educational experiences is skirted around in the emphasis on getting them 'back on track' (DCSF, 2008). The problem is either with the young person, the quality of AP, or schools' commissioning and overseeing of AP. The problems that lead to formal exclusion and the commissioning of AP are absent, even though 'school exclusion raises economic, political, social and historical issues which go to the heart of questions about an equitable and just society' (Ashurst and Venn, 2014: 1).

We are also concerned that the direction of current quality governance is promoting a narrow conceptualization of quality that risks narrowing and instrumentalizing the characteristic flexibility of AP. Our concern is about a process of governing quality and practice in AP, through mainstream understanding and processes, which ignores the role these very processes have played in alienating some learners in the first place.

Historically, AP has been the space where young people are educated who have been most negatively affected by education reforms. Critical perspectives on the intersections between education policy, and the culture this creates in mainstream schools, and exclusionary practices are missing. Current policy silences the reality that AP is needed because of the culture of mainstream schools, and the way these are governed and accountable. Contributing factors that are aligned with mainstream schooling such as curriculum and assessment are, unproblematically, used as a gauge of quality in AP. Accountability is presented as the answer, with no recognition of its role in exacerbating exclusionary practices.

This logic of making sense of AP through mainstream systems and notions of quality is important because it frames the possibilities for practice in AP, and for thinking otherwise about the role of AP. If AP is necessary because some young people cannot get on in mainstream school, then what happens to these young people if APs become aligned with, and accountable to, mainstream systems and notions of quality?

Policy as problematization revisited

Bacchi suggests the importance of evaluating the different interpretations and solutions that are offered by policy (Bacchi, 1999). In order to evaluate the effects of the current problematizations of AP we draw on our 2014 UK-wide study of AP (Thomson and Pennacchia, 2014) and make specific reference to the Scottish context to problematize the 'inevitability' of the current configuration of quality AP in the English context.

Quality and accountability in England

In 2014 we undertook a UK-wide study of quality in AP, including case study research in 17 provisions. During this we saw some of the practice implications of the policy focus on governing AP through systems and notions of quality that are aligned with mainstream schooling. The implications appeared strongest for full-time AP providers in England, as these were provisions that were formally registered with the Department for Education and inspected by Ofsted. We noted the strongest shifts to align with mainstream schools in provisions that were presented as successful case studies by government stakeholders. We have offered an extended critique of this practice, considering the way the effectiveness logic of mainstream schools has played out in AP (Thomson and Pennacchia, 2016). Here we offer a brief summary.

The full-time APs we researched developed mechanisms to support young people to become less risky. Quality APs had robust processes for documenting individual student achievement according to key data thresholds. Behaviour, and the methods being used to improve this, was meticulously documented and levels of surveillance were high. It was clear that these systems were responding to the need for progress in behaviour to be measurable and easy to produce for external auditors. This coheres with the demands to keep the mainstream school informed of whether or not a pupil has been sufficiently transformed to return.

In addition, the 'quality' movement resulted in practices that restricted the flexibility that has traditionally characterized the work of AP. The emphasis was narrowed to prioritize behaviour improvements above the social and emotional work associated with AP in the literature. The move to align AP outcomes with those of mainstream schools led to increased focus on provable outcomes in a narrow range of subjects and qualifications. The subjects most likely to be lost were social sciences and humanities, the very areas that might enable young people to develop a better understanding of the structural issues that contributed to their difficult time in school and/or other areas of their life (Thomson and Pennacchia, 2016).

In this context, the emphasis was on 'fixing' the child. Attempts to support the needs of young people were geared more towards ameliorating the risk they posed through the development of compliance, than to addressing the more complex foundations of their vulnerability to exclusion. Meanwhile any emphasis on changing the mainstream schooling context was diminished. Young people's educational entitlements were denied, including those that would help them to make better sense of their social situations. We argued that these processes might be read as ways of producing young people as compliant citizens and workers, which fits with the neoliberal demand for a precariat (Standing, 2011) – a workforce which will take up unstable work, in harsher disciplinary conditions that require a responsibilized self.

By contrast, in the part-time and complementary provisions we visited there continued to be a focus on more flexible curricular and social and emotional well-being (Pennacchia and Thomson, 2016). These provisions remain beyond the scope of current legislation for being a registered provider. If registration is the locus of increased accountability criteria, then part-time and complementary provisions may continue to operate with the higher levels of flexibility and autonomy traditionally associated with AP. This suggests opportunities for future research to compare the accountability regimes operating in different kinds of AP: those where the government has positioned it as reasonable that the education on offer is the same as that of mainstream schools and those where there is less pressure. There is an important question here about if and how quality and accountability might be accomplished in different ways. It is to the idea of other possibilities that we turn now, to conclude our analysis.

The Scottish context

Bacchi's style of analysis usefully highlights the contingent nature of policy, which could be other than it is. Bacchi suggests working with the opportunities provided by comparisons – across time, contexts and cultures – to bring to the fore other possibilities. We can consider how responses might differ if the 'problem' was 'thought about or represented differently' (Bacchi, 1999: 13). Neighbouring UK countries, with their own devolved education systems, offer one possible point of reference for English AP policy. They can usefully alert us to what dominates and what is missing in the English system of thought, and encourage analysis of the points of departure and what can be learnt from these. This reminds us that exclusion arises out of and in relation to 'the needs and demands of a given culture' (McNay, 1994: 18).

Since the end of the Second World War, Scotland has made clear attempts to demarcate a specific Scottish vision of education that is distinctive from the English vision (Jones, 2016). This is part of a wider attempt to develop an 'alternative social model', within which inclusion and equity are distinct priorities (Jones, 2016: 191). Scotland's provision of AP differs from the English context. It does not have pupil referral units or a market of eclectic AP providers. Instead AP, along with special schools, is part of a continuum of educational provision overseen by LAs. Rather than 'AP', the terminology of inclusion bases or units is used.

The Curriculum for Excellence, implemented in 2010, has been developed to apply to all young people across this continuum of provision. This is a flexible curriculum that provides young people with opportunities to develop as successful learners, confident individuals, responsible citizens, and effective contributors (Kidner, 2013: 4). Eight curriculum areas are intersected with crosscutting foci on literacy, numeracy, health and well-being (Kidner, 2013: 3). Student achievement takes into account formal learning and informal learning outside of the classroom, including programmes like the Duke of Edinburgh Award (Kidner, 2013: 3). The Curriculum for Excellence was 'plausibly claimed to represent a move away from a prescriptive top-down model of curriculum design and delivery, to one which encouraged schools to develop their own ways of implementing broad consensual principles – the opposite of the English model' (Jones, 2016: 193). LAs and schools are responsible for designing their own curriculum policy and explaining how it meets the needs of the Curriculum for Excellence and their pupils (Kidner, 2013: 4).

All young people are included in this curriculum, albeit at different levels. It offers an opportunity for parity of esteem across all schools. The focus on formal and informal learning as a point of commonality for all young people creates a less clear demarcation between both the value placed on different forms of learning, and where these happen. At the same time it provides an opportunity for AP to retain its characteristic flexibility. Curriculum areas and broad principles can be integrated in different ways depending on the needs of students, but the outcome can still be understood as part of the curriculum framework that all young people follow. Entire curriculum areas seem less likely to be sidelined in such an approach, while health and well-being are fundamental curriculum development areas for all young people.

Scottish teachers are employed by LAs, and may be seconded from mainstream schools to inclusion bases and special schools. This is a method of sharing knowledge and expertise between sites, and means that the idea of a continuum of provision is not only theorized but can also be practised. It is significant that such a reform would be increasingly difficult in the English context, where academization has left the role of the LA greatly diminished and ambiguous in relation to AP. This highlights how different cultures engage in different theoretical organization of the same concepts and areas of provision (McNay, 1994).

Conclusion

In this chapter we have analysed AP policy in the English context, paying attention to its current problematizations. As Hart notes, 'understanding education policy is crucial because policies give voice to government interpretations of the way educational institutions may be used as instruments of the state' (Hart, 212: 13). Our analysis shows the ways in which this has recently taken shape in English AP.

We argue that the notions and systems of quality that are being woven into the full-time AP sector are informed by mainstream schooling. Within this, the representations of young people accessing AP are fraught, as vulnerability remains problematically intertwined with notions of risk. Our case study research highlighted a number of concerns proposed by these policy problematizations.

Policy problematizations can be seen as shaping possibilities for action and for being and becoming. Policy can be more or less capacious in discursive affordances and thus legitimate practices that are more or less generous, more or less compliant. A comparison of policy in Scotland and England emphasizes the potential differences. The comparison demonstrates that AP and the young people who attend it are culturally produced in ways that connect with the wider educational and social policy demands of a society (Parsons, 2005).

AP should be ensuring young people's educational entitlement and striving to support each learner to have a positive and fulfilling educational experience. A key question that emerged from our analysis is how the quality of AP can be governed, without losing the particular qualities of AP that have been so valued by, and important to, young people. Reducing AP to a focus on grades is a concern because of the research that suggests that this is part of the reason some young people disengage or are excluded from mainstream school in the first place. This is, in our view, a misplaced approach to quality in AP that lacks the fundamental flexibility that is required. This highlights the problematic nature of the current reform of English AP. The focus on aligning AP with the mainstream, while not heeding the education climate that continues to demand and require AP, risks leaving us without sufficient recognition of what is valuable about AP.

Equity must be balanced with the particular needs of young people, and understandings of quality must retain a recognition of the fact that AP necessarily needs to be different from mainstream school. The Scottish example provides one model for balancing diversity with equality, basing education around broadly framed principles that focus on the social and emotional development of all children as well as academic credentials. Here, those aspects characteristically associated with AP are included as core educational principles for all.

References

Ashurst, F. and Venn, C. (2014) *Inequality, Poverty, Education: A political economy of school exclusion*. Basingstoke: Palgrave Macmillan.

Bacchi, C.L. (1999) *Women, Policy and Politics: The construction of policy problems*. London: SAGE Publications.

Bacchi, C. (2012) 'Why study problematizations? Making politics visible'. *Open Journal of Political Science*, 2 (1), 1–8.

Ball, S.J., Maguire, M. and Braun, A. (2012) *How Schools Do Policy: Policy enactments in secondary schools*. London: Routledge.

Blyth, E. and Milner, J. (1993) 'Exclusion from school: A first step in exclusion from society?'. *Children and Society*, 7 (3), 255–68.

Cameron, D. (2011) 'PM's speech on the fightback after the riots'. 15 August. Online. www.gov.uk/government/speeches/pms-speech-on-the-fightback-after-the-riots (accessed 18 March 2016).

Crossley, S. (2016) 'Realising the (troubled) family, crafting the neoliberal state'. *Families, Relationships and Societies*, 5 (2), 263–79.

CSJ (Centre for Social Justice) (2011) *No Excuses: A review of educational exclusion*. London: Centre for Social Justice.

DCSF (Department for Children, Schools and Families) (2008) *Back on Track: A strategy for modernising alternative provision for young people*. Norwich: The Stationery Office.

DfE (Department for Education) (2013) *Alternative Provision: Statutory guidance for local authorities*. London: Department for Education.

DfE (Department for Education) (2015) 'Policy paper – 2010 to 2015 government policy: Children outside mainstream education'. Online. www.gov.uk/government/publications/2010-to-2015-government-policy-children-outside-mainstream-education/2010-to-2015-government-policy-children-outside-mainstream-education (accessed 16 October 2016).

DfE (Department for Education) (2016a) *Educational Excellence Everywhere*. London: Department for Education.

DfE (Department for Education) (2016b) 'Provisional GCSE and equivalent results in England, 2015 to 2016'. Online. www.gov.uk/government/statistics/gcse-and-equivalent-results-2015-to-2016-provisional (accessed 25 October 2016).

DfE (Department for Education) (2016c) 'Schools, pupils and their characteristics: January 2016'. Online. www.gov.uk/government/statistics/schools-pupils-and-their-characteristics-january-2016 (accessed 2 November 2016).

DfE (Department for Education) (2017) *Permanent and Fixed Period Exclusions in England: 2015 to 2016* (SFR 35/2017). London: Department for Education. Online. www.gov.uk/government/uploads/system/uploads/attachment_data/file/633365/SFR35_2017_text.pdf (accessed 4 August 2017).

DfE (Department for Education) and Department of Health (2015) *Special Educational Needs and Disability Code of Practice: 0 to 25 years: Statutory guidance for organisations which work with and support children and young people who have special educational needs or disabilities*. London: Department for Education.

DfES (Department for Education and Skills) (2001) *Inclusive Schooling: Children with special educational needs*. Nottingham: Department for Education and Skills.

Evans, J. (2010) *Not Present and Not Correct: Understanding and preventing school exclusions*. Ilford: Barnardo's.

Foucault, M. (1990) *The History of Sexuality* (Vol. 1). Trans. Hurley, R. London: Penguin Books.

Foucault, M. (2003) 'Polemics, politics, and problematizations: An interview with Michel Foucault'. In Rabinow, P. and Rose, N. (eds) *The Essential Foucault: Selections from essential works of Foucault, 1954–1984*. New York: New Press, 18–24.

Gillborn, D. and Youdell, D. (2000) *Rationing Education: Policy, practice, reform and equity*. Buckingham: Open University Press.

Hallam, S., Rogers, L., Rhamie, J., Shaw, J., Rees, E., Haskins, H., Blackmore, J. and Hallam, J. (2007) 'Pupils' perceptions of an alternative curriculum: Skill Force'. *Research Papers in Education*, 22 (1), 43–63.

Hart, C.S. (2012) *Aspirations, Education and Social Justice: Applying Sen and Bourdieu*. London: Bloomsbury.

IOE (Institute of Education) and NFER (National Foundation for Educational Research) (2013) *School Exclusion Trial Evaluation Research: Interim report*. London: Department for Education.

IOE (Institute of Education) and NFER (National Foundation for Educational Research) (2014) *School Exclusion Trial Evaluation: Research report*. London: Department for Education.

Jonathan, R. (1997) 'Educational "goods": Value and benefit'. *Journal of Philosophy of Education*, 31 (1), 59–82.

Jones, K. (2016) *Education in Britain: 1944 to the present*. 2nd ed. Cambridge: Polity Press.

Kidner, C. (2013) *Curriculum for Excellence*. Edinburgh: Scottish Parliament Information Centre (SPICe).

Lumby, J. (2012) 'Disengaged and disaffected young people: Surviving the system'. *British Educational Research Journal*, 38 (2), 261–79.

Maguire, M., Perryman, J., Ball, S. and Braun, A. (2011) 'The ordinary school – what is it?'. *British Journal of Sociology of Education*, 32 (1), 1–16.

McCluskey, G., Riddell, S., Weedon, E. and Fordyce, M. (2016) 'Exclusion from school and recognition of difference'. *Discourse: Studies in the Cultural Politics of Education*, 37 (4), 529–39.

Mckenzie, L. (2015) *Getting By: Estates, class and culture in austerity Britain*. Bristol: Policy Press.

McNay, L. (1994) *Foucault: A critical introduction*. Cambridge: Polity Press.

Mills, M., McGregor, G., Baroutsis, A., te Riele, K. and Hayes, D. (2016) 'Alternative education and social justice: Considering issues of affective and contributive justice'. *Critical Studies in Education*, 57 (1), 100–15.

Mills, M., Renshaw, P. and Zipin, L. (2013) 'Alternative education provision: A dumping ground for "wasted lives" or a challenge to the mainstream?'. *Social Alternatives*, 32 (2), 13–18.

OCC (Office of the Children's Commissioner) (2013a) *'They Go the Extra Mile': Reducing inequality in school exclusions*. London: Office of the Children's Commissioner.

OCC (Office of the Children's Commissioner) (2013b) *'Always Someone Else's Problem': Office of the Children's Commissioner's report on illegal exclusions*. London: Office of the Children's Commissioner.

Ofsted (2011) *Alternative Provision*. Manchester: Ofsted.

Ofsted (2016) *Alternative Provision: The findings from Ofsted's three-year survey of schools' use of off-site alternative provision*. Manchester: Ofsted.

Ogg, T. and Kaill, E. (2010) *A New Secret Garden? Alternative provision, exclusion and children's rights*. London: Civitas.

Ozga, J. (2009) 'Governing education through data in England: From regulation to self-evaluation'. *Journal of Education Policy*, 24 (2), 149–62.

Parsons, C. (2005) 'School exclusion: The will to punish'. *British Journal of Educational Studies*, 53 (2), 187–211.

Pennacchia, J. and Thomson, P. (2016) 'Complementing the mainstream: An exploration of partnership work between complementary alternative provisions and mainstream schools'. *Pastoral Care in Education*, 34 (2), 67–78.

Perryman, J., Ball, S., Maguire, M. and Braun, A. (2011) 'Life in the pressure cooker: School league tables and English and mathematics teachers' responses to accountability in a results-driven era'. *British Journal of Educational Studies*, 59 (2), 179–95.

Pirrie, A., Macleod, G., Cullen, M.A. and McCluskey, G. (2011) 'What happens to pupils permanently excluded from special schools and pupil referral units in England?'. *British Educational Research Journal*, 37 (3), 519–38.

Standing, G. (2011) *The Precariat: The new dangerous class*. London: Bloomsbury.

Taylor, C. (2012) *Improving Alternative Provision*. London: Department for Education.

Taylor, C. (2016) *Review of the Youth Justice System: An interim report of emerging findings*. London: Ministry of Justice.

Thomson, P. (2014) *Literature Review: What's the alternative? Effective support for young people disengaging from the mainstream*. London: Prince's Trust.

Thomson, P. and Pennacchia, J. (2014) *What's the Alternative? Effective support for young people disengaging from mainstream education*. London: Prince's Trust.

Thomson, P. and Pennacchia, J. (2016) 'Hugs and behaviour points: Alternative education and the regulation of "excluded" youth'. *International Journal of Inclusive Education*, 20 (6), 622–40.

Thomson, P. and Russell, L. (2007). *Mapping the Alternatives to Permanent Exclusion*. York: Joseph Rowntree Foundation.

Thomson, P. and Russell, L. (2009) 'Data, data everywhere – but not all the numbers that count? Mapping alternative provisions for students excluded from school'. *International Journal of Inclusive Education*, 13 (4), 423–38.

White, R., Martin, K. and Jeffes, J. (2012) *The Back on Track Alternative Provision Pilots: Final report* (Research Report RR250). London: Department for Education.

Chapter 5

Alternative schooling in Australia: Policy and practice

Martin Mills and Glenda McGregor

Introduction

Current education policies in Australia have led to an increased focus on alternative provision in that country. While there has been an historical concern with alternative schooling in the form of democratic education that falls outside of the state sector (see Waters, Chapter 14 in this volume), there is a new focus on alternative schooling that is subsidized by the state and is designed to meet the needs of young people who often come from marginalized backgrounds, sometimes referred to as second chance or flexi-schooling (see Murray and Shay, Chapters 8 and 9 in this volume). The chapter will focus on this latter type of school. (We have covered democratic schools elsewhere, see Mills and McGregor, 2014.) In Australia, the policy framework around alternative provision is a work in progress. The alternative education sector is regarded as highly unregulated and varying in quality. As such, various governments have sought to explore the way in which these schools meet the needs of highly disadvantaged young people who have struggled with the expectations of mainstream schooling (see te Riele *et al.*, 2017). According to te Riele in work published in 2014 there were then 70,000 students in such schools; the number is likely to be much larger now. This chapter will outline the policy context around alternative schooling and will draw on data from two alternative schools in Australia in order to highlight practices in these schools. These data primarily come from interviews with teachers and students in flexi-schools – schools designed to support those young people who have rejected or been rejected by the mainstream sector. The chapter argues that any analysis of alternative schooling requires a commitment to ensuring that *all* students regardless of background receive a quality education.

There is widespread interest in alternative education across many locations (see, for example, Abelmann *et al.*, 2012; Aron, 2006; Aron and Zweig, 2003; Kim, 2011; Wrigley *et al.*, 2012; McCluskey *et al.*, 2015; Woods and Woods, 2009). Australia is no different (see, for example,

Baker, 2016; Fish, 2017; Lewthwaite *et al.*, 2017; Mills and McGregor, 2014; te Riele, 2007). In Australia, a variety of policy pressures have led to an increase in the provision of alternative education, sparking interest by governments, philanthropic organizations and think tanks (see, for example, KPMG, 2009; Mills and McGregor, 2010; Mills *et al.*, 2012; te Riele, 2012). As other contributors to this volume have noted, the term 'alternative' is, however, quite slippery. What is meant by 'alternative'? And 'alternative' from what? In this chapter we use the term 'alternative' to describe those schools that appear to trouble what could be called the 'grammar of schooling' (Tyack and Tobin, 1994). That is, we are interested here in those schools which are clearly not like mainstream schools; in particular, we are concerned with flexi-schools that are attempting to meet the needs of highly disadvantaged students who appear to have either rejected or been rejected by mainstream schooling. These schools are known by a variety of terms, such as flexible schools, learning options and second chance schooling (Gallagher, 2011; Raywid, 1999; Ross and Gray, 2005; te Riele, 2007). For consistency we use flexi-schools throughout. The vast majority of these schools in Australia are independent and sit outside the jurisdiction of state authorities. However, they are supported through state funding, are subject to a variety of government controls, and students do not pay fees to attend them. Many of these schools are a recent addition to the education landscape and appear to be a response to recent policy pressures. In this chapter we outline the policy context in Australia as it relates to alternative schooling and then draw on examples of what this means for students who have entered into flexi-schooling. Various policies, practices and processes in these schools will be outlined.

Policy context

As many of the chapters in this book indicate, current educational reforms are shaped largely within a neoliberal paradigm. These reforms, referred to as GERM (global education reform movement) by Pasi Sahlberg (2011), are based on the assumption that the market, accountability and competition are all critical to the improvement of schools. The impacts of these reforms are evident in government concerns with league tables based on exam results, including international league tables, ensuring that parents (as consumers of education) have detailed information on schools that enable them to make comparisons between schools, and giving schools more autonomy to address the needs of the local market. In Australia, such processes are evident in the creation of the Australian Curriculum, Assessment and Reporting Authority's (ACARA) *My School* website (ACARA, 2017), which lists a school's results on national literacy and numeracy tests against national averages and also the school's performance measured against sixty 'statistically similar schools' across the nation on a socio-economic scale (Index of Community Socio-Educational Advantage – ICSEA) developed by ACARA. The impact of these policies in Australia has worked to put significant pressure on principals, teachers and students to ensure that they are competitive in this education marketplace.

Schools are thus often judged by the quality of their exam results and by the impression that they can create of themselves in the marketplace. This has meant that teachers and students are under enormous pressures to ensure that exam results are good. In some cases this has meant that there has been a narrowing of curricular choices to focus upon important core subjects such as literacy, numeracy and science, and a narrowing of pedagogical strategies in favour of direct instruction so that test achievements can be maximized. These problematic outcomes of current policies have been well documented (Ball, 2006, 2012; Lingard, 2011; Lingard and Sellar, 2013; McCluskey, 2017). At the same time, students who are perceived as being damaging to the school's overall performance on these exams, having behaviours that impact on others' performance levels or project an image of the school which will deter high-performing students from attending, are often not wanted at the school. In those instances where schools have a high degree of autonomy such students may be discouraged from attending or asked to leave (McGregor and Mills, 2012; Mills *et al.*, 2013).

At the same time as this reform agenda has been taking place, so too has there been one that has had a social justice aim. There is a recognition that schools have not always served the needs of the most disadvantaged students well and that something needs to be done to improve the outcomes of such students. For instance, the 'earning or learning' agenda in Australia (Australian Department of Social Services, 2014) sought to reduce the number of young people not in education, employment or training by raising the compulsory school leaving age. This aligns with government commitments to keeping young people in full-time education. For example, in 2008 all State and Territory Ministers of Education, with the Commonwealth Minister for Education, meeting as the Ministerial Council on Education, Employment, Training and Youth Affairs (MCEETYA), agreed on the Melbourne Declaration on Educational Goals for Young Australians (MCEETYA, 2008). MCEETYA set a goal over the next ten years of 'Improving educational outcomes for Indigenous youth and disadvantaged young Australians, especially those from low socio-economic backgrounds', and the Council on Australian Governments (COAG) agreed on a range of targets to improve the school retention of marginalized young people. This is important because, as reports published by the Organisation of Economic and Co-operative Development (OECD) show, in Australia school completion rates are low for Indigenous students, and improvement has been slow for young people from the lowest socio-economic status (SES) compared to a national completion rate of young people from the highest SES backgrounds (COAG, 2013). Data provided by the OECD also indicate that while it is improving, the relationship between SES and educational outcomes is still stronger in Australia than in countries such as Canada, Norway and Japan (OECD, 2012). As part of the Melbourne Declaration on Educational Goals for Young Australians, all Australian States made a commitment that all young people under the age of 25 would be entitled to an education or training place, subject to course requirements and availability. One of the main goals was to lift Year 12 retention rates to 90 per cent by 2015 (COAG, 2009). However, recent data from the Australian Bureau of Statistics indicate that this ambition has not been realized:

> Between 2015 and 2016 the Apparent Retention Rate from Year 7/8 to Year 12 for all full-time students rose marginally, from 84.0% to 84.3%. The rate was 87.8% for females and 80.9% for males .... For Aboriginal and Torres Strait Islander students, the Apparent Retention Rate to Year 12 rose slightly between 2015 and 2016, from 59.4% to 59.8%. The rate for females (64.1%) exceeded that for males (55.7%). (ABS, 2017)

Such statistics continue to drive governments in Australia to raise retention rates for all students, particularly for Aboriginal and Torres Strait Islanders.

One way in which retention targets can be met is through the provision of a range of schools that sit outside of the mainstream. The rapid growth of this alternative sector has been identified as a key issue for education departments, leading to a number of government inquiries and investigations into alternative schooling in Australia. Indeed, as we were writing this chapter we were invited to a whole-day forum being organized by Queensland's Director General of Education to discuss issues related to the upsurge in these schools. The Department of Education and Training in Queensland has recently launched a raft of promising policies in respect of schooling engagement that builds on much research that has been undertaken in that State in recent years. Notably, the Queensland government has made a 'pledge to collaborate across government and with non-government partners to ensure that every child and young person is equipped with the tools and support they need to succeed professionally and personally'. This promise is being supported by the establishment of youth engagement hubs that bring local communities together to assist schools in crafting local solutions to educational disengagement (for a full set of policies see Queensland Government Department of Education, 2017).

Te Riele *et al.* (2017) have provided an analysis of considerable 'grey literature', i.e. reports for government, on alternative schooling in Australia, to which we have contributed (these include Mills *et al.* (2012) and a currently embargoed report for the QLD Department of Education and Training). The extent of this literature is evidence of the interest by government in the alternative education space. However, as their analysis shows, there is a clear intent on the part of government to determine the outcomes and hence value-for-money of investing in these schools. It could also be argued, though, that the commissioning of these reports is an indication of the commitment by government to maximizing schooling retention. However, as suggested by Bills and Howard (2017) in their policy analysis (using Bacchi, 2009; 2012; see also Pennacchia and Thomson, Chapter 4 of this volume) of the state-sponsored system of Flexible Learning Options (FLO) in South Australia, government support for this reform may well be based on improving their school retention data, rather than an attempt to ensure that all students receive a 'meaningful education' (McGregor *et al.*, 2015).

While attempts to improve school retention suggest an agenda that is supportive of marginalized young people, some are sceptical of such attempts. For instance, Wyn and Woodman (2006), argue that various retention measures have been designed 'to coerce young people into remaining in education and training and to limit the proportion of young people who are eligible for government income support' (505). Regardless of the motivation, the setting of targets necessitates schools having to demonstrate how they are performing against a particular set of performance indicators. This has meant that schools that do not want certain students need to have alternatives to offer them. The development of the alternative education sector catering to these students can be seen in this light. It is also important to note that clearly there are many social, economic and cultural factors that influence schooling retention that are beyond the control of schools (McCluskey *et al.*, 2016; McGregor *et al.*, 2017). However, there are also institutional practices and policies that work against retaining marginalized young people. For young people who are homeless (which includes drifting from one friend's house to another), or who live in high poverty families, completion of assignments and compliance with assessment dates may be very challenging. Such young people often struggle to conform to standards of dress and presentation and this sets them up for likely conflicts with teachers who are required to enforce such rules. Understandably, young people are likely to react defiantly as they become overwhelmed by the stresses and strains of their personal circumstances, and the current political climate is not on their side. This too can contribute to high suspension and exclusion rates.

Bills and Howard (2017) also argue that in South Australia the FLOs entrench disadvantage by facilitating 'passive exclusion' (69). However, they also concede that these schools can make a difference if there is 'a more encompassing FLO (Flexible Learning Option) policy approach that is inclusive of a variety of interventions including school redesign and more parental involvement in redesigned schools … not just geared to those students deemed to be "at risk"' (70). They also argue that the Southern Australian FLO system is very much about changing the young person rather than changing schools. As such, these schools leave the mainstream unchallenged. The problem is seen to be the student. Hence, sometimes approaches to students in these schools can take a therapeutic turn whereby efforts are made to 'fix up' the student, rather than considering what changes could be made to the schooling environment (Fish, 2017). We are not suggesting that all therapeutic work is without benefit, since we are aware that many students have experienced various kinds of trauma. However, in our view such trauma may be exacerbated by intransigencies within some mainstream schools and hence there needs to be change in systemic responses to these young people.

Plows *et al.* (2017) indicate that attending alternative education sites can lead to stigma and further marginalization for young people, who are not being exposed to a mainstream curriculum and are receiving 'less-valued' credentials than their mainstream counterparts. Thomson and Russell (2007) have been critical of such alternatives in England that primarily offered a narrow curriculum, usually based on vocational skills (see also Dovemark and Beach, 2015). While they also found evidence of good practice they suggested that it was largely an 'unregulated market' which lacked quality control. This is supported by the former Labour government's white paper *Back on Track* which suggested that: 'The accountability framework for Pupil Referral Units and alternative provision is seriously under-developed compared with mainstream schools' (cited in Ogg and Kaill, 2010). Similar concerns about the lack of quality control in alternative schooling sector have been expressed in the USA (Martin and Brand, 2006).

However, many of those who offer alternative educational provision have been driven by a commitment to social justice and to an attempt to ensure that those who would have missed out on an education are able to still obtain formal qualifications. The schools that are considered here are run as independent schools, as part of a religious chain of such schools, or as an off-site campus of one or more government high schools. What is important here is that the primary purpose of the schools was not to change the young person, but to change the schools into places attractive to students who could be supported by a multitude of services that would allow them to establish learning pathways and achieve educational goals. Plows *et al.* (2017) also argue that these schools can be places of resistance to the mainstream, or 'counter-spaces', whereby a more expansive vision of education is made possible (see also Riddle and Cleaver, 2017). We agree, but also argue strongly that this should not let the mainstream sector abrogate its responsibility towards highly marginalized young people (Mills and McGregor, 2014).

From policy to practice: Flexible learning in Australia

Young people who access flexi-schools are often faced with severe economic marginalization, which makes it difficult for them to attend. For example, in the research considered here it was not uncommon to meet young people who were homeless, could not afford regular meals and struggled to get by from day to day. It was also common in these schools to find students who had been compelled to leave their previous schools or had been unable to find a school that would accept them. Many of these young people also indicated that they had been forced out of their mainstream school because they were perceived to be 'different' or because they had been marginalized by cultural factors such as race/ethnicity, sexuality or gender. Australian flexi-schools also have a disproportionally high Indigenous population for both students and staff (Shay and Heck, 2015). Within Australia there has been significant concern over the ways in which Aboriginal and Torres Strait Islander students have not been served well by mainstream schooling (Dreise and Thomson, 2014). This has led to policy responses, most notable of which is 'Closing the Gap' (Australian Government, 2017). However, this response has not taken into account the large numbers of Indigenous young people in flexi-schools. We agree with Shay and Heck (2015), who suggest that the mainstream might like to look towards what these flexi-schools are doing to support young Indigenous people in order to improve their practices (see also Skattebol and Hayes, 2016).

In our research, flexi-schools' concerns about student welfare were often addressed by ensuring that food was available throughout the day and by ensuring access to services that would cater to the most basic needs of young people, including accommodation, legal aid and social and emotional issues. The intent was to ensure that the barriers that prevented the young people from participating fully in schooling were minimized – what we have referred to elsewhere as 'clearing the path for learning' (McGregor *et al.*, 2017). The importance of relationships with teachers and other workers was emphasized. Many of these schools sought to ensure that their curricula and organizational structures took into account marginalized cultures. For example, we have seen places in Australia that were infused with Indigenous knowledges and incorporated consultation with local Elders or engaged with the community and families; although as Shay indicates in this volume (Chapter 9), this has not occurred unproblematically. In a number of locations there was also support for pregnant young women and for new parents. Flexible arrangements also ensured that the 'different' adversities that many of these young people faced could be accommodated within the educational expectations of the school. There was also a set of processes in place to ensure that the types of conflicts that had driven them out of their previous schools were addressed in supportive ways.

Methodology

The remainder of this chapter draws on data from two examples of flexi-schools that took part in a major study of a range of alternative schools across three Australian states and one territory. Data comprised written observations, educational artefacts and interviews with a variety of students and staff (teachers, workers, parents, volunteers and administrators). In the broader study, there were multiple visits over a period of three years (2012–14). We sought to explore a range of themes that included the following broad areas, as relevant to teachers, workers and students:

- previous experiences
- a pathway into the alternative site
- reasons for staying
- what works (relational, material, pedagogical and curricular elements) and why
- resourcing and sustainability issues.

In the analysis of our data we looked for thematic commonalities and contradictions across texts in respect of prior and current educational experiences of students and workers in alternative schools, and practices and philosophies of alternative schooling sites.

Initial visits were conducted at each site according to when the schools could accommodate us and lasted for approximately one week. As much as possible we continued to maintain contact with subsequent short-term visits. In the construction of narratives and synthesis of data we included a variety of stages of drafting and cross checking of data sets collected at different stages of the research.

Given the relatively small size of the schools and the intimate nature of some of the classes, we found we had considerable time to observe and interact with the participants. We conducted interviews with a range of students at each site and gathered school documents. Interviews were carried out individually or within the context of focus groups, depending upon the personal preferences of the young people involved. The availability of adult personnel for interview depended upon the nature of the site and included teachers, workers, parents, volunteers, administrators and social workers. Interviews lasted from 30 to 90 minutes and were electronically recorded. Pseudonyms are used for all sites and participants. In this chapter we explore the experiences of teachers and students in two of these flexible learning sites: Victoria Meadows and Fernvale.

The schools

Victoria Meadows began life in a park for homeless young people and was originally staffed by youth workers. With support from a major city council, this alternative option moved into the premises of an old school. It has since developed into one of Queensland's most successful flexi-schools and is now part of the Youth+ network (see Murray, Chapter 8 in this volume). Fernvale began as a space in a house for young mothers or pregnant young women, and the students were primarily Indigenous in background. Over time the numbers grew significantly and eventually an independent girls' school was created, with a separate crèche attached for young mothers. This flexi-school has very close links to local Aboriginal Elders.

Victoria Meadows Flexi School

At Victoria Meadows, the vast majority of the young people indicated that both teachers and other students were accepting of individual differences. Milly, for example, had chosen Victoria Meadows because of the way she could 'be herself' at the school. In her searches, she had been to both a private and a government school and had found them not too dissimilar:

> I was in a mainstream school – Catholic education, for three years from Year 8 till Year 10. I was having complications with bullying and stuff like that, just wasn't really finding it easy to do my work ... so I decided to go to a state school for two months and I realised that it wasn't the school it was just the whole *system*. I just couldn't deal with the way that they were teaching

the kids. I wasn't getting enough attention and so I stopped going to school.

Milly was dressed in gothic black when we interviewed her, and noted problems in relation to uniforms at previous schools; she told us that, for her, being 'different' was important to her sense of being a 'free spirit':

> I didn't like the uniforms and stuff (slight laugh) definitely because I'm more of a free spiritual person like, today I'm wearing this, I mean tomorrow I'll be wearing something completely different! Like I'll be wearing, I don't know, colours and stuff like I'm not really into having a set way of looking and being because I don't believe that a school should teach you how to look or how to be; they're just there to teach you how to do maths, English and the subjects you need in order to make it; the rest of it is your choice in life.

This view was shared by the teachers and workers. For instance, George, a teacher at Victoria Meadows Flexi School, commented:

> I think the other strength that this place offers is a place where difference is accepted, where alternative viewpoints are accepted, alternative lifestyles are accepted in a safe and respectful environment where your ability to succeed in academic endeavours isn't the be all and end all of you as a person.

We also heard stories from young people about feeling alienated by school curricula and being unable to meet the inflexible arrangements of the school due to their caring responsibilities or other life events. For example, we met young women with babies for whom mainstream schools would not change their practices.

Many of the young people in these schools related stories of how they had experienced a form of injustice and had no avenue of appeal, often leading them to leave the school. For instance Julie, a student from Victoria Meadows, told us about her previous experience:

> I got into trouble for things that I didn't do. Like a text message that was sent from somebody else's phone and I just got suspended for that and I was like, 'Nah, I don't want to be here anymore' so I left.

The vast majority of our research schools had a policy of not suspending or expelling students. Instead, teachers at Victoria Meadows told us how young people were sometimes asked to go home as a 'circuit breaker' but that they were always welcomed back. Victoria Meadows Flexi School operated via a framework of 'Rights, Respect, Responsibility and Relationships'. Both workers and students at the schools emphasized to us that their relationships were based on trust and that when students were asked to take some time out they later returned to the school and the issue was addressed as a community. There were also strategies for dealing with interpersonal conflicts in ways that left all parties' dignity intact. As a student, Leanne, from Victoria Meadows explained:

> They do the community group meetings and stuff, bringing everyone together and sorting out conflicts and everyone having their say. And these little meetings is a really good thing they do because it lowers the chances of anyone having any sort of fights or arguments so everyone has their own opinion – so it brings people together as one community.

In all our research flexi-school teachers and students spoke about the importance of relationships. In each instance everyone on site addressed each other by first names. Justin, a student from Victoria Meadows, explained the importance of this:

> You know it's not Sir, Madam, it's not Mr and Mrs whatever. I couldn't even tell you what half the teachers' last names were ... Yeah pretty much, they're all you know, like, – George, or Angela and, you know, you don't really know their last names. It makes you feel equal not below, like it's not 'yes sir, no sir, three bags full sir'.

What is interesting here is that Justin, who had had a very difficult time at his previous school, was fully engaged in learning and that the practices that 'make you feel equal not below' were seen as central to supporting this engagement. For example, he went on to explain to us that:

> Like, in English ... we'll discuss something or we bring up a topic and we'll actually sit down and have a full class discussion about it.... It's more what your opinion is about stuff and they're not going to beat you down on every opinion.

Fernvale Flexi School

Fernvale commenced in 1997 in a house in suburban Brisbane as an initiative of a Christian organization. The programme was designed originally to provide a range of services, including education, to young women who were in care and protection or who were at risk of coming into care of the Department of Families. The programme started with seven young women, a teacher and a part-time youth worker. The young women were enrolled with the Brisbane School of Distance Education. As well, an education programme, life skills, personal development and recreational activities were offered. In 2002 the school relocated to its current location and the following year a charitable organization provided a crèche near the school to support pregnant girls and young mothers who wished to complete their secondary education. In order to facilitate the work of the school, the Christian organization purchased property next to the school's current location. Fernvale had also been one of the schools that we had researched for a previous report (Mills and McGregor, 2010), and we draw on some of the data from that work. At the time of the current research, plans were being finalized to move into the new building mid 2014 in order to accommodate the addition of Year 7 students who commenced in 2014. In 2014 Queensland moved Year 7 from the primary sector into high schools in line with the rest of Australia.

Fernvale demonstrated a very strong philosophical base that was derived from an ethos of care and democratic principles. According to its founding school principal:

> We drew on an eclectic mix of research. Democratic Education Theory and the Community Access School concepts were central to our approach. All students at the school are treated with *unconditional positive regard.* The success of this model is based on the development of trusting relationships with these young people who have been let down so often by other significant adults in their lives. Our challenge was to create a democratic school with a warm and friendly atmosphere where young people felt welcome and where their input into curriculum development and school organization was valued.

Such sentiments were echoed by the students, as noted here by Carol:

> We are like a big family here.... Like, here it's like, 'Oh, yeah, we are all – like, we are all human, we all make mistakes'. So we just have to find a way together to get along, eventually, we will connect. I don't know … we are just like family.

This school for girls had a very high proportion of Indigenous students and/or mothers or soon to be mothers. The stories about the racism they experienced and lack of support they received at their previous schools are damning of the mainstream sector (both private and public). However, at Fernvale, things were very different. There was a crèche with childcare workers; there were opportunities to meet and discuss parenting issues with other mothers and with social workers; and there was support to help them find accommodation or to leave abusive relationships. Sienna, a student, told us:

> They've got a crèche which makes it awesome ... youth workers that will help you with Centrelink ... can get you counsellors, if like you have a problem with your parents or your partner or you need a home or something she'll help you do that.... I had help to leave a domestic violence relationship.

The school also employed Indigenous workers to support Indigenous students. The school ensured that Indigenous knowledges and understandings were incorporated into the curriculum and pedagogies. One of the teachers, Nerissa, viewed her Indigeneity and cultural background as important aspects of her practice:

> I really believe that a lot of the teachings of my old people, the Elders that I grew up with and worked with, the lessons, the knowledge, the information, the respect that they taught me, have helped me to establish myself here and I think that even though the girls may come from homes, how can I explain this, even though we think that the girls don't understand about some of those things, I think that deep down inside there, there's ninety-nine per cent of them understand the key concept of *respect* ... and I think that we're able to tap into it. We have, the girls go to the Elders' sewing circle on Wednesdays. They've got that connection there and this year's theme for NAIDOC [National Aboriginal and Islander Day Observance Committee] is honouring our elders, 'honouring our elders – nurturing our youth'. So we're really tapping into that whole philosophy here at the school.

At the same time Fernvale offered the standard curriculum and was expected to participate in all of the national and state testing regimes.

Many of the young women at the school indicated that if it were not for this school they would not be in education. And as testament to their commitment to this school, many of the students travelled up to an hour and a half to attend. There was a flexible approach to participation so that students became engaged when they were ready. One student, Marie said:

> Well, they would really love for everyone to participate but if you don't want to participate, they are fine with that anyway. And, like, even if you just sit and watch, they are happy with that.… They just make you, like, you want to be there. They will encourage you. But if you don't want to go to class, you can just go out and do a different subject.

The positive relationships evident at this school underpinned the pedagogical approaches of the teachers as noted by student Amy: 'They'll come (teachers/ workers) and talk to you and check up on how you're doing. Like if you don't understand something they'll come and help you and it's just, they're more supportive'. The opportunity to provide such personal attention, however, was facilitated by the size of the school and its classes. As is the case in most other alternative schools, lower than mainstream numbers allowed for smaller class sizes: 'Like, the classrooms are half the size from a normal school. So you get more one-on-one time with the teacher. Because the classes are smaller, you also get to know more people and know how they are feeling and – yeah' (Marie, student).

Like Fernvale, the vast majority of flexi-schools have a very strong focus on social and pastoral care. They wanted to ensure that the students' social and emotional well-being were priorities. However, they also recognized that they had to provide a quality education. This is vitally important to the long-term well-being and academic progression of the students. In our research projects we have occasionally had cause for concern if particular alternative education sites fail to engage students in learning, work with deficit understandings of the students and/or continue to reproduce stereotypic behaviours. This has been widely recognized (Dovemark and Beach, 2015; Choi, 2012; Kim, 2011; Thomson and Russell, 2007).

Conclusion

The relatively recent upsurge of flexi-schooling in Australia has received mixed responses from educators and researchers. While these schools are very different from 'behaviour schools' (Graham *et al.*, 2015), or England's pupil referral units (PRUs), of central concern is whether or not these alternative schools will benefit some of the most marginalized students in schools or will reproduce disadvantage. As we have indicated, students who attend these programmes tend to be young people from poor backgrounds, many of whom have experienced discrimination on the basis of race/ethnicity, sexuality and/or gender. If these programmes act purely as 'holding pens' or 'dumping grounds' for students deemed to be unteachable in the mainstream then they will indeed continue to reproduce the social status quo. Furthermore, if little attention is paid to the professional learning of the staff in these schools then this too will impact upon their ability to provide viable educational alternatives. Plows (2017) suggests that the quality of educational provision is tied very closely to the quality of staff in each institution. She also argues that a lack of concern with the professional learning of staff works to marginalize teachers and workers and to further damage the education of the students in such schools. How to determine success is a quandary for flexi-schooling (te Riele *et al.*, 2017), and is closely tied to questions about their purpose. However, in an era of schooling obsessed with 'outcomes' their existence and funding is often dependent upon demonstrating the 'gains' that they produce. We are not opposed to flexi-schools being made accountable. However, we do want to consider to whom and for what they should be made accountable.

Our research into these schools in Australia has revealed highly committed teachers and young people attending meaningful education programmes after having become alienated from mainstream schooling. These schools have support structures such as crèches, housing and legal assistance, enabling the young people to attend (Mills and McGregor, 2014; te Riele *et al.*, 2017). From this research it was clear that many of the young people in these schools would have not been in education if it were not for the existence of such alternatives.

There are, however, vast differences amongst flexi-schools within Australia. In terms of those that appear to be making the most difference in the lives of the young people they support, the evidence points to a range of common signature practices that supersede context; they are practices that work to effectively re-engage marginalized and severely disadvantaged young people, who are often struggling with a range of economic, social and mental health issues in education. In sum they include the following:

1. Realistic recognition of the challenges of the material and personal circumstances of each student
2. Provision of a wide range of basic necessities for young people with few resources, for example childcare or access to it, food, transport, learning materials, access to second-hand goods, access to showers, etc.
3. Strategies to connect their students to the external services that they need to progress their lives, for example social security, health and welfare agencies, legal aid, childcare and child welfare services

4. Provision of staff to prepare students for, and to accompany them to, external agencies, for example court hearings, other educational providers, job interviews or work experience

5. Flexibility in requirements for completion of schoolwork, attendance, dress, pathways and ways of working towards personal and educational goals

6. Provision of programmes of learning that are individually crafted for each student, address individual gaps in knowledge and skills, target the interests and connect to the lives of these young people, and provide them with meaningful pathways to further training or employment

7. Non-hierarchical social structures that foster a set of relationships among staff, students and workers whereby all people, regardless of age, are addressed by their first names and accorded the right to express themselves

8. Giving and receiving respect as a fundamental right and responsibility for all who work or study at the schools

9. Provision of a safe, nurturing and supportive environment that is premised upon unconditional regard, positive reinforcement and validation of difference; an environment within which it is safe to 'fail' and learn from it; an environment that teaches young people the fundamentals of respect and responsibility and thereby facilitates the development of self-worth, self-esteem and hope.

Thus, in any move towards supporting alternative provision of education, we would argue that there must be a policy framework that takes into account the needs of students beyond the immediate demands of schooling: a policy framework that enables schools to create a positive climate in which meaningful learning can take place in flexible ways. While this will inevitably require a significant funding commitment, it will also necessitate a re-visioning of the nature and purpose of schooling itself.

References

Abelmann, N., Choi, J. and Park, S.J. (eds) (2012) *No Alternative? Experiments in South Korean education*. Berkeley: University of California Press.

ABS (Australian Bureau of Statistics) (2017) '4221.0 – Schools, Australia, 2016'. Online. www.abs.gov.au/AUSSTATS/abs@.nsf/Lookup/4221.0Main+Features1 2016?OpenDocument (accessed 6 May 2018).

ACARA (Australian Curriculum, Assessment and Reporting Authority) (2017) 'My School'. Online. www.myschool.edu.au/ (accessed 23 February 2018).

Aron, L.Y. (2006) *An Overview of Alternative Education*. Washington, DC: Urban Institute.

Aron, L.Y. and Zweig, J.M. (2003) *Educational Alternatives for Vulnerable Youth: Student needs, program types, and research directions*. Washington, DC: Urban Institute.

Australian Department of Social Services (2014) 'Budget fact sheet – Working age payments'. Online. www.dss.gov.au/about-the-department/publications-articles/corporate-publications/budget-and-additional-estimates-statements/2014-15-budget/budget-fact-sheet-working-age-payments (accessed 23 September 2017).

Australian Government (2017) *Closing the Gap: Prime Minister's report 2017*. Canberra: Commonwealth of Australia. Online. www.pmc.gov.au/sites/default/files/publications/ctg-report-2017.pdf (accessed 6 May 2018).

Bacchi, C. (2009) *Analysing Policy: What's the problem represented to be?* Frenchs Forest, NSW: Pearson Australia.

Bacchi, C. (2012) 'Why study problematizations? Making politics visible'. *Open Journal of Political Science*, 2 (1), 1–8.

Baker, A.M. (2016) 'The process and product: Crafting community portraits with young people in flexible learning settings'. *International Journal of Inclusive Education*, 20 (3), 309–30.

Ball, S.J. (2006) *Education Policy and Social Class: The selected works of Stephen J. Ball*. London: Routledge.

Ball, S.J. (2012) *Global Education Inc.: New policy networks and the neo-liberal imaginary*. London: Routledge.

Bills, A. and Howard, N. (2017) 'Social inclusion education policy in South Australia: What can we learn?'. *Australian Journal of Education*, 61 (1), 54–74.

Choi, J. (2012) 'A second-chance high school: Students' second-class internalization and stratification'. In Abelmann, N., Choi, J. and Park, S.J. (eds) *No Alternative? Experiments in South Korean education*. Berkeley: University of California Press, 47–62.

COAG (Council of Australian Governments) (2009) 'COAG National Partnership on Youth Attainment and Transitions'. Online. https://web.archive.org/web/20110422132217/www.socialinclusion.gov.au/LatestNews/Pages/COAGNationalPartnershipYouthAttainmentandTransitions.aspx (accessed 6 May 2018).

COAG (Council of Australian Governments) Reform Council (2013) *Education in Australia 2012: Five years of performance*. Sydney: COAG Reform Council.

Dovemark, M. and Beach, D. (2015) 'Academic work on a back-burner: Habituating students in the upper-secondary school towards marginality and a life in the precariat'. *International Journal of Inclusive Education*, 19 (6), 583–94.

Dreise, T. and Thomson, S. (2014) *Unfinished Business: PISA shows Indigenous youth are being left behind* (ACER Occasional Essays). Camberwell, VIC: Australian Council for Educational Research.

Fish, T. (2017) 'Therapeutic responses to "at risk" disengaged early school leavers in a rural alternative education programme'. *Ethnography and Education*, 12 (1), 95–111.

Gallagher, E. (2011) 'The second chance school'. *International Journal of Inclusive Education*, 15 (4), 445–59.

Graham, L.J., Van Bergen, P. and Sweller, N. (2015) '"To educate you to be smart": Disaffected students and the purpose of school in the (not so clever) "lucky country"'. *Journal of Education Policy*, 30 (2), 237–57.

Kim, J.-H. (2011) 'Narrative inquiry into (re)imagining alternative schools: A case study of Kevin Gonzales'. *International Journal of Qualitative Studies in Education*, 24 (1), 77–96.

KPMG (2009) *Re-engaging Our Kids: A framework for education provision to children and young people at risk of disengaging or disengaged from school*. Melbourne: Department of Education and Early Childhood Development.

Lewthwaite, B., Wilson, K., Wallace, V., McGinty, S. and Swain, L. (2017) 'Challenging normative assumptions regarding disengaged youth: A phenomenological perspective'. *International Journal of Qualitative Studies in Education*, 30 (4), 388–405.

Lingard, B. (2011) 'Policy as numbers: Ac/counting for educational research'. *Australian Educational Researcher*, 38 (4), 355–82.

Lingard, B. and Sellar, S. (2013) '"Catalyst data": Perverse systemic effects of audit and accountability in Australian schooling'. *Journal of Education Policy*, 28 (5), 634–56.

Martin, N. and Brand, B. (2006) *Federal, State, and Local Roles Supporting Alternative Education*. Washington, DC: American Youth Policy Forum.

McCluskey, G. (2017) 'Closing the attainment gap in Scottish schools: Three challenges in an unequal society'. *Education, Citizenship and Social Justice*, 12 (1), 24–35.

McCluskey, G., Riddell, S. and Weedon, E. (2015) 'Children's rights, school exclusion and alternative educational provision'. *International Journal of Inclusive Education*, 19 (6), 595–607.

McCluskey, G., Riddell, S., Weedon, E. and Fordyce, M. (2016) 'Exclusion from school and recognition of difference'. *Discourse: Studies in the Cultural Politics of Education*, 37 (4), 529–39.

MCEETYA (Ministerial Council on Education, Employment, Training and Youth Affairs) (2008) *Melbourne Declaration on Educational Goals for Young Australians*. Melbourne: Ministerial Council on Education, Employment, Training and Youth Affairs.

McGregor, G. and Mills, M. (2012) 'Alternative education sites and marginalised young people: "I wish there were more schools like this one"'. *International Journal of Inclusive Education*, 16 (8), 843–62.

McGregor, G., Mills, M., te Riele, K., Baroutsis, A. and Hayes, D. (2017) *Re-imagining Schooling for Education: Socially just alternatives*. London: Palgrave Macmillan.

McGregor, G., Mills, M., te Riele, K. and Hayes, D. (2015) 'Excluded from school: Getting a second chance at a "meaningful" education'. *International Journal of Inclusive Education*, 19 (6), 608–25.

Mills, M. and McGregor, G. (2010) *Re-engaging Students in Education: Success factors in alternative schools*. Brisbane: Youth Affairs Network Queensland.

Mills, M. and McGregor, G. (2014) *Re-engaging Young People in Education: Learning from alternative schools*. London: Routledge.

Mills, M., McGregor, G. and Muspratt, S. (2012) *Flexible Learning Options/ Centres in the Australian Capital Territory (ACT)*. Canberra: ACT Education and Training Directorate.

Mills, M., Renshaw, P. and Zipin, L. (2013) 'Alternative education provision: A dumping ground for "wasted lives" or a challenge to the mainstream?'. *Social Alternatives*, 32 (2), 13–18.

OECD (Organisation for Economic Co-operation and Development) (2012) *Equity and Quality in Education: Supporting disadvantaged students and schools*. Paris: OECD Publishing.

Ogg, T. and Kaill, E. (2010) *A New Secret Garden? Alternative provision, exclusion and children's rights*. London: Civitas.

Plows, V. (2017) 'Reworking or reaffirming practice? Perceptions of professional learning in alternative and flexible education settings'. *Teaching Education*, 28 (1), 72–87.

Plows, V., Bottrell, D. and te Riele, K. (2017) 'Valued outcomes in the counter-spaces of alternative education programs: Success but on whose scale?'. *Geographical Research*, 55 (1), 29–37.

Queensland Government Department of Education (2017) 'Youth engagement'. Online. http://advancingeducation.qld.gov.au/youthengagement/Pages/default. aspx (accessed 6 May 2018).

Raywid, M.A. (1999) 'History and issues of alternative schools'. *Education Digest*, 64 (9), 47–51.

Riddle, S. and Cleaver, D. (2017) 'Working within and against the grain of policy in an alternative school'. *Discourse: Studies in the Cultural Politics of Education*, 38 (4), 498–510.

Ross, S. and Gray, J. (2005) 'Transitions and re-engagement through second chance education'. *Australian Educational Researcher*, 32 (3), 103–40.

Sahlberg, P. (2011) *Finnish Lessons: What can the world learn from educational change in Finland?* New York: Teachers College Press.

Shay, M. and Heck, D. (2015) 'Alternative education engaging Indigenous young people: Flexi-schooling in Queensland'. *Australian Journal of Indigenous Education*, 44 (1), 37–47.

Skattebol, J. and Hayes, D. (2016) 'Cracking with affect: Relationality in young people's movements in and out of mainstream schooling'. *Critical Studies in Education*, 57 (1), 6–20.

Te Riele, K. (2007) 'Educational alternatives for marginalised youth'. *Australian Educational Researcher*, 34 (3), 53–68.

Te Riele, K. (2012) *Learning Choices: A map for the future*. Bondi Junction, NSW: Dusseldorp Skills Forum.

Te Riele, K. (2014). *Putting the jigsaw together: Flexible learning programs in Australia. Final report*. Melbourne: The Victoria Institute for Education, Diversity and Lifelong Learning

Te Riele, K., Wilson, K., Wallace, V., McGinty, S. and Lewthwaite, B. (2017) 'Outcomes from flexible learning options for disenfranchised youth: What counts?'. *International Journal of Inclusive Education*, 21 (2), 117–30.

Thomson, P. and Russell, L. (2007) *Mapping the Alternatives to Permanent Exclusion*. York: Joseph Rowntree Foundation.

Tyack, D. and Tobin, W. (1994) 'The "grammar" of schooling: Why has it been so hard to change?'. *American Educational Research Journal*, 31 (3), 453–79.

Woods, P.A. and Woods, G.J. (eds) (2009) *Alternative Education for the 21st century: Philosophies, approaches, visions*. New York: Palgrave Macmillan.

Wrigley, T., Thomson, P. and Lingard, B. (eds) (2012) *Changing Schools: Alternative ways to make a world of difference*. London: Routledge.

Wyn, J. and Woodman, D. (2006) 'Generation, youth and social change in Australia'. *Journal of Youth Studies*, 9 (5), 495–514.

Chapter 6

Alternative schooling for disadvantaged young people in Indonesia

Ila Rosmilawati, Carol Reid and David Wright

In Indonesia, poverty forces students to pursue alternative pathways to an education. These students have dropped out of mainstream schooling for several reasons. They include lack of financial resources, distance to school and having to work to support their family. However, the provision of alternative education opportunities has meant they are now returning to re-engage with education. This creates a challenge for the Indonesian government: to accommodate a diverse group of non-traditional learners in the context of international pressure to increase education levels. For Indonesian disadvantaged youth, the choice is often not between an alternative or mainstream school, but between an alternative school or no school. Using Mezirow's (Mezirow and Associates, 2000) theory of transformative learning, this chapter draws on the experience of students from two public alternative schools in Indonesia to problematize the challenges and tensions that individual students face and how they work against mainstream assumptions to transform their opportunities.

Equivalency Programs (EP), as the alternative education system in Indonesia is known, work to meet the needs of disadvantaged learners and their communities. These construct educational orientations and philosophies particular to the social-ecological (Wright and Hill, 2011) relationships that define those communities. Some students approach this learning experience reluctantly, unconvinced of its competitive merit. Most, however, learn to live with the contradictions and conflicts inherent in the alternative experience. Evidence drawn from participants suggests that success in these systems enables students to develop new perspectives on possible futures. These new perspectives are drawn from the background they bring to their learning and the new learning they experience. Overall, this study of the school-based learning experiences of participants in the EP system sought to uncover the value students place on this learning.

In this chapter, educational experience is explored through the notion of transformative learning, shaped through critical (Freire, 1993) and ecological consciousness (O'Sullivan, 2012). Critical consciousness emerges in the increased capacity to question the broader social construction of alternative and mainstream education. Ecological consciousness is a broad form of learning that transforms students' perspectives upon the social and physical relationships that sustain life. It is a systemic analysis (Capra and Luisi, 2014) constructed from a personal perspective: an analysis that is always mediated through the assumptions that predicate that analysis. The chapter concludes with a discussion of the ways in which the students' resistance to, and reflection on, their EP experience constitute a systemically driven transformation of learning.

Introduction

The assumption that effective systems of education are essential to national success creates significant challenges to the government of Indonesia. As a nation, Indonesia suffers long-term inequalities related to poverty and access to education. In 2014, the number of Indonesian people who lived below the poverty line (less than US$2 per day) reached more than 28 million, that is, 11 per cent of the Indonesian population (OECD and ADB, 2015: 59). In the education sector, the OECD and ADB (2015) reported that the dropout rate for students in primary school was 1.09 per cent in 2011/12, and 4.7 per cent did not continue to junior secondary school. In the junior secondary school context, 1.7 per cent of students dropped out, and 10 per cent did not continue to senior secondary school. In addition, the total dropout rate for senior secondary school is 3 per cent per year. These numbers do not include children who have never attended school. In Indonesia, there are no consequences for families who do not send their children to school. Even though the primary years are compulsory there is no legal enforcement. Given the limit to the resources the Indonesian government can apply to formal schooling programmes, poverty forces an increasing number of Indonesian students to find alternative ways to gain an education. By law, the first nine years of compulsory schooling are free for all citizens (this covers the annual enrolment fee and monthly tuition fees). Beyond those years, at senior secondary level, fees are levied. These fees are a major impediment to poorer students. In the EP at senior secondary school level tuition fees are minimal and in some instances non-existent. In 2010 throughout Indonesia, 829,776 EP students attended 23,210 EP learning programmes. Of these programmes, 20,907 were managed by the Ministry of Education and Culture and 2,303 were managed by the Ministry of Religious Affairs and based on the Islamic faith.

The provision of access to education for previously excluded groups of young people is an important first step to greater equality of opportunity. However, while Indonesia has worked towards the development of an alternative education system, there has been strong critique of the system and the schools within it. Much of this is formulated in terms of outcomes. EP in Indonesia is classified by some as having a low quality of education with low performance by students compared to students from mainstream schooling. This deficit construction of EP in Indonesia raises one crucial question. How can this form of education tap into the potential of its large and diverse group of non-traditional learners?

For Indonesian disadvantaged youth, EPs give young people, primarily from disadvantaged backgrounds, the opportunity to achieve education through other than mainstream pathways. The EP comprises Package A (equivalent to primary school), Package B (equivalent to junior secondary school) and Package C (equivalent to senior secondary school). This approach is not only a feature of Indonesian education; it is being utilized throughout South and Southeast Asian nations to improve basic educational standards and provide 'Education for All' (EFA; see UNESCO, n.d.).

The Indonesian model of EP is flexible in terms of length of time, period, curriculum, pedagogy, venue and language (UNESCO, 2013). Flexibility enables inclusive interventions that support young people ordinarily excluded from acquiring the learning competencies that meet their needs and circumstances. The flexible approach can include teaching in the 'mother tongue' and the use of diverse teaching methodologies such as mobile learning, distance learning, multigrade teaching and flexible hours of teaching and learning. A multiple entry system also provides flexibility for students wishing to transfer to an EP after dropping out from mainstream education. It also enables learners to leave an EP and re-enter at a later stage and it evaluates and documents learning achievements realized during their absence.

EP works to meet the needs of disadvantaged learners and their communities. These construct educational orientations and philosophies particular to the social-ecological (Wright and Hill, 2011) relationships that define those communities. However, the impact of learning in EP cannot be demonstrated solely through reference to traditional learning processes: those involving students in set tasks grounded in an objectivist understanding of experience (Zyngier, 2008). It is through students' transformative engagement in their own learning – a critical, self-reflective perspective upon self and institutional learning – that an effective base for relevant, effective and equivalent learning is constructed. Arguably, this has the potential to become the foundation of each student's future learning, a form of learning derived from participation in the EP, which amounts to more than absorption of the taught content. It has also been used as the basis for the argument that 'different' processes and outcomes may in fact be 'deficient'.

Importantly, the EP is provided through a separate formal school system: separate physical structures and separate curriculum structures. Its principal concern is the provision of schooling for a specific target group. The location of an EP is often a temporary site with non-permanent buildings and facilities. The site is organized through a community-learning centre (CLC) and is deliberately situated in a location where its students are located. Thus in order to meet their students in urban areas an EP may be set up in a location near a transport station to attract students currently working as street singers or snack peddlers, or near a riverbank for displaced urban poor people, or near a marketplace so as to be accessible to beggar children or toy sellers, or in middle-class community areas to serve domestic cleaners and housemaids. In rural areas, EPs can be situated specifically to attract, for example, minorities living in isolated areas, students of Islamic boarding schools who have received religious but no formal education services, or in fishing communities to provide education to those who have grown up learning only to make a living from the sea. Some EPs are also set up in prisons to allow young offenders to get an education. By contrast with formal schools that generally require students to come to them, the EP school system is designed to go to the students. A lack of money to pay for transportation is one of the major barriers to schooling for the disadvantaged.

It is clear that EP offers an alternative to a diverse range of young people when formal education is not available, accessible or suitable. Little is known of the experiences in such settings, but given the growth in this sector and the current desire to increase national education participation and the hitherto focus on equivalency of outcomes only, it seems timely to ask the young people who participate in the system what they think.

Equivalency programmes

This study utilizes the notion of transformative learning (Mezirow, 1991), shaped through critical (Freire, 1993) and ecological consciousness (O'Sullivan, 2012). O'Sullivan argues that ecological consciousness reshapes a learner's views, understanding and actions, thereby enhancing appreciation of the relationships upon which learning is founded. This brings with it reflection upon how individuals contribute to their social ecology: their social relationships and their ecological relationships.

O'Sullivan argues that transformative learning may benefit from going beyond Mezirow's conception of humans' focused reflections upon themselves and their social relationships, to incorporate an understanding of the relationship between individuals, societies and the physical world. Thus, O'Sullivan argues that transformative learning through ecological consciousness:

> involves experiencing a deep, structural shift in the basic premises of thought, feelings and actions. Transformative learning is a shift of consciousness that dramatically alters our way of being in the world. Such a shift involves our understanding of ourselves and our self-locations; our relationships with other humans and with the natural world; our understanding of relations of power in interlocking structures of class, race and gender; our body awareness; our visions of alternative approaches to living and our sense of possibilities for social justice and peace and personal joy. (O'Sullivan, 2002: 11)

This is a broad and expansive extension of the concept. It is a powerful emancipatory vision. Here ecological consciousness is less to do with ecological science and more to do with the social-ecological construction of knowledge (Wright and Hill, 2011). This concept can be seen as a vehicle that allows a deep understanding of how young people in EP can come to understand their education and the circumstances within which it occurs. The conception of transformative learning through ecological consciousness contributes three ideas to educational processes: (1) education for survival; (2) education for critical understanding; (3) education for integral creativity (O'Sullivan, 2012: 166). It builds on the concept of critical consciousness developed by Freire (1993) where place, learning and social connection are central to the development of education initiatives, particularly among the poor and disenfranchised. It recognizes their locations in their communities and the practices and resources community and learning are built on. Freire argued that understanding the forces shaping your world is pivotal in the movement towards liberation.

With these ideas, transformative learning for disadvantaged youth in EP can be seen to construct a mode of negotiation, resistance and critique, and creativity and vision through educational processes and experiences. This requires that the EP students recognize their marginalization, educationally and socially, through critical reflection on their position as students at EP, in the shadow of the mainstream. To achieve this sort of consciousness, the disadvantaged student needs first to recognize the relationship between their limitations (such as poverty) and conventional educational opportunities. Such insight creates a consciousness of how to negotiate and learn in the broad educational arena. In such circumstances a student might face the dynamics of denial, despair and even grief, especially when the learning process in the EP does not meet their educational expectations or when their life circumstances (such as pressures imposed by employment) do not integrate well with the schooling process. Such awareness requires a student to engage in critical reflection upon the relationship between their educational position and their larger social relationships, including their relationship with the educational community and the community within which they live. This can contribute to a critical consciousness through which the student comes to critique the hegemonic culture of mainstream education and the society (Freire, 1993), which places more value on mainstream education than it does on alternative education. This critique is then a basis from which change can be imagined. From the perspective of ecological consciousness, transformation is a process of learning that creates conditions for sustainable futures (O'Sullivan, 2012).

This theoretical framework is used to discuss the case studies of two alternative schools, which belong to local government authorities: Wijaya Learning Centre and Nusantara Non-formal Education Centre. These two have been chosen from a larger study of alternative schools in Indonesia (Rosmilawati, 2016) because they are alternative government schools that operate in different locations. One is in a rural setting, the other in an urban setting.

Wijaya Learning Centre is located in an urban-metropolitan area of Jakarta, the capital city of Indonesia. Jakarta has long been the main destination for people seeking a better life. This includes youth from across Indonesia. Young people who leave school early often migrate to Jakarta without their parents because they believe that economic opportunities are unavailable in their village or city of origin. Most arrive in Jakarta with the hope of gaining employment. Typically, young females establish themselves in jobs as domestic servants, while males often start out as workers in small-scale factories or as street sellers. In general, they work casually or are self-employed. They work long hours for low wages in low-level occupations. They are prepared to work hard because, while in the city they lack family support, they still carry responsibility for their families, who remain in their village. In addition to those who have migrated from the countryside, an additional group of students also seek out EP. These are local students who have dropped out of, or been excluded from, mainstream schools and yet still recognize value in further learning. Therefore, the combination of transience, poverty and demanding working conditions requires that the school must be dynamic if it is to meet the learning needs of this very diverse range of students. In this study, six students were interviewed and nine students were involved in a focus group discussion. The participants comprised nine females and six males aged from 16 to 25.

Figure 6.1: Wijaya Learning Centre students

By contrast Nusantara alternative school lies in a poor, rural region. Its students see the EP as the only available and affordable educational pathway. It offers places to disadvantaged students who need education but cannot enrol in a mainstream high school due to poverty. Most Nusantara students are similar in age and background: aged between 15 and 18 years and from families of farmers working in the informal agricultural sector or as seasonal community labourers. In Pandeglang district, where Nusantara is located, agriculture is the principal activity of 62.25 per cent of the community. Nine Nusantara students were interviewed and ten were in a focus group discussion. The participants comprised nine females and ten males.

Figure 6.2: Nusantara Non-formal Education Centre students

Most Nusantara students left mainstream schooling after graduating from junior secondary schooling. By law, public junior secondary schooling is free for all citizens in Indonesia. However, senior secondary schooling is not free and school fees and associated educational expenses are a major obstacle to poorer students. Poverty therefore limits access to schooling. For Nusantara students, participation in the EP is not a choice, it is their only opportunity to extend their education and to enjoy the access to opportunity that is taken for granted by those who are more financially secure. In other words, financial cost and affordability are the basic reasons for students to participate in EP at Nusantara. Participation in the EP, even though it is seen by some as not the ideal option, provides these young people with some measure of opportunity. Thus, their actions arise out of an aspiration to improve opportunities while the necessity to do this through EP provides confirmation to them and others of their marginalized circumstances.

These two schools, Wijaya and Nusantara, have specific purposes as a consequence of their location. Both serve out-of-school children in the area while catering also for different learning needs. For example, Wijaya provides afternoon classes, since the majority of its students are working in the morning. Nusantara has morning classes and utilizes some mainstream educational structures such as timetables, formalized school rules and uniforms. Both schools also labour with the recognition that many of their students approach learning in EP reluctantly, less than convinced of its competitive merit. EP schools and EP students, of necessity, live with contradictions and conflicts inherent in the alternative. However, evidence drawn from participants in this research (Rosmilawati, 2016) suggests that success in these systems enables students to develop alternative perspectives on possible futures. This is a powerful form of learning that provides insight not available through mainstream schooling.

Initial learning experiences: Uncertain and reluctant

The EP provides educational access for young disadvantaged students: it enables such students to access the benefits that further education can bring to life. It can take the form of a first-chance and second-chance avenue to learning and this can be the vehicle for personal and social transformation and future opportunity. However, young people studying in the Indonesian EP often report that they are seen as – and they often see themselves as – subordinate or inferior to those students who access mainstream schooling. For some students this can be very troubling.

> If I compare, mainstream school is more standardized. It has more subjects to learn, more knowledge for students. In contrast, we learn little here because we only study three hours a day. (Tedjo, male, 14 years old, Wijaya)

> In a mainstream school, we are serious students. In contrast, I found that the learning process in the EP is more relaxed than in the mainstream school; there is no punishment for whatever students do. But one thing is the students do not pay attention to the lessons. (Dwipa, male, 16 years old, Wijaya)

The flexible learning systems that are often central to critiques of the EP program allow EP schools to work through flexible scheduling. This enables students to negotiate the learning hours that are best suited to their circumstances. For example, Wijaya school offers between three and five days of schooling per week in the afternoon. These afternoon classes include both workers and non-workers. For reasons discussed above, Nusantara sets up a morning school, with shorter learning sessions than in mainstream schools. In both schools, attendance requirements are not as strict as for mainstream schools. Students can obtain permission from their teachers to attend class irregularly or at particular times after explaining the reasons for doing so. Flexible scheduling, in effect, allows school staff the latitude to attempt to best meet student needs and work towards their students' success. However, students have varying responses to this flexibility. For some Wijaya students, this is welcome. Neneng and Widi are two such students:

What I am thinking about this school is useful for us, is because its system helps worker-student, in managing their time. In the formal school, the learning hours are too long. Furthermore, they are not flexible on the learning process. Therefore, this school supports me so much better. (Neneng, female, 22 years old)

In the school days, I start work earlier. I wake up at 4.30 a.m. and do the household job because I am a housemaid. I wash dishes, prepare breakfast for all family members, and clean the house; I have to make sure that my duties are done before I go to school … I get home at 7.30 p.m. Sometimes I continue my work after that, such as doing gardening until 9 p.m., after that I sleep. (Widi, female, 17 years old)

However, some Nusantara students argue that a flexible learning schedule leads to a feeling of uncertainty. Students do not understand how such a school provides appropriate learning when it does not seek to regulate attendance. Irfan says:

What makes me lazy at this school is everybody knows that EP is a flexible school. Even though some students do not come to the school for several days or even a month, they still continue to the next grade. (Irfan, male, 18 years old)

The flexible learning environment expands beyond the classroom, allowing learning to take place in a variety of off-site locations. These include the home or other places where students spend a lot of time. This strategy aims to increase involvement in schooling and reduce dropout rates. However, for some Wijaya and Nusantara students, this has a negative impact. Some students want to spend more time at school, especially if they do not have work or family responsibilities to attend to:

When I was in Grade 10 here, we studied four days a week, but now only three days a week. The teacher said that students could only focus on subjects that will be included for the national examination. However, these new rules make the students feel bored. I want to learn more about other subjects just like at the mainstream school, such as art, language and computer. (Sinta, female, 17 years old, Wijaya)

Times of learning are too short. I wish the head of school gave (more) time for students to study at school. (If so), we will get more from here. (Rara, female, 17 years old, Nusantara)

The physical school environment and the educational resources of EP schools also influence students' learning experiences. Wijaya and Nusantara have limited equipment and resources in comparison to mainstream schools. EP students often feel further disadvantaged because they feel frustrated from reaching their potential because of these sorts of limitations:

> In my opinion, [the] learning experience in this school is still limited. We do not have good facilities. Even for sport, we have to go to city courts, because we do not have [our own]. Moreover, several computers are also broken, so the students have to take a turn if we want to use it. The teacher told us the government will provide additional life skills programme for the EP, but until now, it has not happened. (Susi, female, 16 years old, Nusantara)

Some Nusantara students could be described as 'reluctant stayers'. This is generally because their main reason for studying at EP is a lack of choice. The fact that they are poor means they face economic barriers to education. As some encounter the limiting and constraining factors in the EP system, they unconsciously downgrade any earlier intentions to be 'good students'. They become reluctant stayers, determined simply to wait out the period until they finally graduate. Since there are no external forces (apart from their families' expectations) to encourage students to stay in the EP, some feel a mismatch between their expectation of schooling and what the schools actually offer. Some students who may be seen as using the EP just to fill in time, could be using the EP as a shelter from unemployment. For example, they consciously choose to stay at EP rather than become unemployed, as the rural area they live in offers few job opportunities. This challenges the EP teachers to focus their teaching in the EP to best support those school-age students who are more fully engaged learners.

The discourse around transformative learning suggests that students can be seen to have transformed their situation by their capacity to critique and challenge EP policy through the expression of what Illeris (2007: 188) calls 'ambivalent tolerance'. This is an understanding that students arrive at by themselves: in effect it means that they face contradictions, yet develop agency. This condition influences the subjectivities of young people as EP students. At a personal level, the vulnerability constructed through this position can be distressing but it can have positive consequences. Mezirow (1991) terms this a 'disorienting dilemma', and describes it as a necessary element in the transformation of learning. Through this learning process students can be seen to demonstrate their awareness of context by opening their eyes to a wider world. As a consequence, the viewed world is changed, as is the viewpoint of the students or conscious participant-learners. The students recognize that they have become reluctant stayers and are therefore participants in a new way of learning. There is a metaphorical link between this and O'Sullivan's (2012) planetary or ecological perspective. O'Sullivan argues that this is how we are required to negotiate life on this planet: as conscious participant learners working through our 'ambivalent tolerance'. Recognition by learners of their ambivalent tolerance is a necessary stage in Mezirow's (1991) formulation of learning transformation. It is the stage where learners come to appreciate that their difficulties are not theirs alone. They are shared with others. Such recognition enables learning to become a social experience: a gradual process of finding meaning in a newly understood environment. This is a potent space for learning. It invites students to become actively involved in their education and the way it prepares them for adult life and the workplace. When these issues are resolved, self-development is signified. From Mezirow's (1991) perspective, transformation occurs when students have sufficient self-orientation to perceive and address problems caused by limitations to their education. This changes their understanding of their social-ecological relationship and the opportunities that appropriately focused learning makes available to them.

Key tensions in transformation: Resistance and appreciation

Learning can be transformative if there is a shift in understanding of the relationship between humans, the self and the natural world (O'Sullivan, 2012). Applying O'Sullivan's thesis to Wijaya and Nusantara students can reveal how this emerges in the context of the EP. Two forms of learning, resulting from such a shift in consciousness, deserve discussion: learning through resistance and learning through appreciation.

Learning through resistance

In the previous section, it was possible to see that there is a period of resistance to learning for many students. This stands in direct relationship to their capacity to negotiate the educational arena. Limitations to life-fulfilment for Indonesian disadvantaged youth, especially those related to the need for learning and education, is an existential condition that few can escape. Student recognition of being 'trapped' is a major element in the transformation of learning.

At Nusantara and Wijaya, many students learn through resistance. This means that these students are faced with something that they find very difficult to accept regarding their expectations around schooling and learning. However, to maintain their status as a student and not drop out, the students remain at school: they set their learning expectations to fit the learning culture and environment. They do this because they believe that the EP protects them from 'downward mobility' (Shavit *et al.*, 2002: 9):

> We are now [able] to integrate with this learning culture and environment, even [if it is] different [from] what we experienced in the previous school. (group of Nusantara female students)

> It is absolutely irrelevant experience for me, but I will keep staying at this school so I can get future engagement in mainstream school once I graduate from EP. (Tedjo, male, 14 years old, Wijaya)

The students learn to take more responsibility for their own learning. The transformation of these learners involves emancipation from unnecessary deference and self-denial, which is culturally embedded in the wider society. Students understand the learning situation in the EP and learn to live with its contradictions and conflicts. This part of their learning involves the capacity to deal with both personal expectation and social reality. It can also involve:

> an understanding of ourselves and our locations, our relations with other humans and with the natural world; an understanding of the relations of power in the interlocking structures of class, race and gender; body awareness; and our visions of alternative approaches to living. (O'Sullivan *et al.*, 2002: xvii, 11)

From an ecological perspective, transformation is a process of learning that creates conditions for recognition of participation in, and ongoing contribution to, the relationships required to ensure the continuation of life (O'Sullivan, 2012). It is learning that is less concerned with trying to find fixed facts and more concerned with identifying what is needed to learn to adapt to change and live responsibly in relation to challenges presented by social conflict and personal doubts.

Resistance learning can create a space for learning. It can be a legitimate expression of learning, and it can challenge EP institutions to engage with students to promote meaningful learning. For example, although Tedjo from Wijaya is resistant to his current learning, he understands it will build a 'bridge to future engagement', stating, 'I will re-enrol at mainstream senior high school after I get Package B certificate.' Eva plans to gain the pre-requisites to attend university even though she is uncertain about her current learning situation: 'I will hire a private tutor for preparing me … to get into university.' To identify the potential for future learning that results from the current experience, students have to be able to accommodate the limitations they perceive in their current learning (Freire, 1993).

Learning through resistance can be a source of the most far-reaching potential for learning. In terms of learning for transformation, this is part of a strategy of negotiation between learning and social situations. It is a defence mechanism that prevents students from being overwhelmed by the deeply problematic nature of life (O'Sullivan, 2012). A resilient attitude needs to be developed in a process of learning. It requires students to develop self-control and justification for what they feel, know and believe, and to act upon that knowing. Students who learn through resistance in this group of Wijaya students are different from those students who achieve transformation in learning through their valuing of family and community, as discussed in the next section.

Learning through appreciation

Learning is not limited to the classroom; it also arises in relationship to society. By connecting with society, learning can assist students to avoid being overwhelmed by the deeply problematic nature of student life (O'Sullivan, 2012). In the social environment of Indonesia, family and close community groups tend to construct ideals: social rules and structured relationships that each individual is expected to understand and conform to. Indonesians value loyalty to family and friends above all else. For example, Javanese ethnic Indonesians have a saying: '*Mangan ora mangan asal ngumpul*', which means 'whether we have food or not, the most important thing is that we are together'. Through fundamentals of this kind, children and young people are taught to obey and respect parents and to honour and respect social expectations. These then form the basis of interpersonal behaviour. As a result, many Indonesian children are committed to their parents and grow up with a desire to make their parents' life easier. This also applies to parents, who are mainly strongly committed to their children and, if circumstances allow it, tend not to let children live separate from the family until they marry. In other words, Indonesia is a collective society and maintaining harmonious relationships is extremely important. For those living in rural areas those relationships extend into the community and towards surrounding land and water systems that provide sustenance and require nurturing. Here, informed participation in ecological networks, central to which is responsibility for family, demonstrate learning of a transformative kind. O'Sullivan extrapolates upon this and discusses it as a relationship to the more expansive entities of the cosmos and the biosphere (O'Sullivan, 2012).

Various explanations are given by those students who continue to study at EP. Interviews suggest that these students appreciate learning in part through the way they value certain aspects of their lives, especially family and community. They act co-operatively in learning and schooling, they come to class regularly and their involvement with learning stands in direct relationship to their emerging understanding of opportunities available to them in family and community life. This type of appreciation is another form of transformative learning. It addresses the experience of students who have learnt to function as individuals in relation to the larger experience of family and community.

> My parents always ask me to go to school even though my school environment is like this. They (say) that I have to stay at school until graduation day comes. (Dedi, male, 18 years old, Nusantara)

> In the very beginning, I do not like to study here. I feel like this school is different from another school, especially for learning experience and environment. But I have to stay here until [I] finish, because I don't have money to transfer to another school. (Syarif, male, 18 years old, Nusantara)

> I do not enjoy to study here because [there are] many bad students. But, my sister said that I have to stay until graduating from Grade 12. (Irfan, male, 18 years old, Nusantara)

In this respect students can be seen to look at, appreciate, and learn from cultures that honour learning processes as much as the product of learning. This sort of participatory consciousness comes from students' understanding of the role that social values play in Indonesian life. It comes from students' insight into their family and kinship obligations. These obligations extend, in some situations more than others, into relationships to the natural world: plant and animal life, seasonal influences, tides and other patterns of nature that construct the context of sustainable life. The role of a flexible educational institution, able to work with the patterns of community life to provide learning opportunities for those seen as disadvantaged, can both affirm and encourage an understanding of learning in relationship to the patterns, processes and responsibilities that systematise the life of disadvantaged students.

In the context of an urban school, the EP school climate generally separates disadvantaged students from difficulties they may have experienced in mainstream schools: difficulties characterized by and resulting in disruption, truancy and threatening behaviours. The flexible characteristics of EP schools, the relationships that are fostered and the small size of classes facilitate students' learning and influence students to value the school experience. This allows young students to understand and to make a connection between self-needs or interests and their social-ecological relationships. From an ecological perspective, there is no way the learning of a person can be detached from the community and the physical environment within which it occurs. The value of such understanding lies in a person's ability to reflect upon and appreciate their relationship to those elements. Dwipa said:

> The students do not fight each other; they do not have an enemy. So, I feel like this school environment is suited for me. It is relaxed environment actually, maybe because of a small school community. I do not want to go back to my previous school. I promise to myself, even though I am studying at EP, I will stay here until I graduate from high school. This school suits me. (It gives me) peace and quiet, and most importantly, I do not have any problem with other students. (Dwipa, male, 16 years old, Wijaya)

Learning through appreciation involves the construction of a transformed understanding that is guided by values and norms that integrate with school, its circumstances and the society it serves. Ideally it results in engaged wisdom: a life contributing to the common good of family and social and environmental relationships. This facilitates discourse upon the qualities and capacities of citizenship (Parker and Nilan, 2013).

Conclusion

EP provides a transformational educational space for many disadvantaged students. EP also challenges the deficit constructions of young, disadvantaged Indonesian students to enable shifts in educational perspectives. There are students who are able to engage with learning in the EP context, to improve themselves as individuals and to transform their educational orientation into new (alternative) educational goals. Indonesian disadvantaged youth engage with a different process of transformative learning in EP. Students often approach this learning experience reluctantly, unconvinced of its competitive merit. Most, however, learn to live with the contradictions and conflicts inherent in the alternative experience. This study argues that this experience can assist students to critically examine assumptions and become more reflective, open and inclusive.

The Indonesian alternative system is different from that which operates in high-income countries, where young people may attend alternative schooling through a desire to search out what they consider to be more appropriate curriculum and pedagogy (te Riele, 2007). The focus in Indonesia is on ongoing participation in education for disadvantaged young people. It is very important to sustain these needs by providing an equivalence of educational outcomes. EP challenges students who are willing and able to engage with learning, whatever their educational aspiration. Success in the EP can require a shift in educational perspective. At their best, teachers in the EP system work to help students reflect upon their learning experience, to allow them to discover that learning is something they do rather than something that is done to them. It arises through dialogical and dialectical relationships between educators and students. At their best, students in the EP network change the communities they participate in because they understand that communities are constructed, consciously or unconsciously, by the contribution of its participants.

References

Capra, F. and Luisi, P.L. (2014) *The Systems View of Life: A unifying vision.* Cambridge: Cambridge University Press.

Freire, P. (1993) *Pedagogy of the Oppressed.* New rev. 20th anniversary ed. Trans. Ramos, M.B. New York: Continuum.

Illeris, K. (2007) *How We Learn: Learning and non-learning in school and beyond.* London: Routledge.

Mezirow, J. (1991) *Transformative Dimensions of Adult Learning.* San Francisco: Jossey-Bass.

Mezirow, J. and Associates (2000) *Learning as Transformation: Critical perspectives on a theory in progress.* San Francisco: Jossey-Bass.

OECD (Organisation for Economic Co-operation and Development) and ADB (Asian Development Bank) (2015) *Education in Indonesia: Rising to the challenge* (Reviews of National Policies for Education). Paris: OECD Publishing.

O'Sullivan, E. (2012) 'Deep transformation: Forging a planetary worldview'. In Taylor, E.W. and Cranton, P. (eds) *The Handbook of Transformative Learning: Theory, research, and practice.* San Francisco: Jossey-Bass, 162–77.

O'Sullivan, E., Morrell, A. and O'Connor, M.A. (eds) (2002) *Expanding the Boundaries of Transformative Learning: Essays on theory and praxis.* New York: Palgrave.

Parker, L. and Nilan, P. (2013) *Adolescents in Contemporary Indonesia.* London: Routledge.

Rosmilawati, I. (2016) 'Disadvantaged Youth in Alternative Schooling: Investigating Indonesian young people's re-engagement with education'. Unpublished PhD thesis, Western Sydney University.

Shavit, Y., Ayalon, H. and Kurlaender, M. (2002) 'Schooling alternatives, inequality, and mobility in Israel'. In Fuller, B. and Hannum, E. (eds) *Schooling and Social Capital in Diverse Cultures* (Research in the Sociology of Education 13). Amsterdam: JAI Press, 105–24.

Te Riele, K. (2007) 'Educational alternatives for marginalised youth'. *Australian Educational Researcher*, 34 (3), 53–68.

UNESCO (United Nations Educational, Scientific and Cultural Organization) (2013) *Asia-Pacific End of Decade Notes on Education for All: EFA Goal 3 – Life skills and lifelong learning*. Bangkok: United Nations Educational, Scientific and Cultural Organization.

UNESCO (United Nations Educational, Scientific and Cultural Organization) (n.d.) *Education for All Movement*. Online. www.unesco.org/new/en/ education/themes/leading-the-international-agenda/education-for-all/ (accessed 3 July 2018).

Wright, D. and Hill, S.B. (2011) 'Introduction: The emerging field of social ecology'. In Wright, D., Camden-Pratt, C.E. and Hill, S.B. (eds) *Social Ecology: Applying ecological understanding to our lives and our planet*. Stroud: Hawthorn Press, 1–14.

Zyngier, D. (2008) '(Re)conceptualising student engagement: Doing education not doing time'. *Teaching and Teacher Education*, 24 (7), 1765–76.

Chapter 7

Free school systems in Denmark

Lars Erik Storgaard and Maren Skotte

Introduction

In this chapter, we review the underlying principles of Danish free schools, their structures and systems as well as their distinctive ways of working with parents. We also consider the pressures on the free schools system today and how they are seeking to respond to these pressures. In this discussion, we draw on our knowledge of the Danish education system overall and of free schools in particular. Lars is a former Educational Consultant at the Danish Ministry of Education, with direct experience of supervision and inspection of Danish free schools. He is currently a vice-principal at Bernadotteskolen, a free school in Copenhagen. Bernadotteskolen was the first Danish international school and is inspired by the thinking of Summerhill School among others. Maren has been head of policy and communication for the Dansk Friskoleforening (Danish Free School Association) since 2004.

Bringing up and educating children poses major questions for parents and for society. In Denmark we focus on the notion of compulsory education in a broad sense, rather than compulsory schooling. In so doing, we aim to acknowledge the key role and responsibility of parents in their child's education. Danish parents are free to choose whether they send their child to a state school or to one of the many types of free (alternative) schools subsidized by the state. They may also choose to get together and set up a new free school of their own, based on mutually agreed principles. They may, if they wish, teach their children at home, though this is still rare in practice. All that is demanded of private education is that it offers the same high quality as municipal schools (*folkeskole*). About 18 per cent of all children at primary school level from preschool to ninth grade currently attend free schools.

The principles of free schools

In the mid-nineteenth century Denmark first introduced a unique dual system of education in which state-provided education and 'free' school education were regarded as equal partners rather than competitors. This system has prospered so that today's free schools and state schools continue to function as complementary and often mutually supportive systems in Denmark.

The idea of 'freedom' espoused by free schools means both freedom *from* being subordinate to the power of the state and also the freedom *to* establish schools and offer education on their own terms. This idea of freedom is also allied with key principles of ideological freedom, pedagogical freedom, financial freedom, and freedom of employment.

Ideological freedom is seen as important because it recognizes the rights and responsibilities of parents to decide how their children are to be brought up and educated. Essential to this principle is the freedom to foster diverse viewpoints through education and upbringing, and this in turn implies the freedom to oppose other viewpoints – as long as this takes place in ways that do not contravene the law of the land.

The second key principle is that of pedagogical freedom. In Denmark, the state has only general requirements as regards educational content and none as regards methodology. In practice, schools are given considerable freedom with respect to the choice of educational content and the organization of school life. This is why there is a great variety of different methodologies within free schools. Some schools mix students across grades, some educate mostly outside in nature, many schools gather all students and staff for a morning assembly with music, storytelling and performance, many schools prioritize visits outside school.

The third important principle is one of financial freedom. Although state funding for education is relatively high in Denmark, parents are expected to contribute financially for their child to attend a free school. The fees vary from school to school, but because free schools do not want financial considerations to prevent parents from sending their child to a free school, they try to keep the payments at a low level. The majority of free schools have school fees of less than €3,000 per year. Parents may also apply to the school board for a subsidy to reduce the school fee based on household income.

The fourth principle within the free school movement refers to the principle of freedom of employment, meaning that no one outside the school, whether the state, the unions, or any other external authority, has the right to determine the type of educational background and training their teachers should have. Ideological freedom and pedagogical freedom mean that the schools themselves determine whether a teacher has the appropriate qualifications to teach their pupils, an issue returned to later in this chapter. Finally, schools also hold to a principle of freedom to enrol or admit pupils.

Just as no authority outside the school can intervene in the employment of teachers, there is no official authority that can require a particular child to be admitted to the school. It is assumed that those parents who seek to enrol their child in the school agree with and will conform to the school's ideology.

The diversity of free schools in Denmark

Since 1849, when the democratic constitution was ratified in Denmark, the rights of minorities have been enshrined in legislation. Denmark's famous pastor, philosopher and teacher N.F.S. Grundtvig and his political allies fought for this principle, insisting that the minority should not only have the right to think and act as they wish in opposition to the majority, but that the majority (the state) should also provide them with economic support to live in accordance with their minority opinions. Here, in essence, is the approach to minorities adopted by Danish democracy. The protection of the minority is a right of the minority, and is particularly relevant to school legislation. It holds that the minority should not be subordinated to the majority but must be able to uphold both their political and their economic rights – and even to make use of this right to oppose the majority. This view of democracy ensures considerable freedom to schools that are established by minority groups.

Free schools today in Denmark are of many different kinds, including small free schools, typically in rural districts, but also larger free schools often in urban districts, as well as religious or congregational schools, progressive free schools and other schools such as the Waldorf schools. Some cater for the elite, some for new minority populations and others for immigrant groups. Currently around 15 per cent of all Danish pupils attend some kind of free school. Overall, free schools tend to be smaller than state schools. The majority have pupils from preschool classes up to 9th-form level (around 15–16 years old), though some only have pupils up to 6th-, 7th- or 8th-form level. Pupils from these schools must then attend another public or free school or be home schooled in order to fulfil their compulsory education (9th-form level).

The rights of parents

The concept of parents' rights has had a profound influence on Danish school legislation, again influenced originally by the thinking of Grundtvig and then later Chresten Kold. However, over time, and influenced by the Enlightenment's emphasis on education and liberalism as means of developing a new, free, civil society, the movement firmly established the idea that the state should have no authority in matters of personal belief or religion. It is for this reason that, as noted above, the ideas of compulsory education, rather than compulsory schooling, and the idea that education is a parental responsibility, came to be seen as paramount. The term 'the rights of parents' first emerged as a matter of faith in Denmark and can be traced back to the first School Act of 1814 and reinforced by subsequent legislation in the later nineteenth century. From 1908, when free schools were first assured state grants, the state began to pay for the right of all parents to decide how their children would be educated, regardless of their economic situation. This notion of parents' rights was developed and formed through public debate and controversy about the teaching of Christianity in state municipal schools, and was based on the broader right of ordinary people to stand up to the authorities and demand the right to teach their own children in ways that allowed them to stay true to their faith or belief. Over time, the debate extended from the religious to the cultural sphere and revolved around the state's regulation of pedagogic, economic and social conditions and the political authority gained through the struggle of ordinary people to gain self-determination in these areas. The fact that the government regularly updates the laws regarding educational subsidies reflects the strength of the continuing commitment to the rights of parents in the Danish educational system.

The structure and systems of the free school

In order to establish a free school, the founders need to give 12 months notice to the Ministry of Education, draft a set of 'statutes' or rules for the school which are also presented to the Ministry and pay a deposit of approximately €4,000. No other approvals are required. In order to receive grants from the state, a new free school must have at least 14 pupils in its first year (preschool to 9th-form level combined), 24 pupils in its second year (preschool to 9th-form level combined), 32 pupils by the third year and so on, as the school grows.

All free schools are non-profit institutions, meaning that a private person may not own a school, and the school must not be run for private gain. If there is a surplus, this is held in the school's account. Today, free schools receive 75 per cent of the per capita funding given to state schools. The governors of a free school must submit annual accounts to the Ministry of Education, and they must pay their teachers on a nationally agreed scale. Apart from this, the free schools may administer their funds in almost any way they wish – provided they use the money for the benefit of the school. The actual grant per pupil varies from one school to the next depending on three factors: the school roll, the age of the pupils (pupils over the age of 13 attract a higher subsidy) and the location of the school. Urban schools receive higher levels of subsidy as it is recognized that the living costs are higher in urban areas.

All schools must have a board of governors as the primary arbiter of all the school's activities. Many free schools have a 'School Circle', consisting of the pupils' parents and others who wish to support the school. From this circle, a board of governors is elected. The board of governors is responsible to the Ministry of Education for the running of the school as a whole. Although parents play an important role in free schools, they are not involved directly in teaching. Quite a number of parents, however, attend daily morning assembly or help out during classes. It is also very common for parents, teachers and the school board to meet annually to discuss possible pedagogical developments and ideas. It is characteristic of these free schools that parents are actively involved in the school, by participating, for example, in the maintenance and cleaning of the school. In general, staff, parents and heads aim to work closely together for the common good and to ensure the best possible education for each individual child.

The parents and the board of any free school are also responsible for choosing how to supervise the teaching. They must choose either to elect one or more supervisors or, alternatively, carry out school self-evaluation. If a school chooses to supervise teaching via a supervisor they must elect a supervisor who is an independent individual with a teaching background in primary or lower secondary school. To become a supervisor it is necessary to attend a course leading to certification by the Ministry of Education. Elected supervisors must check the following: the pupils' levels of achievement in Danish, Mathematics and English; whether the overall teaching of the school is equal to what is generally achieved in the municipal school; and whether the school prepares its pupils for a life in a society based on freedom and democracy. If these requirements are not met, the supervisor must give the school an injunction or subsequently report to the Ministry of Education. The supervisor is also required to report to parents annually and the report's conclusions must be made public via the school's website homepage.

If the parents and board choose to carry out the supervision by means of school self-evaluation, the model of self-evaluation must be certified by the Ministry of Education. At present there are two certified models. Self-evaluation must ensure the meeting of the same requirements as the supervisors, and the models have explicit and detailed checkpoints. At present less than 5 per cent of all free schools have chosen self-evaluation.

At a national level, the Ministry of Education also carries out its own supervision of free schools in three different ways: risk-based supervision, thematic supervision and individual case supervision.

Risk-based supervision identifies free schools for closer supervision through screening of all free schools based on indicators of quality. These include grades achieved in the Leaving Examination of the Primary and Lower Secondary School and the percentage of pupils who, after having finished basic school, continue into upper secondary school, vocational school or other types of youth education. This screening takes account of the socio-economic background of its pupils. In this way, schools that are identified as struggling to meet the required teaching standards will come under risk-based supervision.

Thematic supervision is carried out when, for example, free schools declare that they will not hold the Leaving Examination of the Primary and Lower Secondary School in general. This may include schools that only teach up to the 8th-form level. Thematic supervision is also used when free schools choose to carry out their own supervision by means of self-evaluation.

Individual case supervision mainly originates from information presented to the Ministry of Education by parents, supervisors, board-members, teachers, members of the media, etc. A recent example arose when parents believed a school leader had intimidated a number of pupils. The parents were unsatisfied with the School Board's response, so they contacted both the media and the Ministry of Education. The Ministry was asked to comment on the case and subsequently decided to initiate a supervision. This type of supervision initiated on the basis of the information mentioned is relatively rare (it occurs from about 5 to 10 times a year). It can ultimately decide that a free school cannot exist within the law and must therefore lose its grants. It is important to note here that the Ministry of Education is not an appeal body, but that dissatisfied parents have the right to appeal to the School Board or take the matter to court.

Academic standards and attainment

Free schools must give teaching of equal quality to that generally on offer in the municipal school (*folkeskole*). While the latter have a set number of lessons per subject, the free schools are not bound by this requirement. Instead, they can choose to state that their objectives are the same as 'Common Objectives of the *Folkeskole*' (COF) or produce objectives of their own. Again, these objectives must lead to teaching equal to that generally achieved in the municipal school. The COF cover every subject in the municipal school and are set out in law. The subjects are divided into three blocks:

- humanities: Danish, English, German/French, History, Christian studies and social studies
- science: mathematics, natural sciences/technology, geography, biology and physics/chemistry
- practical/creative subjects: physical education and sport, music, visual arts, crafts and design, home economics and optional subjects (form levels 7 to 10).

These subjects give a framework to what is taught in the *folkeskole*. The objectives of each subject describe areas of competence and the stages of progression throughout the form levels. There is considerable freedom as to which topics, books and materials to choose, as well as how to organize and carry out the teaching.

If a free school chooses to declare that its objectives are COF, the subjects of the school must be the same as the compulsory subjects of the *folkeskole*. The free school then has the same freedom in topics, books, organizing etc. as the *folkeskole*. Where the free school chooses to produce objectives of its own, there are multiple ways to organize and carry out the teaching. The school may, for example, choose to give teaching in two or more subjects combined, to define subjects of their own or to give non-subject-divided lessons. However, some subjects must be identifiable by way of part-objectives at certain form levels: Danish, English, maths, physics/chemistry, geography and biology. A free school may also choose to declare that its objectives are COF in some subjects, while in other subjects the school has objectives of its own. The freedom of objectives is taken to its full extent if a school chooses to have one common objective for each of the three subject blocs: humanities, science and practical/creative subjects.

When it comes to academic achievement overall, free schools at primary level are more successful than state schools (Danish Ministry of Education, 2016). Overall, pupils in free schools score generally almost one score point higher than pupils at state schools. Research also indicates that there are no significant differences in the socio-economic status of families attending free schools and municipal schools. Pupils from free schools are also more successful when they enter high school level and go on to formal education at college and university. Many factors could be said to contribute to this success: the high level of professional skill, teacher commitment, the strong co-operation between school and parents, pupil autonomy and responsibility, and the nurturing of independence and responsibility, of interdependence and collaboration and mutual respect between teachers and pupils, and so on. The success of Danish free schools is in large part due to having their roots deep in a culture that nurtures and sustains such elements, and that values the shared freedoms and responsibilities that are at the heart of the Danish constitution.

Changing times?

The number of pupils enrolling in free schools has increased following national reforms undertaken in 2007. One of the main reasons for this is that state schools are changing. Over recent decades, smaller local public schools – with pupil numbers below 200 – have been closed or amalgamated by local authorities in favour of larger schools. When the local state school closes, parents often look to establish free schools instead, in order for their child to attend a small local school and benefit from all that it has to offer.

However, free schools also face some major challenges in these changing times. Many free schools are popular and waiting lists are common, so that parents may need to apply for admission of their child at a very early age. Some parents who may wish their child to attend a free school can face financial and other barriers, even with the option to request reduced fees. A further issue relates to school transport costs. The municipality is obliged to provide school transport for pupils attending public schools and living in rural districts, but this obligation does not extend to pupils attending the free schools and may inadvertently prove to be a further barrier for poorer parents. It is also worth noting that free schools have complete autonomy with regards to decisions to enrol or expel pupils, raising further important questions for free schools, for example in relation to the obligations of the UNCRC and its requirement to involve children and young people in decisions directly affecting them.

More generally, in Denmark, education is increasingly on the political agenda. Despite Denmark having one of the most expensive school systems in the world, results in maths, science and reading are only about average according to international comparisons through PISA (Programme for International Student Assessment). This leads to a range of questions, for example about teachers' educational background and training. These most recent PISA results (2015) also show continuing issues for the achievement of immigrant pupils in Denmark. Schools are seen as a place where the socialization of marginalized groups can take place and where immigrants and their descendants can learn the values and practices of Danish liberal democracy. However, there also has been an increasing concern that new levels of extremism within Danish society might lead to the radicalization of young people in schools set up without government oversight. These issues have led to the state introducing over the last 15 years a number of new regulations for free schools and especially in relation to faith schools in Denmark. These regulations have seen a shift to more systems of testing and more 'quality control' of teaching. These changes and the pressures driving them, are felt by many to challenge the fundamental commitment to parents' rights which has developed so strongly in Danish education over the last 150 years, and to also challenge key educational values held high by many Danes, such as courage, working together, respect for diversity, responsibility, emancipation, creativeness and innovation. These are challenging times for education in Denmark and also for the free schools.

References

Danish Ministry of Education (2016) *Primary School Attainment*. Online. https://uvm.dk/statistik/grundskolen/karakterer-og-test/karakterer-i-grundskolen (accessed 3 August 2017).

PISA (Programme for International Student Assessment) (2015) *Denmark*. Online. www.compareyourcountry.org/pisa/country/dnk?lg=en (accessed 9 July 2018).

Part Two

Alternative education in international context

2

Chapter 8

Flexi-learning in Australia: The Youth+ approach

Dale Murray

> Education is the belief in possibilities. It is a belief about knowledge systems. It is a belief in the capacities of ordinary humans. We as educators must refuse to believe that anything in human nature and in various situations condemns humans to poverty, dependency, weakness, and ignorance. We must reject the idea that youth are confined to situations of fate, such as being born into a particular class, gender, or race. We must believe that teachers/youth workers and students can confront and defeat the forces that prevent students from living more fully and more freely. Every school is a site of reproduction or a site of change. In other words, education can be liberating, or it can domesticate and maintain domination. (Battiste, 2013)

For over 30 years, I have worked in flexible education, first as a teacher, then principal and more recently as Director of Edmund Rice Education Australia Youth+ Institute. The privilege of this career has been the establishment of 20 flexible learning centres (FLCs), in consultation with their communities across the Australian continent, and the opportunity this has created in influencing education systems. It has included a body of research with international colleagues who are working together to deepen the epistemologies of flexible learning.

In this chapter, I will argue that it is at the 'edges' of educational landscapes, such as FLCs, where we find evidence of innovation and advocacy for social justice and educational change. The spaces that cater for those outside the mainstream are spaces that by necessity are experimental, challenge dominant paradigms and offer habitats of learning inclusion, decolonization, justice and equity. Many first-world nations have and continue to develop these spaces because of the alienation and exclusion brought about by a model of education that continues to disenfranchise those caught in poverty and colonial hegemony in countries such as Australia.

In my view, such alienation and exclusion is brought about because the state defines educational progress in terms of neoliberal economic rationalization of human capital that regularly discards a cohort of young people considered to be not meeting the requirements of national benchmarks, standardized testing, social norms and compliance and/or what may be commonly viewed as acceptable behaviours.

My personal view of education contrasts with this. It is one with a clear and intentional focus on relationships, wherein adults and young people engage in the relational business of learning, caring, understanding and growing together. The Youth+ education model we have honed over many years may be characterized by a relational pedagogy wherein young people and adults work in a partnership based on a genuine respect for each other's knowledges and capitals. This pedagogy asks adults and young people to be 'present' to each other in ways that are not normally possible in mainstream education learning environments. This presence is represented in developing a deep understanding of all community members, knowing and respecting each other's stories. This 'knowing' is enabled by intentional community groups, special person relationships, 'big ears' groups wherein an adult has the responsibility of deepening a relationship with a group of young people they are working with. The type of relationships the Youth+ model fosters has its basis in an unconditional positive regard for all who choose to participate in the learning community in which power is shared between all participants. In essence, this is a learning community bound together with values of empathy, care, cultural understanding, willingness to learn, respect and love.

Flexible learning centres reflect my view of schooling. These registered schools have at their core a fundamental aim to provide young people with a safe learning environment that allows them to re-engage with holistic education – safe in the most comprehensive sense of the word: culturally, spiritually, academically, emotionally and socially. Commonly held within flexible learning environments is the view that all young people require equal access to a holistic education that promotes their innate ability. These communities offer learning environments for young people who have often been told they are not capable of reaching their potential, usually in the form of ongoing suspension, time out, organizational neglect and exclusion. Youth+ learning communities resist this paradigm and offer a place to re-engage with a positive education pathway for young people from a variety of backgrounds: urban, rural or remote communities; low socio-economic backgrounds; Indigenous backgrounds; experiencing homelessness, living with refugee status or involved in the juvenile justice system; young parents or those in the care of the state.

The context

Australia is home to an ever-increasing number of young people who for complex cultural, social, historical, political and economic reasons are outside mainstream education environments. Where disenfranchisement of young people reflects the legacy of an education system that acts as a class sorting mechanism, flexible learning communities have emerged to bring equity, social justice and positive education pathways for young people. With some 70,000 young Australians engaged in about 900 flexible or alternative educational environments (te Riele, 2014) and potentially many thousands more disengaged from learning altogether, Australia is in effect being challenged about its commitments under the Melbourne Education Declaration to '[improve] educational outcomes for Indigenous youth and disadvantaged young Australians, especially those from low socioeconomic backgrounds' (MCEETYA, 2008: 11).

Many of these young people, and a wide range of others who are disenfranchised, have the common experience marginalization brings: that is, a sense of being pushed out from mainstream educational environments. Thomson *et al.*, drawing on the 2015 PISA data for Australia conclude:

> On average, students from higher socioeconomic backgrounds performed at a significantly higher level than students from lower socioeconomic backgrounds. Students from metropolitan schools achieved significantly higher scores than students from provincial schools or remote schools. Indigenous students achieved significantly lower scores than non-Indigenous students in scientific, reading and mathematical literacy domains. (Thomson *et al.*, 2016: 60)

Those working in the flexible learning space are dealing directly with the situations reflected in this data. Many of those who are performing 'significantly lower' are the young people experiencing the push out from mainstream education that results in continued disenfranchisement and poor life outcomes. This is picked up in the Dusseldorp Forum's *The Case for Inclusive Learning Systems*:

> It is well accepted at both policy and practice levels that participation in education has significant economic, social and civic benefits for individuals, families and communities. Education plays a critical role in providing young people with the personal, life and vocational skills they need to participate in the workforce. (Wierenga and Taylor, 2015: 42)

The most recent PISA research indicates that highly skilled adults are twice as likely to be employed and almost three times as likely to earn an above-median salary than poorly skilled adults. In other words, poor skills severely limit people's access to better paying and more rewarding jobs. There is also strong evidence that people with qualifications at Vocational Educational Training Certificate 3 level or above (there are four levels of certificates, 1 being benchmarked at junior high school age and 3 and above at senior phase of learning) are more likely to be employed, earn more and be less susceptible to changes caused by economic downturn and industry restructuring than people with lower levels of educational attainment.

Thomson *et al.* (2016) go on to highlight that 'Highly skilled people are also more likely to volunteer, see themselves as active actors rather than as passive objects of political processes, and are more likely to trust others' (65). While Australia has deep and persistent patterns of disadvantage, a 2013 Australian Government Productivity Commission report has identified education and employment as the principal way to shift these patterns:

> Education has positive health and wellbeing outcomes that impact at individual, family and community levels. Building a more inclusive education system that works for all young people allows them to take up constructive roles in society. This is recognised as the most significant mechanism for supporting potential and for breaking cycles of disadvantage. (SCRGSP, 2013)

More recent research unearthing the 'social return on investment' with regard to young people in the flexible learning environments, *Gauging the Value of Flexible Learning*, an Australian Research Council Linkage partnership, draws attention to the economic benefits, in term of dollars spent, with regard to social return (see McGinty *et al.*, 2018). The research estimates that for every AU\$1 spent on a young person engaged in a flexible learning option there is an AU\$25 social return on this investment. Further, it is argued that by keeping young people at risk of disengagement engaged in education there is a 50 per cent reduction in their potential of becoming NEET (not in education, employment or training). The life-time social return on investment in economic terms represents a value of AU\$359,000, which can be broken down to AU\$70,000 in savings in public health cost, 32,000 in savings in youth justice and welfare costs, 207,000 in savings in unemployment costs and 50,000 in macroeconomic saving (additional tax revenue) (see www.youthplusinstitute.org.au).

It is clear that full engagement in education has positive economic, civic and social, cultural, health and individual outcomes for young people, their futures and communities. The cost to the nation is potentially extreme if inclusion of all young people is not a national priority. Building on the *Gauging the Value of Flexible Learning* data referred to above (McGinty *et al.*, 2018), there are 70,000 young people engaged in flexible learning options; generating a social return on investment of AU$359,000 per individual multiplied by the cohort gives the overall benefit to the community of AU$25,130,000,000. The negative costs to the community are evident if 70,000 young people are not engaged in learning.

Full engagement in education is a foundation that improves a person's employment prospects and earning capacity. There is also a clear relationship between education and better health, and between a positive education experience and raised civic and social engagement. Beyond the economics, this is also about quality of life. Education should not only be seen as a pathway to employment, but also to active forms of citizenship. It should play a key role in nurturing an individual's capacity to engage with society and contribute socially and politically.

The 'pushed out'

The Dusseldorp Forum (Wierenga and Taylor, 2015) offers a broad view of the education service models operating nationally and identifies four areas of education service delivery:

1. Mainstream: standard schooling, vocational training and the tertiary education system are offered.
2. Embedded: additional learning options are delivered within and through the schooling system.
3. Complementary: extra-curricular and additional learning options are delivered to complement schooling.
4. Adjacent: flexible learning options are delivered parallel to the schooling system, as a substitute for mainstream school. (Wierenga and Taylor, 2015: 38)

This typology, in the main, reflects the broad landscape of provision in the Australian context and signals potential transitional pathways for young people on their education engagement journey. However, as a result of the push out of young people disenfranchised from mainstream schooling, there is an increasing number of agencies responding to their needs, educational and otherwise, operating in the adjacent section of this model. Edmund Rice Education Australia Youth+ FLCs are examples of this provision.

The practice

Youth+ is the organizational arm of Edmund Rice Education Australia that focuses on those young people in communities who are disenfranchised, homeless, caught in the poverty cycle, caught in recidivist juvenile justice cycles, young parents, and those with a generational history of alienation from school (see www.youthplusinstitute.org.au). For 30 years, Youth+ has responded to the needs of these young people by embedding a culture of compassion and empathy, liberation and relational pedagogy in its FLCs. This response promotes an education model that positions adults as guests in the lives of the young people and families/carers with a responsibility to create positive futures for young people, while focusing on the present. Vadeboncoeur and Murray write:

> Research in afterschool programs, informal contexts and flexible and alternative school programs illustrates the power of adults to imagine futures with children, and imagine them differently from the status quo both in terms of relationships and in terms of institutional structures. Instead of adaptation to an already-existing environment, futures become possible through the transformation of the environment, including the development of new social practices, or new repertoires of cultural ways of seeing, speaking, interacting, knowing, becoming, and valuing. Together, children, youth, and mentor educators imagine futures and then act to organize the futures deemed worthwhile. This joint practice requires the vision of both more experienced and less experienced participants: Through prolepsis, those more experienced draw upon their past experiences to organize for possible futures; those less experienced draw upon their more immediate experiences to expand and push against the ways their experiences are organized. (Vadeboncoeur and Murray, 2014: 643)

The relational space created within the Youth+ FLCs is an intentional effort to create space that offers 'pushed out' students a safe place to reorganize their futures and deal with an often traumatized past with the support of mentor educators. In this way, Youth+ centres offer a challenge to the dominant education paradigm and model good practice, while paving the way for rethinking what educational inclusivity and equity can look and feel like. In this way, a fundamental change occurs whereby the educational landscape adapts to support the young person rather than the young person being required to adapt to the system.

These spaces blend well-being and trauma-informed practice, academic development and social development within a social justice framework, culminating in a positive and accredited holistic education journey for the most disadvantaged young people in the country. The development of educational responses in this space has been profound. It has resulted in many requests from communities that are seeking innovative responses for young people they see as being lost to the system, as well as solutions for the negative community and individual outcomes this alienation brings.

Youth+ development over the past 15 years has seen rapid growth in accredited schools in urban, rural and remote areas of the nation. Acting on invitation from communities seeking more focused engagement opportunities for their young people, Youth+ has grown to 20 schools supporting thousands of young people who for complex reasons are unable to maintain connection with mainstream education services. The overall Youth+ young person population is around 2,000, which includes 35 per cent Aboriginal and Torres Strait Islanders and about 40 per cent young women. All young people engaged with Youth+ are of high school age upwards, with some young people remaining engaged with the services to the age of 23 or 24. In the main, the schools are relatively small, with the average campus serving about 100 young people. There is also a range of outreach and mobile services that support transition programmes into education and on to further education and work.

The Youth+ model

The genesis of practice within Youth+ FLCs has its roots in a number of disciplines that are intentionally combined to develop the Youth+ education model. These include education, social work, outdoor adventure-based learning and trauma-informed practice. This model of education affords young people and adults a common ground where relationships are negotiated within the framework of four principles: respect, safe and legal, honesty and participation. The principles represent the boundaries of our common ground and provide all community members with a space to continually practise at being in relationship.

An essential component of the Youth+ model of common ground is that all who participate do so as a choice. The personal ownership of choosing to engage in this learning community allows for ongoing internalization of behaviour based around its four principles of operation, which thus promotes the conditions of the common ground relationship. The Youth+ model of education sets the engagement/relationship bar high for all members of community as it asks all to operate with respect, honesty, safe and legal, and participation. The principles form the value boundaries of a shared common ground and give young people and adults a language set upon which to negotiate and build/restore relationship.

For many, this space requires deep personal reflection as the model asks adults to embrace the complexities of letting go of authority, and young people to learn to trust adults and take ownership of their behaviour. This, for some young people, given their often traumatic past, is a complex developmental journey and requires a highly skilled and empathic workforce to incorporate the values of being on common ground together while utilizing trauma-informed practice.

The intentional establishment of common ground is paramount for Youth+ learning communities (and for many other flexible learning environments), and is the landscape on which operation by principle occurs. The four principles provide the cornerstone for the relationships and provide a set of values that shape the landscape of common ground. Principles do not define what should happen in any particular relational situation; rather, they help establish a common shared language that helps provide a framework for restorative dialogue between members of the community. The result of committing to operate on common ground is that adults and young people are both accountable and responsible for their individual behaviour.

Learning relationships

Commitment to engaging in effective meeting processes is essential to success of this pedagogy. These meetings take various forms from one-to-one, small group, whole community and extended community. The elegance of operation by principles for group and individual relationship development and maintenance is the requirement for consistent and intentional negotiation of points of view and coming to common understandings about how we will be together as a learning community. Operation by principle then asks us to come together and discuss – often from a point of conflict/ bias – what it is we mean by respect, safe and legal, participation and honesty. We are thus embedding skills of negotiation, agency, self-efficacy and communal discourse, respect for difference and, in turn, community empathy and tolerance.

All learning communities have a responsibility to maintain safe, engaging and meaningful educational pathways for young people. The Youth+ relational pedagogy promotes a common ground ethic of managing learning so that learning can be self-paced, respectful of previous experience and provide an intentional learning environment that promotes holistic development. This model offers a challenge to the dominant paradigm of an authoritarian rule-based education environment and requires adults to 'deschool' themselves of a consequence/punishment behaviour management technique and engage with young people as guests, guides and mentors in relationship. Vadeboncoeur and Murray have made this point about FLCs previously:

> Every child/young person exists in relationships with others, surrounded by adults and peers, and it is these people who mediate her or his experiences. To argue that children/young people be placed at the centre of our work is to acknowledge that engagement may not occur, or it may not be sustained, without relationships that, in a sense, bind the participants together in a learning community. The social role of more experienced others, more experienced learners, in learning–teaching relationships compels us to think about the social roles and responsibilities of adults in these relationships, as well as the recognition that these relationships bestow various privileges alongside obligations. (Vadeboncoeur and Murray, 2014: 634)

The complexities of relearning relationships based on common ground for all come about because it challenges adults to enter a new relational space, in essence a new moral landscape that redefines traditional teacher–student relationships. This new landscape is contradictory to traditional education environments, where adults are authorized with the responsibility to manage participants' behaviour and as such invest enormous amounts of time, energy and emotional commitment into generating and implementing solutions for young people's behaviour when complexity arises. This can lead to adults feeling an obligation to 'making it work' and having a sense that they have some type of control over a young person's behaviour. There is a danger here in reducing the amount of responsibility young people have for their own behaviour and the decisions they make about that experience. Within the Youth+ landscape, adults are challenged not to embrace responsibility for what young people do but rather be part of the negotiation process and implementation of the expectation that the group/individuals have agreed to within a collaborative problem-solving conversation.

Working agreements

Working agreements form an integral part of this practice. In essence, these agreements are a negotiated space and record group consensus based on the outcome of the process in order to provide individuals and groups with:

- empowerment
- a non-punitive approach
- internalization of responsibility for self and group
- models and practice for young people to learn to manage their actions and behaviours
- negotiation skills
- a shift from adults managing young people's behaviour to young people managing young people's behaviour.

Working agreements can take many forms, for example:

- Formal – written, agreed to and displayed. This model is useful for establishing group expectations, and can be used to repair school culture after an incident.
- Symbolic – putting your name or other symbol up when you enter a learning space that means you are ready to operate by the principles or working agreement. It represents a recommitment at the start of the term, day or lesson.

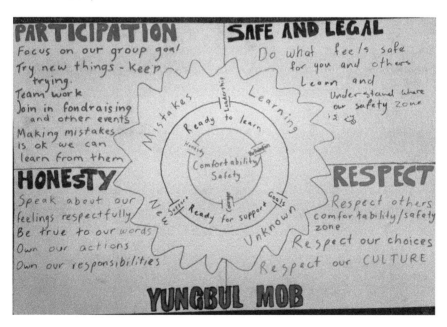

Figure 8.1: Youth+ working agreement from Alice Springs (taken from Yungbul Mob, 2016)

Figure 8.1 shows the working agreement of the Yungbul Mob (a group of Aboriginal young people from Alice Springs Central Australia) in its final published presentation. This agreement documents the negotiated journey of a common ground discussion using the four principles as the guiding value sets. The central focus of this agreement, 'safety and comfortability', symbolically locates the Mob's starting points and potential distance that may be travelled on the learning journey, while the principles define the actions and values that the Mob have determined will guide their relationships.

One of the most important aspects of mentoring individuals and groups with working agreements is for the group/individual to remain committed to the agreement. This requires the group to be faithful to the intention of the agreement and to revisit, recast, or renegotiate if the agreement is no longer meeting the needs of the activity. The constant renewal of agreement reflects the ongoing developmental nature of relationships and the need for intentional focus on the group or individual commitment to the agreement.

Negotiation through problems and conflicts are opportunities for growth of agency and the internalization of responsibility of self. The Youth+ model of operating by principle provides learning communities with a language framework that opens the door to internalization of responsibility for both young people and adults. This democratization of the educational landscape provides young people and adults with a common ground on which to develop relationship and build community. This space, however, requires workers to have professional skills in dealing with the complex traumatic lives our young people have experienced.

Trauma-informed practice

Early life adversity can make it harder for young people to learn, connect with others and have happy, meaningful positive lives. Many young people who disconnect from mainstream education have experienced trauma and/or significant adversity. Trauma's impact on stress responses can cause students to become highly emotionally dysregulated and disassociated from education. Dysregulation and disassociation often take the form of acting out or withdrawal from the learning environment. However, these responses are more often triggered by stimuli that are a result of ongoing trauma. Within Youth+ trauma is summarized as:

- adverse experiences that overwhelm an individual's ability to cope
- chronic stress that can affect brain patterning
- acute trauma – a single event
- complex – cumulative or multi-faceted
- may be direct – affect the individual person
- may be vicarious – that is, the person sees others affected by traumatic events.

The types of trauma most commonly experienced by disadvantaged young people are:

- historical/cultural trauma, e.g. intergenerational trauma, removal from family, removal from land-homes
- community trauma, e.g. substance abuse, racism, multiple deaths
- family trauma, e.g. intergenerational trauma, discrimination, domestic violence
- individual trauma, e.g. child abuse, witnessing violence, negative school experiences.

The Youth+ education model embraces a trauma-informed practice framework based on an understanding of the influence that various types of trauma have on development. The framework has a strong focus on:

- establishing safety through calm and predictable staff; a predictable timetable; staff skilled in de-escalation; negotiated and clear boundaries; working agreements; circle time; cultural safety
- building relationships supported by positive and nurturing connections; professional boundaries; cultural connections
- engaging learning choices at the assessed level of each young person: project-based; accredited and non-accredited; embedded Indigenous perspectives
- learning to manage emotions through operation by principles; collaborative problem-solving, young person self-regulating skills; brain breaks; time in vs time out
- setting up rhythm and repetition with a predictable and structured timetable – daily/weekly/term/year; circle time; rhythmic patterned activity; celebrations.

It is the blending of our common ground approach and operation by principle within a trauma-informed practice that Youth+ embraces, that sets us apart from more traditional education models. It provides staff and young people with common ground on which to live out holistic relational learning.

The challenge

There are many challenges facing flexible learning, including increasing government regulation, union regulation, curriculum development, community resistance and staff turnover.

The challenge of government regulation

In intentionally locating the Youth+ education model within a highly-regulated government-funded school system, FLCs walk a challenging path between on the one hand organizational compliance, audit and review, and on the other innovation and advocacy. The implementation of school improvement legislation, compliance documentation and increasing systems of control over curriculum, coupled with the growing number of high-stakes testing regimes, audit and accountability technologies, as well as the narrative of slipping standards and declining standardized outcomes, heighten the demands in terms of governance of public funds.

Like all endeavours of a frontier nature, acts of political advocacy and challenges to a dominant paradigm grounded in a Eurocentric colonized education system, flexible learning options face increased monitoring, regulations and resistance from authorities, particularly as they continue to grow in response to community invitation. This is demonstrated in the form of increased demand for measurement of academic gain of young people, transition to employment and/or further education outcomes, coupled with data regarding attendance and engagement. This is not, in essence, an unreasonable demand on publicly funded education services. However, I would argue that to lay mainstream performance measure lenses over these education environments will not capture the real gains young people make educationally, socially, culturally, psychologically and emotionally.

The question most often asked of flexible learning environments is, 'how do you measure success?' The most obvious response is that young people are here. That is to say that the vast majority of young people attending FLCs had not been attending any school. These young people, as previously discussed, had felt the 'push' and disengaged from education environments that were not meeting their needs. My experience tells me if young people have made a choice to attend – that is, to face the sometimes overwhelming challenges their lives often have: homelessness, substance addiction, poverty, fear of 'shame' in an education setting, lower levels of literacy, parenting, juvenile justice connection and so on – then they have made a significant choice to enter into relationship with trusted adults and in turn engage in learning for a positive future.

Beyond the fundamental significance of attachment of young people to the learning environment there are success measures that involve the following: completion of senior phases of learning resulting in state and nationally recognized certification and the transition to further education and training environments. Moving to 'soft' measures, such as overcoming anxiety and fear of community and education institutions, breaking the recidivist cycle of juvenile detention, minimizing the harm of substance use, becoming competent parents, and positively engaging with peers and leading a positive, happy life, can represent some of the gains that engagement with education can bring.

Flexible learning options are in the early stages of responding to increasing compliance frameworks. Some responses to date include modification and reinterpretation of standardized school improvement measures coupled with data sets that move beyond traditional academic measurements to embrace well-being development, civic engagement and relational capacity. The Youth+ Fidelity Factor School Improvement Tool (see www.youthplusinstitute.org.au) (knowledge exchange) is an example of such development. Another measure of community relational development is the process and publication of working agreements. As described, these agreements act as guides and reminders of negotiated community expectations. Increased non-academic evidence-based outcome measures that include cultural and relational capacity and well-being measurement rubrics are currently used to develop individual learning plans for young people and will in time form the basis of more public data sets for measurement of 'soft' outcomes related to individual 'distance travelled' for young people. These data sets will form the basis of measures that provide flexible learning communities with data to build upon improvement cycles.

The challenge of union regulation

With the expansion of flexible learning environments has come an increasing scrutiny of employment and industrial conditions for workers. State-based independent education unions, on behalf of their members, have opened up dialogue on employee conditions within the flexible learning environment. This dialogue will need to remain cognisant of the difference in education practice from mainstream education. These conversations are in early stages of negotiation, with expansion to other states and territories flagged. We will need to ensure these conversations do not lose sight of the vision of flexible learning's aspirations, while responding to some of the legitimate needs of the expanding work force.

The challenge of the curriculum

The complexity of appropriate curriculum offerings in flexible learning environments is a chapter in its own right. However, I will table some fundamental challenges that present to all educators working in this space. The first is the vast diversity of capitals young people bring to the learning environment and our ability to positively recognize the value of these capitals – cultural diversity, knowledges learnt, social/civic understanding and a sense of place and history. As mentor educators, our role is to understand the starting points for each young person in our education partnership and then build upon this. This requires deep understanding of the young person's histories of learning and how to enhance their multiliteracies and numeracy development. Many young people who engage with flexible learning present with gaps in their literacy and numeracy development due to long periods of absence from school. The time and content required to catch up with the fundamentals of literacy/numeracy is a challenging and complex process and requires deep commitment from educators to support this development. This highlights the importance of literacy development in all its forms. The key ingredient for agency in cultural, employed, political and social life is the ability to engage with adequate levels of literacy. Without such, young people will continue to be disenfranchised.

Developing a meaningful and engaging curriculum that has high interest for young people, given their experiences of being turned off learning, is a key task that we continue to develop. This is especially challenging when we are confronted with the increased demands of a national and state-based curriculum framework that assumes young people have progressed through year levels with the skills necessary to cope with what is mandated in subsequent years. The complexity arises in scaffolding literacy development with high interest so as to not further marginalize the young person from learning. In short, how do you support a teenager to engage in the fundamentals of language and literacy acquisition while maintaining high levels of interest? Some answers exist in online cultures, some in the space of music culture, some in enquiry-based projects that afford young people greater ownership of the learning space. The ongoing issue is to ensure that all young people who choose to be part of a flexible learning community leave with the literacy and numeracy skills necessary to navigate the world; to do any less would mean flexible learning has disadvantaged the young person.

The challenge of community resistance

Finally, there is the challenge of the social settings where the centres are located. The development of an FLC begins with an invitation from a community who seek to provide their young people with a suite of education options. Many communities, in my experience, have at their core a deep desire to ensure that all their young people are on pathways to positive futures. This is evidenced by the growth of flexible learning options in Australia. However, while this positive view of FLCs exists, there is also a negative view that we have experienced in the developmental phase of establishing centres in some places. Our organization has experienced a number of communities pushing back on the development of infrastructure to support the most disenfranchised young people in their communities. On one occasion the push back resulted in a council development application being denied, even after significant political and community support brought to the appeal process. The development of this service is still on hold while we seek another potential site. The issues the young people of this community face also remain on hold and the complexity of their disassociation with their community remains. Another school's application resulted in the centre not being allowed to be built on the designated council land, as the local residents became very concerned by the prospect of such a facility in their neighbourhood. The result was a shift of location to a less adequate site. The site has now been constructed and operates with over 100 young people. The engagement of young people is high, but the facility struggles to cope with the needs the community brings to the centre because of the less than ideal site.

The challenge of staffing

Australia is a very large country, with most of the population clinging to the coastal fringe, mainly on the east coast. This distribution of population creates complex staffing issues for FLCs that are not situated in these more populated regions. Attracting a workforce with the appropriate qualifications in some of the more remote areas of the nation is challenging, as is maintaining their commitment to remote centres. Many staff commit to a community for only a few years and then move back to bigger cities, which results in a consistent staff turnover and ongoing induction and training requirements for new workers. One result of this churn is the loss of relational trust established with young people; workers have the capacity to move from the community while young people often do not (even if they have the means or inclination – which often they do not). More work on supporting young people's resilience through change will need to be developed as we progress growth of services nationally.

Conclusion

Vadeboncouer writes:

> Alternative educational programs will continue to exist, not because youth 'choose' an alternative program, and not because of the amazing epistemological, ontological, and axiological

work that is undertaken, but as a necessity wrought by capitalism. (Vadeboncouer, 2009: 296)

I agree. If a nation's maturity is measured on how it treats its vulnerable (younger and older Australians; those with less access to economic security; differently abled; those with diverse cultural backgrounds and sexual orientations), then our nation, since colonization, may be classified as very young. Continued leadership, research and advocacy are called for, to claim the freedoms and educational equity that should be the right of each young person, no matter their postcode. The establishment of these freedoms will bring continued innovations in flexible learning and the mainstream that will in turn benefit all on their education journey.

References

Battiste, M. (2013) *Decolonizing Education: Nourishing the learning spirit.* Saskatoon, SK: Purich Publishing.

McGinty, S., Wilson, K., Thomas, J. and Lewthaite, B. (eds) (2018) *Gauging the Value of Education for Disenfranchised Youth – Flexible Learning Options.* Boston: Brill Sense.

MCEETYA (Ministerial Council on Education, Employment, Training and Youth Affairs) (2008) *Melbourne Declaration on Educational Goals for Young Australians.* Melbourne: Ministerial Council on Education, Employment, Training and Youth Affairs.

SCRGSP (Steering Committee for the Review of Government Service Provision) (2013) *Report on Government Services 2013.* Canberra: Productivity Commission.

Te Riele, K. (2014) *Putting the Jigsaw Together: Flexible learning programs in Australia: Final report.* Melbourne: Victoria Institute for Education, Diversity and Lifelong Learning.

Thomson, S., De Bortoli, L. and Underwood, C. (2016) *PISA 2015: A first look at Australia's results.* Camberwell, VIC: Australian Council for Educational Research.

Wierenga, A. and Taylor, J. (2015) *The Case for Inclusive Learning Systems: Building more inclusive learning systems in Australia.* Sydney: Dusseldorp Forum.

Vadeboncoeur, J.A. (2009) 'Spaces of difference: The contradictions of alternative educational programs'. *Educational Studies*, 45 (3), 280–99.

Vadeboncoeur, J. A. and Murray, D. (2014). Imagined futures in the present: Minding learning opportunities. *National Society for the Study of Education*, 113 (2), 633–652.

Yungbul Mob (2016) *Aboriginal young people from St Joseph's Catholic Flexible Learning Centre Alice Springs. Northern Territory, Australia.* [Photograph.]

Chapter 9

Leadership in flexi-schools: Issues of race and racism in Australia

Marnee Shay

Introduction

I am an Aboriginal Australian educator and researcher. In this chapter, I will report on findings from a study undertaken in Queensland, Australia, with education leaders of flexi-schools into how they are working with Aboriginal and Torres Strait Islander (Indigenous Australian) students. Indigenous Australians, like many First Nations peoples internationally, are amongst the most researched and observed groups in the world (Tuhiwai Smith, 2012). It is only recently that we have seen Indigenous researchers claim our rightful place within the academy after colonialism and imperialism ensured our exclusion from knowledge production (Tuhiwai Smith, 2012). Our presence means we are now able to speak for ourselves and contribute to knowledge production that we consider to be serving our interests, as well as pose new questions from an Indigenous experience or standpoint (Tuhiwai Smith, 2005). Indigenous standpoint and experience offer new perspectives on the educational leadership required to shift deficit notions associated with Indigenous learners. Such a change may provide practice alternatives about education leadership for all cultural and racial minority groups.

Australia has a rich multicultural society (Hickling Hudson, 2003). Yet, the majority of the education workforce are White, middle-class women (Santoro and Allard, 2005). McKenzie *et al.* (2011) outlined how poorly represented Indigenous peoples are in the education workforce. In their national scan, they illustrated that not only are Indigenous teachers critically underrepresented, but Indigenous representation among leaders is also concerning. A scan of Indigenous representation in school leadership found that just 0.1 per cent of leaders in primary schools are Indigenous. Indigenous representation of leaders in secondary schools also comprised just 0.1 per cent (McKenzie *et al.*, 2011). In Australia, Indigenous students experience educational deficit across areas such as literacy and numeracy outcomes and year 12 completion rates (Australian Government, 2014). As an Aboriginal researcher and educator, I saw the need, in seeking to explain the educational disparity that Indigenous students face, to shift the gaze from Indigenous students towards an examination of the work practices of educational leaders. I chose to focus on flexi-schools because of my professional experiences in teaching and leading in this context, as well as knowing that there are disproportionately high numbers of Indigenous students interacting in this model of schooling (Shay, 2015). Flexi-schools are defined more fully later in the chapter, but are schools that provide young people who have been disenfranchised from education the opportunity to re-engage in education. Flexi-schools are also sometimes called alternative schools, flexible learning programmes or non-traditional schools in Australian literature (see also Murray (Chapter 8) and Mills and McGregor (Chapter 5) in this volume; te Riele, 2012).

Critical race theory underpinned the research design and data analysis (Ladson-Billings, 1998; Solórzano and Yosso, 2001). Critical race theory in education is used to 'analyze the role of race and racism in education' (Dixson and Rousseau, 2005: 8). When used in education contexts, critical race theory has the potential to 'define, expose and address educational "problems"' (Parker and Lynn, 2002: 7) that are largely avoided in education research (Haney López, 2013). This qualitative study used an online survey methodology (Mertler, 2002) to explore how education leaders of flexi-school settings described their practices and leadership for Indigenous education. In this chapter, I will argue that further studies that explicitly explore the role that constructs race and issues of racism within flexi-schools are of particular importance, because many young people who attend flexi-school experience intersections of disadvantage, including issues that are connected to race and culture (Shay, 2015). Focus on race and racism is of particular relevance in countries where the cultural backgrounds of the education workforce do not adequately reflect the cultural background of students in classrooms (Santoro and Allard, 2005).

Indigenous Australia: The continuing effects of Australian history

In Australia, there are two Indigenous groups: Aboriginal and Torres Strait Islander peoples. Aboriginal peoples are the First Nations peoples of mainland Australia. Torres Strait Islander peoples (originally from islands located off far north Queensland) are also recognized as Indigenous Australians and First Nations peoples of the Torres Straits since the islands were annexed by Queensland in the late 1800s (Davis, 2004). Aboriginal and Torres Strait Islander cultures are diverse: they vary from each other, and also vary within cultural groups.

The invasion of Australia has caused mass trauma for First Nations people (Aboriginal and Torres Strait Islander Social Justice Commissioner, 2000). Racist policies such as assimilation in the 1900s saw thousands of Indigenous peoples herded onto missions, having their lives controlled and living in appalling conditions (Blake, 1998). Indigenous Australians survived these dark times in Australian history, though many of our people live with the consequences (Cummings, 1990; Smallwood, 2011). Indigenous Australians currently experience poorer health outcomes and education outcomes, are grossly over-represented in the prison systems and continue to experience racism in a wide range of contexts (Australian Government, 2014; Weatherburn and Holmes, 2010). Considering the level of trauma Indigenous Australians have experienced and the racist policies designed by the Australian Government to 'breed out' Aboriginal peoples (Cummings, 1990), we have a strong presence in contemporary Australia. Approximately 3 per cent of the population in Australia in 2011 identified as Aboriginal and or Torres Strait Islander (ABS, 2013).

There have been some positive Indigenous education policy changes and initiatives in Australia in the past decade. The specific inclusion of national teacher standards mandates that all teachers must demonstrate respect for Indigenous Australians and know how to teach Indigenous students (AITSL, 2013). Aboriginal and Torres Strait Islander content is now a cross-curriculum priority area in the national curriculum (ACARA, 2014). There is also a national strategy called 'MATSITI' (More Aboriginal and Torres Strait Islander Teachers Initiative) that has been working on multiple approaches that aim to increase the numbers of Indigenous teachers in Australian classrooms (MATSITI, 2017). Although these changes are positive, there is still much more that needs to change if we are to see genuine improvements to outcomes in Indigenous education broadly. The study reported in this chapter examines how school leadership can influence such change in flexi-schooling contexts.

Flexi-schools in Australia

Flexi-schools are an emerging schooling context in Australia. Flexi-schools or alternative schools are providing many young people (up to Year 12, or 18 years of age and under) who have been disenfranchised from education the opportunity to re-engage in formal education (Morgan *et al.*, 2015; Shay, 2015). Flexi-schools have three broad structural categories:

'programs operating within mainstream schools, programs operating within TAFE (Technical and Further Education) or ACE (Adult and Community Education) and separate (stand-alone) programs' (te Riele, 2014: 12). Earlier work by te Riele (2007) differentiated flexi-schools as being either focused on changing the provision of education or focused on changing the young person to meet the needs of the education system. She further concluded that these could either be short-term or longer-term opportunities for young people to engage. Te Riele's scholarship has been influential in identifying the participants for the study described in this chapter. The study focused on flexi-schools that describe themselves as changing the provision of education to meet the needs of young people and are longer-term engagement opportunities.

Flexi-schools in Australia have received increasing interest from education scholars over the past decade. Several studies have concluded that they are playing a crucial role in supporting young people who have been excluded from mainstream education, and are enabling them to re-engage in formal learning (Baroutsis *et al*., 2016; McGregor *et al*., 2015; Mills and McGregor, 2010; Mills and McGregor, 2014). Te Riele (2014) suggests that alternative education settings are a growing sector, estimating that over 900 programmes are operating, working with over 70,000 students every year. Although there are no large data sets that outline the proportion of students who are Indigenous engaging with alternative education settings, there is evidence that there are high numbers of Indigenous students and staff engaging with alternative schools (Shay and Heck, 2015).

Vadeboncoeur (2009) outlines the tensions that exist around the role of flexi-schools in the broader education discourse. She argues that the very existence of alternative school sites highlights the contradiction between democratic ideals in education and neoliberal economic shrewdness. The 'sorting machine' (2009: 281) of said neoliberalism has resulted in many young people who lack the social, cultural and economic capital to fit the education system needing alternative schools if they are to have any chance of gaining a formal education. In an Australian context, Indigenous over-representation in flexi-schools can be linked with neoliberalism. However, the role of race in the sorting machine in the context of institutionalized racism is also an interesting and underexplored tension that exists for flexi-schools. Moreover, this important point that Vadeboncoeur makes about the neoliberal sorting machine and the very existence of flexi-schools supports an argument that flexi-schools must be equipped to adequately address issues such as racism that have resulted in young people attending flexi-schools.

Educational leadership and Indigenous learners

Many scholars agree that education leadership impacts on outcomes for Indigenous students (Blackley, 2012; Hughes *et al.*, 2007; Sarra, 2007). However, there are limited studies that explore multiple dimensions of the connection between how school leadership supports the engagement of Indigenous learners. Fitzgerald (2006) discusses the role of ethnocentrism in research that explores the link between school leadership and student outcomes. She argues that when researchers do not identify the cultural standpoint of the principals or school leaders in their leadership research, critical information about the effectiveness of leadership is neglected in the discussion. Moreover, Blackmore (2010) concludes that the resistance within education leadership to discuss race or culture has resulted in discourse that does not recognize schools as racialized spaces, which is highly problematic particularly for other-than-White students. She evaluates that 'rarely do White men or women leaders question their Whiteness, whereas Indigenous and other minority groups, as a consequence of their being "other than White" are expected to explain their exclusion' (2010: 46). More studies are needed that shift this dynamic and the incontestable position of White leaders to avoid such topics (Aveling, 2007). The study reported on in this chapter is a contribution to this important change in leadership research.

The study did not have the capacity to explore all aspects and dimensions of the role leadership plays for Indigenous learners in flexi-schools. However, the study does offer new insights about how leaders of flexi-schools described their leadership practices in schooling contexts that have high numbers of Indigenous learners (Shay, 2015). Moreover, the use of critical race theory in the analysis of the findings provides a deeper exploration of the power of constructs of race and issues of racism, which is often omitted in studies that explore education leadership (Aveling, 2007; Blackmore, 2010).

Indigenous education leadership in flexi-schools: Key findings

The findings reported in this chapter are from a study that included eight flexi-schools in Queensland (Shay, 2013, 2015; Shay and Heck, 2015). Participants were the school leaders of the flexi-school sites. The study did not explicitly ask about each participant's cultural background. However, it did overtly explore the practices of school leaders of a specific group of young people (Aboriginal and Torres Strait Islander) who are racially categorized. There were multiple open-ended questions where participants could contextualize their responses by naming their cultural standpoint. This section will discuss two of the main conclusions that explore the knowledge/understanding and practices of school leaders about supporting Aboriginal and Torres Strait Islander young people.

A strong theme that emerged from exploring the skills and understanding of flexi-school leaders was how emphatic they were about their willingness to engage in self-directed learning about Indigenous cultures. In this particular group of flexi-school leaders, seven out of eight leaders reported self-directed learning as part of their ongoing professional learning. This finding is positive, especially since the requirement for teachers to learn about Indigenous cultures has resulted in documented resistance to learning about Indigenous cultures and challenging white racial normativity, particularly in pre-service teacher education settings (Aveling, 2006). It does appear that in a flexi-school context leaders seem to be less affected by this resistance. This conclusion is evidenced by the data that clearly outlined that flexi-school leaders demonstrated a commitment to ongoing professional development about their learning about Indigenous cultures.

Paradoxically, the second key finding was that there was a limited understanding of Indigenous cultures demonstrated through the responses provided by participants. The survey asked school leaders to give examples of what enabled their practices about Indigenous learners and what the barriers were. The practices were connected directly to the literature on what is reported to engage Indigenous learners in conventional contexts (no substantial literature exists in flexi-schooling contexts). These were synthesized into six themes: schools nurturing the cultural identity of Indigenous young people; awareness and cultural competence of educators; engagement with Indigenous families and communities; the presence of Indigenous cultures in schools; employment and presence of Indigenous staff and the leadership within the school (Shay and Heck, 2015).

Analysis of the responses concluded that there was not enough data to support the notion that school leaders had a good understanding about what engaged Indigenous learners and Indigenous cultures. Rather, the data indicated that there was only a surface-level understanding of what supports Indigenous learners, often linked to essentialist notions of race (Shay, 2015). For example, flexi-school leaders were asked about whether they actively encouraged their staff to support and nurture the cultural identities of Indigenous young people. All of the flexi-school leaders responded 'yes'. However, when asked to elaborate, the responses were predominantly framed around practices of cultural celebrations and cultural activities.

Cultural celebrations such as NAIDOC (National Aboriginal and Islander Day Observance Committee), a national week of cultural celebrations once a year and other activities such as eating bush tucker and art workshops, were all reported as the dominant ways in which leaders were working to address Indigenous education at their flexi-school sites (Shay, 2015).

These practices are positive for Indigenous learners and indeed all young people. However, when cultural celebrations are the only practice, such limited practices can be linked to what is defined as 'multiculturalist' practices in schools (Shay, 2015). Ladson-Billings and Tate (2006) argue that multiculturalist practices can be a distinct form of covert racism that has resulted in superficial practices of schools such as eating ethnic foods and dancing. Blackmore (2010) discerns that multiculturalist practices of leaders in isolation from other more robust practices to support cultural minorities do not effectively disrupt the White cultural norm. Moreover, the essence of multiculturalism is the promotion of tolerance, which in effect produces the status of 'otherness' of cultural minority groups (Ladson-Billings and Tate, 2006). Furthermore, when otherness becomes equal, a competition emerges amongst racial and cultural minority groups to then become included (Ladson-Billings and Tate, 2006). This issue is particularly relevant not only for First Nations peoples in Australia, but internationally, as worldwide diaspora has become a prominent development globally. It may also be a challenge in flexi-schools where young people often have multiple identities and issues that would place them in minority categories such as LGBT (lesbian, gay, bisexual and transgender), young people with disabilities, refugees and those who experience poverty, for example.

Implications for flexi-schools

There was an inconsistency in responses from flexi-school leaders. There was a high level of self-efficacy reported in flexi-school leaders engaging in their self-learning to develop their knowledge and skills in working with Indigenous learners. However, this did not necessarily translate into a demonstration of a good understanding of what is reported in the literature to engage Indigenous learners.

The inconsistencies offered in the responses in this study and the examples above support the need for more critical research and tools for practice. The phenomenon of educators struggling to match their beliefs or values with their practice is not uncommon (Lampert, 2012). In a Western Australian study of how the state's antiracism policy was impacting on the management of the schools, Aveling (2007) reported that most of the principals were quick to dismiss the presence of racism in their schools.

Moreover, the principals consistently claimed that while racism was not a major concern for their school, admissions of any incidents involving racism in some cases resulted in conjecture that the incidences were because of Indigenous young people or reverse racism (Aveling, 2007). She concluded that not only was it problematic that principals did not see racism as an issue in their schools, but that their limited definition and construction of race resulted in problems that undermined the implementation of a statewide policy specifically designed to counter racism (Aveling, 2007). In the context of this study, values such as inclusion, caring and prioritizing of relationships are reported in the literature as key features of the flexi-schooling environment (Mills and McGregor, 2010). It is then critical that flexi-schools, which espouse underpinning values connected with inclusion and social justice, actively address issues of race and racism within their schools in order to match their values with practice.

Lampert (2012) concludes that it can be a matter of 'praxis', of educators matching their beliefs to their actions in their professional roles, and undoubtedly this is a significant barrier for many teachers and leaders. However, when exploring the roles of school leaders in supporting a particular cultural group, such as Indigenous students, constructs of race and issues of racism are implicitly intertwined in such discussions. The resistance of educators in engaging with professional learning that incorporates antiracist content is well documented (Aveling, 2006; Phillips, 2011; Santoro, 2009). Racism in schools is an issue that many authors internationally are raising as a critical and pervasive issue (Brinson and Smith, 2014; Ladson-Billings and Tate, 2006; Solórzano and Yosso, 2002). There is a growing number of critical race education scholars who advocate that race and racism mediate all aspects of society, including schools (Hylton, 2012; López, 2003). Hence, instead of pretending racism does not exist or that its impact is minimized, educators should work to gain a deeper understanding of how race and racism work structurally (Brinson and Smith, 2014; Ladson-Billings, 1998). Racism is commonly misunderstood and defined simplistically by the general population (Aveling, 2007; Bodkin-Andrews and Carlson, 2016). Therefore, it is difficult to see how school leaders can support notions of equity for students who are outside of the dominant cultures, such as Indigenous students, without engaging in a thorough understanding of critical race perspectives. Although this study is limited in how deeply it could examine the prevalence of an over-reliance on cultural activities within flexi-schools, it does provide some insight into how value and practice mismatch can happen in any education context.

Conclusion

This chapter has presented key findings from a study that explored how leaders of flexi-schools reported that they are supporting Aboriginal and Torres Strait Islander learners. The findings presented an inconsistency in the responses from flexi-school leaders. The school leaders reported a high level of self-efficacy and willingness to learn about Indigenous cultures and learners, but they did not demonstrate a good understanding and knowledge of engaging Indigenous learners in their overall school practices. Further analysis revealed that studies such as this that focus on engaging cultural minority groups present complex implications about constructs of race and issues of racism in school settings, requiring leadership on sometimes difficult topics (Aveling, 2007).

The influence that school leaders can have on a school culture on matters such as racism is well established (Brinson and Smith, 2014). However, school leaders must be supported by having access to high-quality learning opportunities, particularly in countries such as Australia, where the education workforce is mainly White and middle class (Santoro and Allard, 2005). The literature on flexi-schools outlines that they are education spaces that are inclusive, caring, and relationships-focused (Mills and McGregor, 2010). Thus, a major challenge for flexi-schools is that they do not neglect to adequately address issues of race and racism through a misguided belief that issues of race and racism could not exist in an education context that is so committed to creating such an inclusive environment. Finally, providing education leaders opportunities to critically reflect on their values and how they are connected to school practices to identify areas for improvement may assist in addressing challenging issues such as race and racism.

References

Aboriginal and Torres Strait Islander Social Justice Commission (2000) *Social Justice Report 2000*. Sydney: Human Rights and Equal Opportunity Commission.

ABS (Australian Bureau of Statistics) (2013) *Estimate of Aboriginal and Torres Strait Islander Australians, June 2013*.

ACARA (Australian Curriculum, Assessment and Reporting Authority) (2014) Australian Curriculum, Assessment and Reporting Authority. Online. www.acara.edu.au (accessed 6 May 2018).

AITSL (Australian Institute for Teaching and School Leadership) (2013) 'Australian Professional Standards for Teachers'. Online. www.aitsl.edu. au/australian-professional-standards-for-teachers/standards/list (accessed 6 May 2018).

Australian Government (2014) *Closing the Gap: Prime Minister's report 2014*. Canberra: Commonwealth of Australia. Online. www.pmc.gov.au/sites/default/files/publications/closing_the_gap_2014.pdf (accessed 6 May 2018).

Aveling, N. (2006) '"Hacking at our very roots": Rearticulating white racial identity within the context of teacher education'. *Race Ethnicity and Education*, 9 (3), 261–74.

Aveling, N. (2007) 'Anti-racism in schools: A question of leadership?'. *Discourse: Studies in the Cultural Politics of Education*, 28 (1), 69–85.

Baroutsis, A., Mills, M., McGregor, G., te Riele, K. and Hayes, D. (2016) 'Student voice and the community forum: Finding ways of "being heard" at an alternative school for disenfranchised young people'. *British Educational Research Journal*, 42 (3), 438–53.

Blackley, G. (2012) *The Necessity for Individual Responsibility to Improve Indigenous Education* (Professional Learning Sabbatical Report). Melbourne: Australian Institute for Teaching and School Leadership.

Blackmore, J. (2010) '"The other within": Race/gender disruptions to the professional learning of white educational leaders'. *International Journal of Leadership in Education*, 13 (1), 45–61.

Blake, T. (1998) 'Deported… at the sweet will of the government: The removal of Aborigines to reserves in Queensland 1897–1939'. *Aboriginal History*, 22, 51–61.

Bodkin-Andrews, G. and Carlson, B. (2016) 'The legacy of racism and Indigenous Australian identity within education'. *Race Ethnicity and Education*, 19 (4), 784–807.

Brinson, J.A. and Smith, S.D. (2014) *Racialized Schools: Understanding and addressing racism in schools*. New York: Routledge.

Cummings, B. (1990) *Take This Child… From Kahlin Compound to the Retta Dixon Children's Home*. Canberra: Aboriginal Studies Press.

Davis, R. (ed.) (2004) *Woven Histories, Dancing Lives: Torres Strait Islander identity, culture and history*. Canberra: Aboriginal Studies Press.

Dixson, A.D. and Rousseau, C.K. (2005) 'And we are still not saved: Critical race theory in education ten years later'. *Race Ethnicity and Education*, 8 (1), 7–27.

Fitzgerald, T. (2006) 'Walking between two worlds: Indigenous women and educational leadership'. *Educational Management Administration and Leadership*, 34 (2), 201–13.

Haney López, I.F. (2013) 'The social construction of race'. In Delgado, R. and Stefancic, J. (eds) *Critical Race Theory: The cutting edge*. 3rd ed. Philadelphia: Temple University Press, 238–48.

Hickling Hudson, A. (2003) 'Multicultural education and the postcolonial turn'. *Policy Futures in Education*, 1 (2), 381–401.

Hughes, P., Khan, G. and Matthews, S. (2007) 'Leaders: Acting to improve outcomes for Indigenous students'. In *The Leadership Challenge: Improving learning in schools: Conference proceedings*. Camberwell, VIC: Australian Council for Educational Research, 40–3.

Hylton, K. (2012) 'Talk the talk, walk the walk: Defining critical race theory in research'. *Race Ethnicity and Education*, 15 (1), 23–41.

Ladson-Billings, G. (1998) 'Just what is critical race theory and what's it doing in a nice field like education?'. *International Journal of Qualitative Studies in Education*, 11 (1), 7–24.

Ladson-Billings, G. and Tate, W.F. (2006) 'Toward a critical race theory of education'. In Dixson, A.D. and Rousseau, C.K. (eds) *Critical Race Theory in Education: All God's children got a song*. New York: Routledge, 11–30.

Lampert, J. (2012) 'Becoming a socially just teacher: Walking the talk'. In Phillips, J. and Lampert, J. (eds) *Introductory Indigenous Studies in Education: Reflection and the importance of knowing*. 2nd ed. Frenchs Forest, NSW: Pearson Australia, 81–96.

López, G.R. (2003) 'The (racially neutral) politics of education: A critical race theory perspective'. *Educational Administration Quarterly*, 39 (1), 68–94.

MATSITI (More Aboriginal and Torres Strait Islander Teachers Initiative) (2017) 'Archive: More Aboriginal and Torres Strait Islander Teachers Initiative'. Online. http://matsiti.edu.au/ (accessed 6 May 2018).

McGregor, G., Mills, M., te Riele, K. and Hayes, D. (2015) 'Excluded from school: Getting a second chance at a "meaningful" education'. *International Journal of Inclusive Education*, 19 (6), 608–25.

McKenzie, P., Rowley, G., Weldon, P. and Murphy, M. (2011) *Staff in Australia's Schools 2010: Main report on the survey*. Camberwell, VIC: Australian Council for Educational Research. Online. http://research.acer.edu.au/cgi/viewcontent.cgi?article=1013&context=tll_misc (accessed 6 May 2018).

Mertler, C. (2002) 'Demonstrating the potential for web-based survey methodology with a case study'. *American Secondary Education*, 30 (2), 49–61.

Mills, M. and McGregor, G. (2010) *Re-engaging Students in Education: Success factors in alternative schools*. Brisbane: Youth Affairs Network Queensland.

Mills, M. and McGregor, G. (2014) *Re-engaging Young People in Education: Learning from alternative schools*. London: Routledge.

Morgan, A., Pendergast, D., Brown, R. and Heck, D. (2015) 'Relational ways of being an educator: Trauma-informed practice supporting disenfranchised young people'. *International Journal of Inclusive Education*, 19 (10), 1037–51.

Parker, L. and Lynn, M. (2002) 'What's race got to do with it? Critical race theory's conflicts with and connections to qualitative research methodology and epistemology'. *Qualitative Inquiry*, 8 (1), 7–22.

Phillips, D.J.M. (2011) 'Resisting Contradictions: Non-Indigenous pre-service teacher responses to critical Indigenous studies'. Unpublished PhD thesis, Queensland University of Technology.

Santoro, N. (2009) 'Teaching in culturally diverse contexts: What knowledge about "self" and "others" do teachers need?'. *Journal of Education for Teaching*, 35 (1), 33–45.

Santoro, N. and Allard, A. (2005) '(Re)examining identities: Working with diversity in the pre-service teaching experience'. *Teaching and Teacher Education*, 21 (7), 863–73.

Sarra, C. (2007) 'Stronger, smarter, Sarra'. *Teacher: The National Education Magazine*, March, 32–41.

Shay, M. (2013) 'Practices of Alternative Schools in Queensland in Supporting Aboriginal and Torres Strait Islander Young People to Remain Engaged in Education'. Master's thesis, University of the Sunshine Coast. Retrieved from https://eprints.qut.edu.au/71023/

Shay, M. (2015) 'The perceptions that shape us: Strengthening Indigenous young people's cultural identity in flexi school settings'. In Ferfolja, T., Jones Díaz, C. and Ullman, J. (eds) *Understanding Sociological Theory for Educational Practices*. Melbourne: Cambridge University Press, 93–105.

Shay, M. and Heck, D. (2015) 'Alternative education engaging Indigenous young people: Flexi schooling in Queensland'. *Australian Journal of Indigenous Education*, 44 (1), 37–47.

Smallwood, G. (2011) 'Human Rights and First Australians' Well-Being'. Unpublished PhD thesis, James Cook University.

Solórzano, D.G. and Yosso, T.J. (2001) 'From racial stereotyping and deficit discourse toward a critical race theory in teacher education'. *Multicultural Education*, 9 (1), 2–8.

Solórzano, D.G. and Yosso, T.J. (2002) 'Critical race methodology: Counter-storytelling as an analytical framework for education research'. *Qualitative Inquiry*, 8 (1), 23–44.

Te Riele, K. (2007) 'Educational alternatives for marginalised youth'. *Australian Educational* Researcher, 34 (3), 53–68.

Te Riele, K. (2012) *Learning Choices: A map for the future*. Bondi Junction, NSW: Dusseldorp Skills Forum.

Te Riele, K. (2014) *Putting the Jigsaw Together: Flexible learning programs in Australia: Final report*. Melbourne: Victoria Institute for Education, Diversity and Lifelong Learning.

Tuhiwai Smith, L. (2005) 'Building a research agenda for Indigenous epistemologies and education'. *Anthrolopology and Education Quarterly*, 36 (1), 93–5.

Tuhiwai Smith, L. (2012) *Decolonizing Methodologies: Research and Indigenous peoples*. 2nd ed. London: Zed Books.

Vadeboncoeur, J.A. (2009) 'Spaces of difference: The contradictions of alternative educational programs'. *Educational Studies*, 45 (3), 280–99.

Weatherburn, D. and Holmes, J. (2010) 'Re-thinking Indigenous over-representation in prison'. *Australian Journal of Social Issues*, 45 (4), 559–76.

Chapter 10

Haedoji School: Supporting refugees in South Korea

Sujin Yoon and Myungsook Cho

Introduction

This chapter examines the role of alternative schools for refugees arriving in South Korea from North Korea. The chapter begins by setting out the background and educational context in North Korea, and the reasons children make such difficult migration journeys. It then describes the educational context in South Korea, the challenges these young refugees face, and the efforts of one alternative school to meet these challenges. The chapter concludes by offering some reflections on potential future directions for alternative education for young refugees, bearing in mind that although small in number, their needs are significant and often long-term.

Background and context

The events leading up to the current situation for North Korean refugees began in the early part of the twentieth century when Korea was ruled by Japan. After Japan's defeat in 1945, Japan's power in the country came to an end. With independence, capitalism became established in the south of the Korean peninsula and socialism in the north, supported by the United States and the Soviet Union respectively. After the tragedy of the Korean War (1950–3), North Korea developed a form of military socialism, based on the '*Juche* ideology', idolizing North Korea's founder Kim Il-sung. (*Juche* is a Korean word that broadly means 'self' or 'subject'. According to Reed (1997: 169), it denotes a modified practice of Marxism and Leninism in the unique context of North Korean culture and politics, strongly emphasizing self-reliance and independence.) Under these two very different political systems, a sense of separation has intensified over recent decades.

Since the cease-fire agreement between the two Koreas in 1953, there have been defectors from North to South Korea. Many of these were soldiers who crossed via the Demilitarized Zone (DMZ). They were described in their new host country as heroes who had turned against the north; a symbol of the victory of South Korea over North Korea via media

(Kim, 2012). Their eagerness to seek freedom and their abandoning of political loyalty to the North Korean regime tended to be highlighted as a way to valorise the democratic values of South Korea.

More recently, from the early 1990s, severe drought, famine and a struggling North Korean economy have driven thousands of ordinary people, rather than just defecting soldiers, to cross the border illegally into neighbouring China in search of food. At first it was mostly males, usually fathers, who made these journeys. However, this began to change as police pressure grew. In North Korea, as a patriarchal society, the head of state was often called the 'Father' and this was mirrored at the level of the family, with fathers having strong authority and control of the household. Food was distributed to each family through the father and food rations would be stopped and police investigations ensue if it was found that the head of the household had left his home in search of food to feed the family (Ministry of Unification, 2014). For this reason, it began to fall to mothers or adult daughters to make the dangerous crossing into China. These women mainly made their way to three provinces with large numbers of ethnic Koreans: Liaoning, Jirin and Heilongjiang in Northeast China. These were areas where there were many more men than women, because a considerable number of ethnic Korean women had left to find work or a husband in South Korea, following the 'Korean Dream'. According to Baek (2002), this led North Korean females in their 20s to 40s to become targets of exploitation and human trafficking, to be sold as 'wives' to local men; a situation that continues today (Do *et al.*, 2016).

This very difficult situation is compounded by China's practice of forced repatriation and North Korea's treatment of people thus returned. They are often treated as political prisoners, stigmatized as traitors and persecuted ruthlessly, particularly if they are found to have had contact with Christian missionaries or to have tried to make the journey on to South Korea. For these reasons, those trying to reach South Korea often opt to make the long and arduous journey through Myanmar, Laos, Thailand, and Cambodia, or sometimes via Mongolia rather than China. According to Do *et al.* (2015), 85 per cent of North Koreans entering South Korea came through Southeast Asian countries in 2009. They are smuggled through these countries with the help of religious institutions, advocacy groups and NGOs, or by paying a fee to brokers. These helpers and organizations provide secret shelters and guide them to reach South Korea via relatively safe routes (Do *et al.*, 2015; Song, 2013).

The current situation for young North Korean refugees

According to the Ministry of Unification in South Korea, the number of North Korean refugees who entered South Korea between 1998 and 2016 stood at 30,212.

Table 10.1: Number of North Korean refugees entering South Korea per year between 1998 and 2016

Year	Number	Year	Number
1998	947	2009	2,914
2001	1,043	2010	2,402
2002	1,142	2011	2,706
2003	1,285	2012	1,502
2004	1,898	2013	1,514
2005	1,384	2014	1,397
2006	2,028	2015	1,276
2007	2,554	2016	1,418
2008	2,803	Total	30,212

Note: No official statistics were published between 1999 and 2000.

Source: Ministry of Unification, 2017

As Table 10.1 shows, the numbers increased steadily from 1998 to 2011, reaching a high point in 2008. The numbers then decreased in 2012, when Kim Jong-un was officially declared supreme leader in North Korea and border security between North Korea and China was strengthened by the governments of both countries. As the number of North Korean refugee children and young people in South Korea has increased over time, they have become a focus of attention for policy makers and research (Kim *et al.*, 2015a). Concerns regarding educational issues were first raised in the 1990s (Park, 1998) and support at this time was largely focused on helping young refugees to adapt to South Korean society, by encouraging them to study at a regular school with South Korean students and providing them with additional support programmes to narrow the educational gap. However, it has become apparent in recent times that this approach, while helpful, is not sufficient and that, for example, the mental and emotional health of these young people needed much greater attention (Lee, 2001). The need to consider alternative educational provision for North Korean young refugees emerged out of such concerns.

Patterns of migration and effects on education

To understand the current aims and potential future roles for alternative schools in this challenging context, it is helpful to understand something of the different patterns of migration, how these are shaped by the availability – or not – of family support in making these journeys, and how this in turn affects the young people involved. Young North Korean refugees can be thought of as falling into three main groups: (1) children who escape North Korea in order to be reunited with parents, usually mothers who have often previously been trafficked; (2) young people who arrive in South Korea with family members; and (3) those who arrive without parents or other care-givers. These groups are described in more detail below.

The most common experience among young refugees from North Korea is where their mothers, who have already settled in South Korea, manage to get their children out from the north using brokers. A majority of these mothers have experienced being trafficked into rural, remote or isolated areas in China and forced to marry there. They have often made a home and have had children with their Chinese husbands. They are still illegal immigrants, however, and the risk of exposure of their identity increases over time. Therefore, they often flee their Chinese home and make their way on to South Korea (Song, 2013). They then contact their children in North Korea to try to help the latter escape and join them. In this situation, the children face multiple challenges. They need to adjust not only to a new society and new school environment, but also to living with a mother from whom they may have been parted for a number of years and new siblings of whom they may have known nothing. In the alternative school we describe later in the chapter, we see that this often leads to issues of emotional confusion and deep anxiety.

The second group, and perhaps the most stable among the young refugees, comprises children who enter South Korea accompanied by their parents and/or other family members (Han *et al.*, 2009). Even here, however, difficulties may arise. North Korean parents have been accustomed to a highly patriarchal family structure where fathers, as noted above, traditionally possess a high level of control and authority. This can lead to tension when children, as is often the case, adapt more readily to their new cultural experiences and the different attitudes to child-rearing in the south (Choi *et al.*, 2007).

This tension is further compounded by the way that children's expectations and perceptions of their parents can alter during their migration and settlement. In our experience of working over many years with these young people, we have seen that some of these children perceive their parents to be 'powerless' and unable to take care of their children. We have listened to them talk about their feelings of confusion at experiencing the same hardships and privations as the adults who they expected to protect and care for them. Young refugees often find themselves in conflict with their fathers as a result (Choi *et al.*, 2006; Lee, 2001). In these circumstances, mothers may often try to act as a bridge between fathers and children, though with limited success (Han *et al.*, 2009). The tension that arises here is often then compounded by young people's feelings of resentment and anger about leaving behind their homes and friends, having to face the challenges of adapting to a new society, and finding it hard to be accepted by their new South Korean peers. Pressures are further increased by the financial difficulties that commonly arise for the new arrivals, as parents often find it hard to get work. In these stressful circumstances, home relationships can be very fragile.

The third main group of young refugees, and the group generally regarded as the most vulnerable, is children and young people who have become separated from their parents and other adult caregivers. These young people have told us over the years about the many ways that this can happen. They may have experienced their parents' death in North Korea or indeed during the long migration journey, or become separated while their parents were looking for food in China, or taken by human traffickers during the journey or when their parents have been forcibly repatriated to North Korea. Sometimes, parents let their children cross the border alone in hope that they can find a different, better life. There are also some young people who arrive in South Korea without parents because they have escaped during a school field trip to explore Mount Baekdu, on the border between North Korea and China.

The South Korean government has recognized the significant impact these dangers and trauma has on these young people and it has developed a system of responses, allocating them on arrival to a group home or orphanage. However, this can create other problems for some in learning to live alongside their South Korean peers in these institutions. As a result of this, we have often been aware that these young people face challenging situations not only at school but also personally and in their home environment. In addition, they commonly have mental and physical health issues. North Korean refugee children are typically shorter and slighter than South Korean peers, due to malnutrition and disease (Lee and Lee, 2013). Although they receive medical treatment after entering South Korea and there are specialized programmes in place, including, for example, support for young women who have experienced human trafficking or sexual exploitation during their journey (Park and Kang, 2011), problems often persist. There can, for example, be further loss of self-confidence in a society that is very appearance-oriented (Yang and Bae, 2010), when North Korean children and young people look different. This is one key reason why a focus on healing and protection are often key aims of alternative schools for North Korean young refugees.

There are many reasons, then, why young North Korean people encounter challenges in adjusting to life in South Korea. Research highlights ways in which these young people experience a variety of difficulties such as discrimination and social exclusion (Kim *et al.*, 2015b), communication problems caused by language differences, cultural gaps and educational gaps in learning (Lee *et al.*, 2011). Often this is also exacerbated by the contrasts between the North and South Korean educational systems.

The North Korean education system

The founder of North Korea, Kim Il-sung, regarded education as one of the main vehicles of social control, expounding his views in 'The Theses on Socialist Education revolution and education in Peoples' Korea' (1977). In his view, the aim of education was to train children and young people to be revolutionaries, members of the working class, and communists, rather than to promote personal development. In the view of North Korea, education is a tool to consolidate and maintain absolute support and dedication to the Communist Party and its organizations (Ministry of Unification, 2014). A free education policy means that students do not need to pay tuition fees. However, students are often mobilized as a labour force. For example, students are expected to work on collective farms for four to ten weeks during the busy seasons, planting rice in May and harvesting in September under the names of 'Spring Battle' and 'Fall Battle' respectively. They are also mobilized for construction projects (Ministry of Unification, 2014) and educated to idolize the founder Kim Il-sung from an early age. Teachers are referred to as 'professional revolutionaries' and given strong authority by the ruling Workers' Party and delegated responsibility for the indoctrination of children (Cho, 2004). The class teacher stays with the same class from the time of entry to school until the student graduates from school, further reinforcing this authority. In addition, the Party sends party members to each school to conduct surveillance of teachers and students.

Teaching methods are premised on a need to inspire students with loyalty to the supreme leader of the country, mainly adopting memory-based approaches in practice (Ministry of Unification, 2014). Students repeatedly read a variety of stories that strengthen idolization of Kim Il-sung and his family. Lessons are teacher-led and focus on rote learning and memorization, so that they attain good grades in tests and exams. Teachers expect students to accept curriculum content uncritically and unquestioningly. When we meet these young people in alternative education settings once they are in South Korea, they tell us that students in North Korean schools are not allowed to express their thoughts and opinions freely; they must learn absolute obedience to their teacher's authority and decision. Due to the influence of this kind of education in North Korea, refugee students from North Korea tend to depend heavily on adult teachers and look to them to make decisions for them, rather than making their own choices and decisions.

From 1975 to 2012, the North Korean education system had a universal 11-year compulsory education system, composed of one year of kindergarten, four years of primary school, and six years of secondary school. This education system was reformed by the third leader, Kim Jong-un, in 2012, when he launched the universal 12-year compulsory education system, comprising one year of kindergarten, five years of primary school, three years of junior secondary school, and three years of senior secondary school (Han and Lee, 2014).

This new system claims to emphasize students' intellectual capacities and creative thinking, but for us, it is questionable whether the new scheme can achieve this within the current political and social structures.

Alternative education for North Korean refugee youths in South Korea

North Korean refugees under age 24 who have been admitted or transferred to a high school are eligible for educational support by the state. The wide age range is intended to ensure good continuing educational support for North Korean refugee students, and acknowledge the significant gaps in their learning (Ministry of Education, 2017). The most recent figures available suggest that the total number of North Korean refugee students in Korean Ministry of Education schools stands at 2,688 (Ministry of Education, 2016) and the number of students enrolled in alternative schools, 242 (Kim *et al.*, 2015). Once North Korean young refugees enter South Korea, they are required to participate in a 12-week resettlement programme at the nominated state education centre for refugees from North Korea, named 'Hanawon'. After this programme, the refugee youth can choose either to enrol in mainstream schools close to where they are housed or opt for alternative education.

Educational success in South Korea is generally seen as the key to social mobility and to a successful adult life, and schools are therefore fiercely competitive (Seth, 2002). There is growing national recognition that such pressures affect many (So and Kang, 2014), not only new arrivals. However, good schools are still measured by strong exam results and rates of acceptance into top universities. A majority of mainstream schools therefore focus primarily on formal learning opportunities, with pastoral needs often overlooked. In these circumstances, North Korean pupils have difficulties in adapting to the new school environment. To resolve this problem, alternative educational provision began to appear in the 1990s, increasing in number since 2000, often founded by religious institutions, and aiming to offer holistic support for North Korean young refugees' adjustment to South Korean society.

One of the main reasons North Koreans choose alternative schooling is because they are often older than the South Korean students at a similar stage of learning. Some choose alternative schools because they know they need to improve their basic academic skills and will not be able to achieve in the mainstream. Unaccompanied refugee young people are more inclined to choose alternative educational settings because this also offers accommodation and financial aid (Park, 2012). However, these decisions are not easy ones because alternative schools are still sometimes stigmatized and associated with failure to maintain mainstream school enrolment, especially if such schools are 'non-accredited', i.e. not able to offer qualifications and accreditations recognized by the South Korean government. Students in such schools must take an extra qualification exam equivalent to a school diploma if they wish to proceed in their education. This is discussed in more detail below, in the description of Haedoji ('Sunrise') School. (Note that this is a pseudonym.)

Around 69.8 per cent of high school graduates go on to higher education institutions in South Korea (Ministry of Education, 2016), and there is significant pressure on North Korean young refugees also to gain a high school diploma or higher qualification if they want to apply for work. To do this, alternative school students must take the national qualification exam equivalent to a regular school diploma. While young refugee students pass the exams for elementary and middle school qualification relatively easily, they often have difficulty in passing the exam for high school qualification. This gives rise to a dilemma for alternative schools and often they now find they have no choice but to focus on more academic subjects, leaving behind their initial, more holistic aims.

So far in this chapter we have outlined the reasons that children and young people make the dangerous journey from North Korea, and described the physical, emotional, personal and social impact of the difficulties they encounter as a result. We have also attempted to explain some of the challenges they often meet as they try to settle into their new lives in South Korea. In the following section we will look in more detail at the experience of one alternative school where staff have tried to maintain a balance between helping students make good academic progress while also supporting their emotional and social needs.

Haedoji ('Sunrise') alternative school

Where do we need to put the emphasis? On the word 'alternative', or on the word 'school'? This is perhaps always a difficult question when we discuss the role of alternative education, but particularly so in the South Korean context. In this section we share with you the story of the first alternative school for North Korean refugee youths to be officially accredited to offer high school (state-accredited) and middle school education (non-accredited). Here, it is important to explain why this school made an effort to be approved by the government as an accredited school.

Established in 2004, this school had provided a variety of educational programmes for North Korean young refugees for around five years. Although as staff we were keen to make time in the school day to address the students' trauma and help them overcome this, the students themselves often did not want to take part in the kinds of extra-curricular activities specifically designed to help them. The older students in particular wanted to achieve the high school qualification and to get working and earning as fast as possible. To do this, they knew that they had to take the national exam for high school qualification as they could not obtain a high school diploma in alternative school settings. Because of this, students regarded alternative school as 'cram school': merely a place to prepare for the national exam. Therefore, teachers inevitably focused on teaching subjects for the exam. We decided that to address this issue, the school needed to be authorized as a school that could give a high school diploma. In this way, we could support and ensure the participation of the refugee students in all aspects of the educational programme offered by the school, without the burden of the additional qualification exam. In 2009, Haedoji School began the process of seeking approval as an accredited school but faced what seemed to be insurmountable obstacles because it did not own its school building, land and playground as stipulated in the relevant regulations. We filed a petition for changes in the regulations and were delighted when eventually it was confirmed that an exception could be made for alternative schools for North Korean young refugees. This means that now our refugee students can receive their high school diploma without taking the national exam and achieve the same academic status as regular school graduates.

A tailored curriculum for students with special needs

At the same time, we are still committed to our main purpose of helping students adjust to South Korea successfully, offering help to the young refugees in three main ways: education, care, and rehabilitation. First, the school has developed a curriculum specific to their needs. This includes teaching by experts, customized textbooks, and a programme of field trips. Second, the school provides comfortable accommodation and support for students who are in need of this, for example for those who do not have family able to care for them. The school also offers life coaching, care programmes and free meals, including breakfast and dinner, to help students keep healthy and to enable them to live in a family-like atmosphere. Third, the school works to heal refugee students' mental and physical wounds from the migration journey and also helps them overcome the many challenges they face in their adjustment process. We provide, for example, music therapy, art therapy, opportunities to get involved in sport, psychotherapeutic counselling for mental and physical rehabilitation, health management, and medical support. Around 60 per cent of our students suffer from diabetes and anaemia as a result of the effects of their migration journey from North Korea.

The school also teaches its students how to manage their finances and develop a sense of responsibility in order to help them learn to live as full members of a democratic society. Students learn about potential future jobs through a work experience programme. Behavioural modification is another important part of the school curriculum. A considerable number of North Korean refugee students have suffered a lack of affection, and they have low self-esteem and are easily stressed. This leads some students to depend on alcohol, tobacco, computer games or drugs as an object of attachment or as a way to relieve stress. Therefore, Haedoji School makes efforts to address this, both through teacher involvement and specific educational programmes.

The role of the teacher

Alternative school teachers, such as those in Haedoji, have a variety of roles beyond simply teaching students in the classroom. Most importantly, teachers act as guardians for students who do not have parents or other caregivers. They go to the police station if their students are in trouble;

they take sick students to hospital. They mediate in disputes between students and their parents and provide special lectures for parents on topics such as improving communication skills or understanding adolescents' development. Nevertheless, the teacher working in alternative education tends to be undervalued in the field of education. Alternative school teachers are poorly paid in comparison with regular school teachers. Many lack stable living conditions because their income is less than the minimum cost of living and they are excluded from the welfare benefits that regular school teachers receive. Under these poor working conditions, it is difficult for alternative school teachers to work with North Korean refugee students for a long period, although they try to devote all their energies to them. Better conditions for alternative school teachers are urgently needed.

Future directions

To date, alternative schools for North Korean refugee youths have tended to aim for their successful adjustment into South Korean society. The prevailing view has been that this is best achieved by young people from the two Koreas being educated together. There has been criticism of alternative schools on the grounds that they deprive these young people of the opportunity to mix with their South Korean peers and thereby hinder adjustment to their new society. However, this view underestimates the considerable number of cases of stress among North Korean youths when they are thrown into South Korean society without a buffer zone. Alternative schools can play a vital role by providing that buffer zone. In the early stages of their adaptation to their new lives, when they are putting down roots in South Korea, they have the opportunity to learn in a supportive environment, where an emphasis on academic success is mediated by attention to care and healing. In this sense, these alternative schools may be seen as helping education to prepare for the future reunification of two Koreas. It is commonly said in South Korea that reunification could happen at any time, and it is important to be ready. We believe that alternative schools have an important part to play, with their expertise and experience in the areas of personal and social growth and integration, in helping this reunification process.

References

Baek, Y.O. (2002) 'Research on the actual conditions of the North Korean female refugees in China and aids policies for them'. *North Korean Studies Review*, 6 (1), 241–64.

Cho, J.A. (2004) 'Between the "professional revolutionist" and "unbelievable intelligentsia": The images and socioeconomic status of teachers in North Korea'. *Review of North Korean Studies*, 7 (2), 127–65.

Choi, D.-H., Lee, I.-S. and Kim, H.-A. (2007) 'The development of parental education program for successful adjustment of child and juvenile defectors in South Korea'. *Journal of Child Education*, 16 (2), 277–91.

Choi, M.S., Choi, T.S. and Kang, J.H. (2006) 'Psychological characteristics of children and adolescents escaped from North Korea and seeing a counselling strategy'. *Korean Journal of Play Therapy*, 9 (3), 23–34.

Do, K., Kim, S.-A., Han, D., Lee, K.-S. and Hong, M. (2015) *White Paper on Human Rights in North Korea 2015*. Seoul: Korea Institute for National Unification.

Do, K., Rim, Y.-J., Lee, K. and Hong, J. (2016) *Human Rights Situation of Women and Children in North Korea*. Seoul: Korea Institute for National Unification.

Han, M.G. and Lee, G.H. (2014) 'An analysis on the educational policy of the Kim Jong-Un regime and the reform of North Korean school system'. *North Korean Studies Review*, 18 (2), 233–54.

Han, M.G., Yoon, J., Lee, H. and Kim, I. (2009) *The Current Educational Status of North Korean Migrant Children and the Development of Educational Support Systems in South Korea*. Seoul: Korean Educational Development Institute.

Kim, Il Sung (1977) *Theses on Socialist Education: Revolution and education in Peoples Korea*. New York: World View Publishers.

Kim, J.W., Kim, J.S., Kang, G.S. and Youn, B.R. (2015a) *White Paper on Education of North Korean Migrant Youth in South Korea*. Seoul: Korean Educational Development Institute.

Kim, M.A., Hong, J.S., Ra, M. and Kim, K. (2015b) 'Understanding social exclusion and psychosocial adjustment of North Korean adolescents and young adult refugees in South Korea through Photovoice'. *Qualitative Social Work*, 14 (6), 820–41.

Kim, S.K. (2012) '"Defector", "refugee", or "migrant"? North Korean settlers in South Korea's changing social discourse'. *North Korean Review*, 8 (2), 94–110.

Lee, H.S., Park, J.H and Choi, D.K. (2011) 'A phenomenological study of the adaptation of lives in South Korea for adolescents refugee from North Korea'. *Journal of Adolescent Welfare*, 13 (4), 309–41.

Lee, K. (2001) *Patterns of Maladaptation to South Korean Society among North Korean Adolescent Defectors: A qualitative approach*. Seoul: Korea Institute for Youth Development.

Lee, S.H. and Lee S.H. (2013) 'Children's mental health in multicultural family and North Korean defectors in South Korea'. *Korean Journal of Child and Adolescent Psychiatry*, 24 (3), 124–31.

Ministry of Education, Korean Educational Statistics Service (2016) *2016 Basic Education Statistics*. Online. http://kess.kedi.re.kr/index (accessed 22 January 2017).

Ministry of Education, North Korea Youth Support Centre (2017) *Understanding of North Korean Migrant Youth*. Online. www.hub4u.or.kr/hub/edu/understand.do (accessed 19 March 2017).

Ministry of Unification (2017) *Data and Statistics*. Online. www.unikorea.go.kr/eng_unikorea/relations/statistics/defectors/ (accessed 23 April 2017).

Ministry of Unification, Institute for Unification Education (2014) *2014 Understanding North Korea*. Seoul: Institute for Unification Education.

Park, J.-R. and Kang, D.W. (2011) 'A study on female North Korean defectors: Trends, controversial issues, and tasks'. *North Korean Studies Review*, 15 (2), 1–24.

Park, K.-T. (2012) 'A study on the management characteristics of alternative schools for North Korean youth defector'. *Youth Facilities and Environment*, 10 (3), 51–66.

Park, S.K. (1998) 'A Study on the School Adjustment of North Korean Youth Defectors'. Unpublished Master's Degree thesis, Catholic University of Korea.

Reed, G.G. (1997) 'Globalisation and education: The case of North Korea'. *Compare: Journal of Comparative and International Education*, 27 (2), 167–78.

Seth, M.J. (2002) *Education Fever: Society, politics, and the pursuit of schooling in South Korea*. Honolulu: University of Hawai'i Press.

So, K. and Kang, J. (2014) 'Curriculum reform in Korea: Issues and challenges for twenty-first century learning'. *Asia-Pacific Education Researcher*, 23 (4), 795–803.

Song, J. (2013) '"Smuggled refugees": The social construction of North Korean migration'. *International Migration*, 51 (4), 158–73.

Yang, Y.E. and Bae, I. (2010) 'A study on the adaptation process of North Korean immigrant youth discontinuing formal education'. *Korean Journal of Social Welfare Studies*, 41 (4), 189–224.

Chapter 11

Making the difference in a primary SEBN Scottish school

Leanne Hepburn

What makes a difference?

It was never my career goal to work within SEBN – an education provision that supports children and young people with social, emotional and behavioural needs. This support can be given in mainstream schools, but where the needs are very great or more complex, separate provision is provided by the government in Scotland. I had always worked in mainstream schools and until I became the headteacher of an SEBN provision in Scotland, I was not fully aware of what social, emotional and behavioural needs actually looked like, what I should expect, or how the young people who attended could be supported. However, an SEBN opportunity was presented to me and I took a chance. This chapter details my experiences of leading change in an SEBN school and some of the tensions associated with this.

Although my knowledge and understanding of SEBN was limited on a professional level, I did have some personal experience. As the mother of a child who was diagnosed with Asperger's Syndrome and severe anxiety and had behaviour issues, I knew what it was like to have a child who did not fit into the mainstream world. There was always an issue of one kind or another that would lead to exclusion from the group, from the classroom and sometimes from school. I knew what it was like to be the parent who is called in for yet another meeting to discuss their child's disruptive behaviour. A lot of the time I had hope. Our local authority had a really good process in place for parents and professionals to meet and develop packages of support to help those with additional needs. However, schools and classrooms are big and very busy places and I always felt that this impacted on the desired supports being fully implemented in a consistent way. The more I saw things go wrong for my own child, the more I began to wonder what other young people who did not fit the mould were going through in terms of the barriers they were facing that stopped them from being able to engage with learning and make progress. With much trepidation, I took up my post as headteacher in 2010, and what follows is the journey that we were all on in order to improve the outcomes for the young people we were working with and to have a positive impact on their social and emotional development.

Situated in a large urban local authority, the purpose-built school provided education for primary aged children with severe and complex social, emotional and behavioural needs. The management team consisted of a headteacher, depute headteacher, and principal teacher whose classified position in Scotland is equivalent, for example, to head of department. The school had a multi-agency approach to working with the children and their families, and focused on building relationships, teamwork, and consistent approaches to understanding and managing behaviour so that we could ensure young people were in school, learning, and working towards achieving their potential.

The school aimed to offer a safe, supportive and stimulating environment to help pupils make good progress in their attainment and aspired to actively engage pupils in their learning and to take responsibility for their behaviour, be proud of their school environment and of their achievements. We wanted to help our young people focus on developing respect for themselves and for others, and ensure they had a good primary school experience. We hoped to give them the opportunity to be reintegrated into a mainstream school and community if it was appropriate. Children attended the school from across the authority and there was a city-wide multi-disciplinary process which acted as gatekeeper for pupil placements at the school.

Beginnings

In my first few weeks of being appointed I could see that there was an energy and commitment from the staff team towards the young people who attended, and that the pupils themselves had tremendous potential. However, I could also see that some aspects of the day-to-day life of the school appeared to be causing difficulties for young people and staff. Most of these difficulties centred on the behaviour management of young people. Therefore the first step would be to work towards creating a positive and nurturing environment that would improve behaviour and be conducive to supporting learning and teaching.

Why nurture? When children were placed with us we read the supporting paperwork, which often highlighted the extreme behaviours we should expect. However, almost without exception, and with varying degrees of severity, the main underlying issue was of poor attachment.

For one reason or another, the children had not had the opportunity to build relationships or to create a bond with a significant adult, and may have experienced a crisis that caused key relationships to break down. Consequently they were often not socially and emotionally ready for school or were failing to cope within the mainstream school setting. Our pupils had often disengaged from learning, and we wanted to make sure that we delivered a curriculum that focused on the interests of the child so that they could be excited about learning again. We therefore felt it vital that 'Nurture and Engage' should be the school's mantra.

Pupils placed at the school were there for a variety of reasons, ranging from chronic non-attendance to those who had committed offences in the local community. No matter the reason for the placement, our focus was to give the required additional support to help them manage their behaviour, build their self-confidence, and teach them how to be more resilient so that they were in a better place emotionally and ready to learn again.

Challenges and change

One of the advantages of having a school purpose-built for children with SEBN is that we benefit from having a physical environment that helps us with these aims. Compared to mainstream school, the school and classes are very small (the child-to-teacher ratio is 6:1). The staff team is interdisciplinary, including nursery nurses, pupil support assistants and behaviour assistants as well as teachers. We also have designated spaces for time-out and 'cool-off' rooms. When I was first appointed I soon realized that these time-out and cool-off rooms were not always used in the best ways, and some aspects of the physical environment required a complete overhaul. At this time, the school had three separate learning and teaching teams, each of which had access to three classrooms, a general-purpose area and a playground. The cool-off area and behaviour base was shared by the whole school, and children had to be taken from their team to spend time in the base. The base had become an area for children to congregate, where difficult behaviour tended to escalate and cause disruption in the corridors. This went against the 'Nurture and Engage' approach we wanted to achieve. We therefore decided that we needed a nurture space and support base within each team. The children were involved in deciding what the base should look like and what would help them stay safe when things had escalated and how to get back on track when they were finding things difficult. Once completed these new bases were put into immediate use. They enabled staff and young people to have a safe space to calm down and an area for reflective discussions to help them re-engage with their learning.

The children responded well to being involved in the development of these areas, and although these spaces were sometimes damaged, the children were often keen to put things right and clear up any mess that had been made and there seemed to be more respect for their shared area.

As a school we then decided to invest in improving the spaces in the corridors. We purchased lockable notice boards so that we could display children's work without the fear of anything being ripped off the wall. It did not take long for the children to start to take pride in seeing their work on the walls and also become more open to sharing their hard work, both in class and at whole-school assemblies, as they felt more valued and respected. As we continued to focus on the changes needed to create the best possible environment for learning, we carried out a variety of audits and identified targets. At this stage these related to behaviour and the care and protection of our young people and our responsibility to them. We focused, for example, on creating individual risk assessments for all pupils so that we could best understand their needs and tailor our staff development and training to meet these needs. One of our audits highlighted that staff and pupils were regularly being assaulted, even though all staff were trained in the use of CALM (Crisis, Aggression, Limitation and Management – Calm Training Services is an independent training provider widely used by schools with pupils with very challenging or destructive behaviour[1]) to help manage these challenging and violent situations. However, the number of 'hands on' incidences was high, and we developed a debriefing policy so that pupils and staff could engage in reflective practice following any major incident or episode of restraint in the school. By doing this we were able to reduce the number of incidents. By improving the recording and monitoring of such incidents we were able to use the data to identify the themes, and then staff could undertake training, e.g. on the theory and de-escalation techniques associated with CALM.

In the same way, and to ensure the care and protection of our young people in terms of legislation, we made sure that all Child Protection concerns were being raised appropriately and followed through using proper processes and procedures. This also helped us take a consistent and structured approach to multi-agency Child Planning Meetings (CPM), which involved the children and their families and included their views, all of which is encompassed within the Scottish 'Getting It Right For Every Child' (GIRFEC) process. (GIRFEC is the national approach in Scotland to improving outcomes and supporting the well-being of children and young people. It is child-focused, based on an understanding of the well-being of a child, based on tackling needs early and requires joined-up working.[2]) We made sure all of our pupils had a case co-ordinator (the headteacher or the depute headteacher) who would lead and chair meetings and follow up any action points. We reviewed the roles and responsibilities of the behaviour support staff and the ways in which to manage the difficult behaviour exhibited by pupils. We examined the physical setting of the classrooms in relation to the number of exits from the building, i.e. how could we use the exits to our advantage as a means of support strategy for the children as opposed to the children using them as a way of getting a member of staff or another pupil to chase them.

Our pupils are transported to and from school on a variety of shared buses and taxis, as is common for most pupils educated outside the mainstream in Scotland. Our audit highlighted that the attitude and behaviour of pupils as they arrived and left school was very disruptive, so the start and the end of the school day were particularly difficult. We therefore reviewed the structure of the school day, the provision of individual transport, and shared information with bus escorts and drivers about how best to support the young people on their journey. We decided that inappropriate behaviour should not go unchallenged and so identified when it was appropriate to take a zero tolerance approach, and what the follow-through procedures and supports should be.

Although there was an awareness that change is a necessary aspect of life and work, the journey that the school was on was a tough one. In the early stages there were often 'we used to' type discussions that were sometimes fuelled by doubt and scepticism as to whether or not the change would be successful. There were uncomfortable moments as things started to change, as there was a small cohort of staff who did not fully agree with the vision for the school. This made the change process more challenging and resulted in there being a period of time where there was a high turnover of staff. However, a culture of consistent self-evaluation was developing and was a key driver in taking forward improvements. This became evident as staff, old and new, became more reflective in their practice and focused on finding solutions to issues within their teams and across the school.

With the combination of changes to the physical environment, a much more consistent approach to behaviour, and putting a range of processes and procedures in place, we felt we had eventually reached a turning point where the school felt much calmer and more relaxed. The corridors were quiet, the atmosphere in the building was not so tense, and school partners were commenting about how comfortable they felt coming into a building where they had once feared to tread. We were seeing more being achieved, no matter how small, and we started to have more good days than bad.

There was a willingness to make decisions and take control and there was a growing confidence amongst the whole school and the wider community.

A really important part of this was giving staff and pupils the opportunity to contribute to the success of the vision and the development of the plan. People were invited to take responsibility by taking on a lead or support role in order to move our targets from paper to reality, and I have no doubt that our success was largely down to the staff that we had. Among the staff there was a huge range of experience, skills and expertise that all contributed to the improvement. For example, my deputy and I both started in our new roles at about the same time, but we came with very different skill sets. My background was in mainstream schools while hers was in SEBN, and I think that we complemented each other well in order to lead the change process and build capacity amongst our staff and create more opportunities for our young people. Staff worked really hard to ensure that all factors that may hinder pupil learning were identified and addressed. Communication improved and there was a flexible approach to working with pupils and being more sensitive to individual needs. The staff really cared about the children and they were able to look beyond the challenging or inappropriate behaviour and work with the pupils to find out what was really going on, respond to their needs and offer additional and shared support where required. There were now strong links with our school family support worker, so that family and home issues could be raised and dealt with promptly. Protected time was given to discuss and share good practice within team meetings and as part of sharing classroom experience. Staff development tasks focused on understanding what influences positive mental health and emotional well-being, and how we can best promote it in ourselves and the children we work with.

Running alongside the improvement of the school environment and change to ethos was the development of the school curriculum and the delivery of learning and teaching. Staff identified areas of strength, which included having shared values, strong approaches in teaching about health and well-being, focusing on engaging active learning and thorough whole-school self-evaluation. These areas of strength were then used to help form a strategic three-year plan, which looked closely at the development of breadth, depth and coherence, and the development of collaborative learning. There was focus on specific curricular areas to allow staff and learners the opportunity to develop knowledge, skills, understanding and confidence across the curriculum. We made sure that the contexts for learning were strongly focused around the interests of the young people – so contexts changed regularly.

Gathering and using evidence about change

We started to record pupil profiles and tracked progress. A range of assessments were developed and used to ensure that formal academic attainment and broader achievements were being recorded, and that we had comparable data as one of our measures of success. Parents were reported to on a regular basis, through formal and informal meetings, work being sent home, and through phone calls. They reported that it was refreshing to be having discussions about their child's progress with learning as opposed to their behaviour.

Throughout our journey we evaluated and reflected on our progress in terms of changes in ethos, attainment and the outcomes for our young people. Although It was difficult to compare whole-school attainment data due to the pupil cohort changing throughout each session, we were able to carry out various assessments to ascertain the value-added attainment and achievement that individual learners made during their time with us. The analysis of all of our assessment information indicated that our learners consistently made good progress in literacy and numeracy. However, due to the complexities of the needs of our young people, only some managed this within their expected curriculum level. As a school we became more skilled at supporting new learners who entered with low prior attainment levels. This was due to the robust process we had in place to assess and identify all needs – social and emotional – and to highlight any significant gaps in learning.

We used the Boxall profile,[3] widely used in schools across the UK, to help gauge where our learners were developmentally. Although success could be erratic for individuals, because scores within the profile can be adversely affected by changes in circumstances, our general trend showed improvement. We knew that good health and well-being and readiness to learn are fundamental to success. Therefore, all of our learners had an Individualized Education Programme (IEP) with long- and short-term targets, which were formulated from the Boxall profile information. These data could be used as another measure of success. PE, outdoor education and opportunities to participate in residential activities gave the pupils an opportunity to meet more of the health and well-being targets within the curriculum. All pupils had a personal chart and all achievements, including school club awards, were collated and recorded in individual pupil profiles within our school tracking system. Other indicators of our success included a reduction in the number of exclusions for violent behaviour as well as a noticeable improvement in attendance levels, bringing our attendance rates into line with national averages: a major achievement given the difficulties facing many of our pupils.

We became successful in utilizing shared placements with mainstream schools and were able to support our learners in accessing mainstream and other specialist provisions through improved transition. Our systematic and timely approach to child planning and the reintegration process enabled a smooth move for a significant number of pupils to be reintegrated into mainstream provisions. Our systematic approaches to self-evaluation helped inform our improvement planning and being more outcome and impact focused which has also had a positive influence on our school.

Overall, our learners demonstrated increased success in attainment, displaying more confidence in their abilities and, with support, were taking more responsibility for their behaviour. In terms of social and emotional progress, more pupils were able to reflect accurately on the reasons they required extra support and they were ambitious and more confident that they would be able to achieve a positive destination back into their communities. Many aspired to return to a mainstream provision.

I took up this post in 2010, but the journey of change and improvement that I have described in this chapter took a period of five years. The process was not easy, and it is important to remember that change takes time if it is to be thoroughly embedded. There were difficulties on the way and our routes to success were ever changing, but there were also a lot of rewards and fulfilment. We persevered and we changed ethos and created a positive learning environment. We ensured that there were robust, consistent and structured processes in place to support our young people and ensured accountability. We created a shared vision, instilled trust and belief, encouraged teamwork, provided opportunities for leadership for all, created a reflective culture, built better relationships with multi-agencies and other school partners, and we were proactive in our approaches. We aimed to give our pupils a voice and actively encouraged them to take responsibility for their behaviour and their learning.

While still in my role of headteacher within this school, I was seconded for a very short time to an SEBN secondary school provision. For the most part, I went through a very similar change process, though on this occasion I was armed with skills and knowledge which could be transferred relatively quickly. Success was limited, but this was largely due to the very short timescale I was working within. I do feel that nonetheless we were able to lay good foundations.

Thoughts about the future

I have very recently taken up a new post as headteacher within a large mainstream primary school in an area where many families live with significant levels of socio-economic challenge. It has four specialist provision classes within the school. These classes are small – again the child-to-teacher ratio is 6:1 – and there is a high level of staffing, which reflects the needs of the pupils. If it is appropriate the young people from these classes will integrate into the mainstream classes for certain activities and subjects, and vice versa if there are pupils in the mainstream who would benefit from some activities within a smaller environment. Something that has struck me as being very positive about having mainstream and specialized support within the same school is that we are teaching our young people about tolerance and acceptance of others without actually having to 'teach', and we are offering regular opportunities for young people with additional needs to develop the skills required for a mainly mainstream world.

While the specialist classes in my new school are not specifically for children with SEBN, some of the young people being offered places within the classes do have very high levels of social, emotional and behavioural needs. Some of these children would have in the past been placed within a specialist provision. I think that this shift is partly due to an overall rise in young people with additional needs, and also a lack of specialist placements due to financial cuts in resources and funding. This means that many mainstream schools are going to be required to embark on a cultural change so that we can truly be inclusive and support the needs of all. I am confident that by embarking on a similar change journey, focusing on the elements of ethos, structure and robust processes, staff training, roles and responsibilities of all, accountability, shared leadership, staff training, and pupil voice, we can look at ways to successfully support more young people within the mainstream.

Historically, mainstream schools have had a primary focus on attainment, but if we, working in an alternative setting such as an SEBN school, were able to raise attainment by focusing on ethos and learning environment and breaking barriers to learning, should this not be our aim within all of our educational establishments? I feel quite privileged to have taught and led in schools in Scotland and within my current local authority, as I do think that there is an acute recognition that there are now more young people with specific needs and requiring an alternative education package, but that this can and will be supported within the mainstream. There is now a greater awareness that we need to address social and emotional needs in order to break barriers to learning and through a national policy emphasis on health and well-being. We are getting better at teaching resilience, focusing on good mental health, social development and creativity so that our young people are better prepared for the skills required for life in the twenty-first century.

Notes

[1] www.calmtraining.co.uk/

[2] www.gov.scot/Topics/People/Young-People/gettingitright.

[3] https://nurturegroups.org/introducing-nurture/boxall-profile

Chapter 12

Making the difference in a Scottish SEBN secondary school

Terri Dwyer

The following is based on my experience working in the SEBN sector in Scottish education over a 16-year period. SEBN is the shorthand term we commonly use in Scotland to refer to the needs of children and young people who have significant social, emotional and behavioural needs. This chapter is not an academic study and is not filled with statistics and data. It is my story of my journey in SEBN and is written from my perspective.

Background

I have been teaching for over 20 years and have spent 16 of those years working with young people who have social, emotional and behavioural needs (SEBN). I started my teaching career at the age of 30 and worked in a mainstream school as an English teacher for the first seven years. I loved teaching English and I loved working in a large mainstream school. When I moved to an SEBN school my friends and colleagues thought I was mad! To be fair I am a little mad. While working in mainstream education I loved working with the young people who were perceived as 'the bad kids'. I found I could inspire these young people and show them the value of education and learning. I then took a huge chance and went to work in a residential SEBN school for boys in the east end of Glasgow. I worked there for four years and those years were the most challenging of my career. To say I was terrified was the understatement of the century. Everything I had learnt had to be re-evaluated and changed. How do you inspire young men to learn who just do not seem to care about school? How could I make English relevant to pupils whose main interests had previously been stealing cars and motorbikes and enjoying risky activities? It took a long time and a few grey hairs but I got there, and loved the challenge and the rewards when the boys succeeded, which they did. I moved from there to another SEBN school in another area as the depute headteacher. I worked there for four years and during that time I was seconded to the Scottish Government and it was at this point that I became a trainer for restorative practice. Restorative practice was to have a major impact on the way I taught and in my professional life. I then became the headteacher of an SEBN secondary school in Edinburgh, where I have been for the last eight years and have acquired a few more grey hairs.

The past eight years have been a journey for myself, my staff and the young people we work with. When I arrived in the school there was no discipline, very little learning and total chaos. The staff all wanted to leave and the young people were having a great time running around the school causing mayhem. The first day I arrived they stole a JCB digging machine and drove up and down a nearby main road with it. A lot of the past eight years has been a difficult journey, but I am now very proud to be the headteacher of my school. I am very proud of the hard work of my staff and I am very proud of the young people we work with. I also feel that the young people we work with are very lucky to have staff who want to put so much effort, care and love into them.

Over the years I have come to see that there are different types of young people in SEBN. There are the young people who have problems due to their social needs and others whose problems are due to poverty and deprivation. There are young people who have emotional problems due to early trauma in their lives. This may be from attachment issues, drug-related problems or trauma within their family lives. Our greatest successes are when we have young people in our care from first year until fourth or fifth year. We know that it has often taken a long time for these problems to develop and that it then takes a long time for them to be fixed or at least to build the necessary skills to go into adult life and succeed. So…

What makes the difference?
Staff
I am often asked what makes the difference for young people who were failing in mainstream schools when we see them succeeding with us. The answer is often simple: staff are what make the difference. In mainstream education you often do not have the time to develop proper relationships with your pupils. Class sizes are huge and the workload is massive. In my school there are only six pupils in each class, working with a teacher and a pupil support assistant (PSA). The school has a maximum role of 60, and so staff have time to develop strong relationships with each other and with the pupils. It is vital that we have the right staff as SEBN is not for everyone. We are still expected to ensure that our young people have the same educational entitlements as young people at mainstream schools, so teaching staff need

to have expertise in all areas of Scottish education. PSAs in my school are the heart of the school. They are patient and kind to the pupils and really care about their well-being. It is important that PSAs are involved in all aspects of the school and feel valued. They are often the ones who teach the vital life skills our young people need to succeed in the outside world.

The Scottish curriculum – the Curriculum for Excellence – has enhanced the role of school support staff such as PSAs, so that they can be actively involved in pupil learning. My school could not function without the support staff. We also have a 'nurture base' which lies at the heart of the school. This base is run by three behaviour support assistants who help young people in crisis or who are having a difficult time. These staff are three of the most patient people I have ever met, and they are loved and respected by all of the pupils in the school.

The greatest quality I look for in staff in SEBN is a sense of humour. It is a very difficult and very challenging job and at times it can be very emotionally draining. A sense of humour and a strong team around you can help when things get too hard. One of the things I love most about my job is the laughter you hear around the school and in the staffroom. Our pupils are very challenging but can also be very funny. Learning to laugh at themselves is an amazing skill for young people with behaviour problems, and sometimes having a wee laugh at yourself helps too. Over time many of our pupils form real and lasting attachments to staff within the school. They come back regularly after they leave. For some these attachments have been the first in their young lives.

People are the key in an SEBN school. If budgets were cut I would give away all of my computers before I would lose a member of staff. These people make a huge difference to the lives of our young people, who fight us, argue with us, scream at us, throw things around, break everything in their paths and when we do not walk away or give in, as often others in their lives have, they eventually respect us and work for us. It is a difficult journey for staff and for the young people but a very worthwhile journey.

Relationships and restorative practice
I spoke earlier about how difficult my present school was when I arrived. My belief is that strong relationships are the key to success in an SEBN school. That can be difficult when you work with very challenging young people who can be violent and aggressive at times. There are many confrontations on a daily basis as young people take out their anger and frustrations on people who are enforcing learning, the curriculum and life skills in every lesson.

At this stage in their lives, learning, qualifications, literacy, numeracy and health and well-being are way down the list of their priorities. Many are more concerned with problems at home or in the community, what they are going home to at night, whether their family is going to be OK, if there will be food in the house tonight, if they will be safe tonight, who actually gives a damn…. We have to show them that we do! It is paramount that we build strong relationships and keep them strong in order for young people to trust us and allow us to teach them both formally and informally.

Our secret weapon, which allows us to do so, is restorative practice (RP). As I am a trainer for RP, the first thing I did on taking up my post was to train all of my staff in RP and to make it school policy. I then developed a personal and social education programme to teach the pupils what RP is and how we would be using it. It took some time to embed, but within a year we were starting to see real changes in the school. It took many more training events and dogged determination before I felt we could say we were a 'restorative school', and we are still on the journey. But that, mixed with a strong steer from the Scottish 'Better Behaviour, Better Learning' policy, had a huge impact across the school. Behaviour and relationships improved, young people started learning, most staff started to enjoy teaching and wanted to stay and be part of the school community. That is not to say we have gone from hell to heaven.

Realistically SEBN is a difficult setting and at times a stressful environment, but RP and strong setting of boundaries has had a huge impact on the learning and teaching and of the successes we see on a daily basis. Eight years later we are old hands at restorative mediations and conversations. This allows us to deal with issues, mend relationships and get young people back to class where they can learn and achieve. We are now at the point where we collate data and use it to highlight success, but even more importantly we are at the point where young people ask for a 'restorative' when they have fallen out with a member of staff or another young person. RP is about teaching young people that they can make mistakes and find a way forward. For our young people this is a valuable skill and one they can take with them in their future lives. Restorative practice is the foundation of my school and one of the things that for me really 'makes the difference'.

The emotional environment

Another important element in a successful SEBN school is that the ethos of the school should be that of a nurturing school. The focus should not be on behaviour, but on nurture and support and meeting the individual needs of the young person. In our nurture base young people will find someone to talk to and someone to help if things are difficult. There is always food and a friendly face and we actively work to try to find ways to change negative behaviour and focus on positive behaviour. Each pupil has two trusted people to help them when they are in real crisis and RP is at the heart of the nurture base. We also have an intensive support base within the school for young people who struggle with their behaviour in the main body of the school. This year we have also introduced an intensive nurture base for our most vulnerable pupils in the school and have seen a real difference for these young people.

The physical environment

For any SEBN school to be really successful it must have the right environment. One of the schools I worked in previously was like an old tin shed. The young people hated coming to school and were embarrassed to be associated with the school. The staff also hated coming to school and this must have transferred itself to the pupils. They had no sense of pride and often voted with their feet. My present school is only eight years old. The authority I work for has invested in all of its special schools and this has made a huge difference to the pupils who attend them. My school is relatively new and the facilities are really good. The young people who come to us are, on the whole, proud of their school. Staff put a lot of effort into displays to highlight pupils' work and educational and social achievements. There is a real sense of belonging, and I smile as I arrive each morning and look at the lovely building before me. I have to say, however, I do not always smile as I leave! When the young people are angry, which they are a lot, they often take their frustration out on the building and this can be heartbreaking for staff who put so much effort into making the school attractive. This is something we have worked on and things are getting better as young people learn to manage their behaviour, but it will always be an issue in SEBN. The secret is to get repairs done as soon as possible and fix displays, etc. The fact that the staff have a real pride in the school helps the young people come to value the school and want to be there. There is still, however, a stigma for young people for being at an SEBN school. Many of them like the school but are embarrassed about being at a 'behaviour' school. There is also the perception that an SEBN school is a bad place to be. Consequently, when we have visitors they are often surprised by how mannerly and pleasant our pupils can be.

The right to mainstream schooling for all

All young people should have the right to a mainstream education. Unfortunately many of our pupils have not coped with mainstream school. We try to get some of our young people back to mainstream school, but many find the size of mainstream schools and large classes very difficult to deal with. From the regular pupil evaluations we do, we know they enjoy a slightly more relaxed learning environment and the support they get at our school. They also like the relationships they develop with staff over a period of time. For some the thought of mainstream is terrifying for them. However, a small number of pupils do want an opportunity to experience mainstream education. In these cases, the school and the mainstream schools work hard to transition the young person into mainstream and so far this has been very successful. We continue to support them and the school for the first year and we make sure that they are ready to return and that we are not setting them up to fail.

Areas of strength in SEBN

My job is very important to me and the young people in my care deserve the best in terms of formal education and skills for life. Many of them have not had a good start in life. Many of them find life very difficult and face huge issues that children should never have to deal with. I believe SEBN education has to have a balance between delivering a formal education and ensuring young people have the support they need to do so. As well as the formal learning process, qualifications and planning to ensure positive destinations after leaving school, our job is also about teaching the skills they require to survive and prosper in life. It is about teaching them to manage their behaviour, take responsibility for their actions and resolve their problems. Many people see our pupils as 'bad kids'. I see young people who have really low self-esteem and very little confidence, some of whom have had a difficult start in life. This is hidden behind the behaviours they display. As we build their confidence and self-esteem the behaviour starts to change. Small classes, the right staff, a voice which is listened to and targeted support, all help to change these young people into amazing young men and women with lots of potential. This process takes time and lots of patience and the school and external agencies working together for the good of the young person.

Areas for development in SEBN

There are, however, areas that could further enhance the SEBN provision and support our young people. As I mentioned earlier, many of our pupils suffer from childhood traumas that have not been properly addressed. We are educationalists who specialize in behaviour, but we do not have the skills or expertise to offer psychiatric support or therapy. I feel for some of our young people this is vital. Many of our young people have had or are going through experiences that affect their lives profoundly. Every day I receive notes from staff that we call 'causes for concern', which include young people self-harming, wanting to commit suicide, hearing voices or suffering from depression. These young people need more access to these types of professional support if they are to deal with their problems and function in the adult world. Due to funding restraints these supports are very limited. While we do the best we can and have a measured impact on the young people, if the underlying problem is not resolved this will follow them throughout their lives. Without access to such supports we are failing them, and I believe this is an area of the highest priority in terms of development. Allowing issues to be resolved would have a massive impact on their lives, their happiness and of their future children as they enter adult life.

Another area for development is that of training staff in mainstream schools to deal with young people with SEBN. Although this has improved greatly in recent years there is still a long way to go. Many of our young people could have stayed in mainstream school if they had had the right supports and staff had the right training. When they are removed from the mainstream setting they feel betrayed, angry and lose faith in adults in education. Considering the difficulties they are experiencing in their day-to-day lives it is no wonder their behaviour is erratic when they come to us. I have been a teacher in a mainstream school and I fully understand how difficult a job it is, but it is our responsibility to teach all of the children and not just the good ones. If there are issues with a young person we need to understand these issues and put strategies in place to support them. Mainstream teachers need training and support to allow more young people to stay within the mainstream setting.

Vision for the future

My vision for the future of SEBN would be one in which there are very few SEBN schools, with small numbers of pupils who benefit from the small classes and targeted support. I would hope that more young people would be able to stay in mainstream school and benefit from the wider opportunities and greater number of subject areas. I do not want to see them stuck in a 'support base' in a mainstream school, but learning alongside their peers, given the help and support they require to do well in mainstream classes. I would like to see teacher education that includes training in behaviour management and perhaps a placement in an SEBN school. I would like that training to be updated on a regular basis as we can forget and become complacent after a period of time. I learnt more in my first year in SEBN that I did in the previous four years. I also became a much better practitioner.

Within SEBN schools I would like to see committed staff who have a real desire to help these young people. They deserve the best in terms of opportunities and teachers, as life has not been too kind to them so far. Personally I am a very lucky headteacher because I have a staff exactly like this, a lovely school and a sense of humour that is infectious to the staff and the pupils and has carried me through many difficult days. For young people who do not have a lot to laugh about it is an absolute joy to see them laughing, learning, playing and having fun with people who care for them. I love my job. It makes me laugh. It often makes me cry, but I learn more from the young people in my care than they will ever learn from me and that for me along with seeing them grow and succeed is magic!

Finally…. Why SEBN?

When I was in Primary 7 there was a girl called Margaret who lived around the corner from me. Margaret was perceived as a 'bad girl': the class clown, always getting into trouble. Every morning we had to write our News from the night before. I myself had a difficult home life so when things were not great at home I made up my News as I didn't want anyone to know. Margaret, however, told her News exactly as it was! She would tell of her father beating her mother over and over again. She would tell of the ambulance coming to take her mum to hospital and the police taking her dad away fighting, kicking and screaming. She would tell of her dad wrecking the house and throwing the TV out of the window. The class would laugh. They loved Margaret's News, which the teacher ensured we all heard every day! I did not laugh.

One day Margaret did not come to school and everyone was disappointed at not getting to laugh at her News. On the way home I found the street was filled with police. Women were crying everywhere and the focus seemed to be on Margaret's house. It transpired that Margaret's father had killed her mother and Margaret had witnessed this tragedy. Margaret never got over this trauma, and her behaviour deteriorated even more over the years but everyone just thought she was 'bad'. No one bothered to give her the support she needed to be 'good'. Margaret died as a young woman after a difficult and traumatic life. Margaret is the reason I went into SEBN. Margaret inspired me to try to offer that help and support to young people who have a difficult start in life. Margaret is what makes me go to work every day even when things get really difficult. Margaret is what makes the small difference to the lives of the young people who pass through my school.

Chapter 13

Waldorf education in Germany

Wulf Saggau

Introduction

In this chapter I will describe my experience of Waldorf schools, in many countries also known as Steiner schools. My reflections are based on my personal experience as a Waldorf teacher for drama and art over the last 24 years, as well as my experiences with Waldorf teacher training in Germany and South Korea.

Since its early beginnings in 1919, Waldorf education has been committed to comprehensive co-education for children across Grades 1 to 13, creative approaches to pedagogy such as thematic learning in blocks of three to four weeks, provision of a broad range of subjects including foreign language learning from a young age, and the sharing of regular feedback on learning with students through detailed textual reports rather than standardized grading. Our approach is founded on a belief that students in a class form a community and that this community works together in ways that can best build skills and strengths. Rather than 'survival of the fittest', we stress joint problem-solving, the benefits of working in groups with mixed abilities and the advantages this brings in terms of preparing students for adult life. For this reason, too, we reject ideas such as grade or year repetition.

The idea for the first Waldorf School was born in the destruction and upheaval of the First World War in Europe. Its founder, Rudolf Steiner, was driven by a belief that humankind needed to change its way of thinking. He was already well known for his theoretical work when a Stuttgart-based cigarette manufacturer Emil Molt asked him to found a school in the Waldorf-Astoria factory for the children of his employees. On 7 September 1919 lessons began. Steiner took on the training and guidance of the teaching staff and was, until his death in 1925, the guiding spirit of the school. For us, this represents one of the first, and certainly one of the most significant ways in which social justice and education were brought together in German education.

The school's founding ideas remain its guiding principles today, asserting that young people should receive a common education irrespective of academic ability, social and cultural background, ethnicity, religion, gender or sexual orientation. Systems of student selection, setting and tracking typical of German education even to this day, are replaced by an educational principle of learning by support. These approaches were based on Steiner's ideas about the different phases of child development and on anthroposophy, a philosophical system developed by Steiner to encourage people to turn their attention to phenomena that point to a spiritual reality beyond the material world. Within his system of anthroposophy, he developed a notion of social life based on the principles of 'freedom' of culture, 'equality' in the political community and 'fraternity' in economic life. These equate with the three well-known ideals of the French Revolution: freedom, equality and fraternity. Steiner developed this further, and suggested a threefold division of the person into spirit, soul and body, with three 'soul skills': thinking, feeling and the will (*'Denken, Fühlen und Wollen'*), each of which demands training within education. Steiner intended this to be practical rather than abstract, so that each lesson, each subject, should focus on achieving a balance of each of these qualities.

Waldorf curriculum

Steiner's ideas about anthroposophy also included a reappraisal of childhood development from birth, through the early years, into the school years and onwards, to age 21.

Steiner education aims to build its curriculum around the needs of the child. A key principle of its curriculum lies in matching teaching content and teaching methods with the child's own learning processes and stages of development in childhood and adolescence. From the outset, teaching is orientated towards encouraging the child's curiosity, making space for individual discovery. The teacher's role then is to create and nurture spaces for exploring and learning with the ultimate goal of inner human freedom. There are, of course, times when we need to learn for a particular purpose. This can be satisfying. But in the Waldorf school, we work on the understanding that exploring is more satisfying and, in the long term, more valuable.

There are no books in the Waldorf primary school. Instead, content is shared through fairy tales, stories and the encouragement of vivid imaginations. The children write and paint their own books so that they learn the value of creativity. Teachers ensure that nobody is forced to read or write in the first years. Later, in the intermediate school and high school this method modifies. Here we try to follow three steps. In physics, for example, we do not begin with teaching content knowledge but, rather, with a focus on perception of phenomena. We let the students research by asking, for example, 'What is beautiful?', 'What is unpleasant?', 'What surprised you?', 'What was most memorable about this?' We find that a phenomenological teaching approach, engaging each child's individual senses and emotions, helps deepen learning experiences. In the classroom, we might ask, for example, 'What does the tuning fork do while it is sounding?' With such a question, we aim to give students the opportunity to begin the learning that will lead them to find out for themselves that the tuning fork moves, that the prongs have to perform a counter-transverse oscillation, that the transition to the longitudinal oscillation of the pedicle may follow, perhaps with graphic representations of the various stages of the longitudinal oscillation of the stem or transverse vibration of the prongs. We combine this dialogic approach with practical lessons in each subject. In technology, for example, students can learn to build a clock or a small processing machine. Later, they may learn to program in html and then to create their own website. In chemistry, they may learn first to make soap, perfume and other things of interest to young people of 15/16 years. Later they move on to learn how to use a microscope. In Class 12 they may be introduced to analysing DNA (for example their own). The students themselves research all this in the lab.

Developing social skills: Internships in high school

For many high school students, pressing questions are often: 'How can I find my place in the world?', 'How can I actively shape the future?'

In keeping with the Steiner approach, older students are encouraged to take up internships to help them find answers to such important questions. Steiner schools encourage students to 'grow by doing'. We believe that this leads them to challenge themselves and to learn from being in the world. To encourage students in this way and help them on their way is the concern of the entire senior class, leading to the formation of good judgement and the skills to deal comfortably with different contexts and people. The structures of the internships are tailored to developmental needs of each age and level. They help the development of important skills of judgement in a sequence of stages.

In Class 9 (14–15 years old), for example, at an age when young people are often facing a range of challenges about themselves and their place in the world, the agriculture laboratory course (with a focus on practical competence) provides solid ground under their feet. This offers a two-week period of work experience on a biodynamic farm and allows the students to experience first hand how much work is involved in producing our everyday food. Students take turns doing a range of tasks such as feeding animals or in the operations around harvesting and marketing. Many return back home freshly motivated. At this stage, there is also an internship that will provide insights into the modern world of work, where our students can work in commercial, trade or industrial work areas for four weeks and thereby enhance their own personal experiences. This helps to develop ideas about careers and aspirations.

The following year we offer an internship in land surveying (with a focus on theoretical competence) for students in Class 10 (15–16 years old). This internship develops mathematical teaching of the principles of trigonometry and its practical use, when, for example, students measure and map terrain using highly sensitive instruments. The internship calls for accuracy, patience and teamwork to produce usable maps at the end.

A 'social internship' (focused on social and emotional competence) follows when students are in Class 11 (16–17 years old) and aims to further deepen empathy for their fellow human beings. Over a series of weeks, the young people take on tasks in a social care institution and support people with disabilities in their daily lives. Here the students get involved in what are often completely new situations that call for new levels of taking responsibility and awareness of others' needs. In this 'lab', students not only contribute within our society, but also learn how significant this is for other people's lives. They come to recognize themselves as part of a social whole and develop increasing awareness of social processes. The experience is documented, evaluated, and there is, as after each internship, a report evening with the parents. Thus, the experience is processed and can contribute to the emotional development of the students.

Finally, I want to say something about the other key subject specific to Waldorf education. Eurhythmy is an art form developed by Rudolf Steiner at the beginning of the twentieth century as an expression of the spiritual qualities inherent in speech and music. Whilst gymnastics works with the basic physical forces of weight and gravity, eurhythmy seeks to bring the inner structure and laws of spoken language and music to artistic expression through bodily movement. The formative and harmonizing qualities of eurhythmy play a significant role in Waldorf education as well as being a valuable therapy. All children in Waldorf schools are taught eurhythmy. Just as the other arts do, eurhythmy finds different ways of expressing itself. This can be very simple or highly complicated and consist of individual components that are interwoven. Eurythmic movements are based on two elements. One of these is speech, from the sounds of vowels and consonants: hence the phrase often associated with Waldorf education: 'They can dance their names'. The other is music in all its elements, from simple tones and intervals up to the laws of harmony and musical form. In primary school, students first learn to perform simple forms, vowels, consonants, rhythms and melodies from the stories told within the classes. Then later, they do the same with grammatical forms, rhymes, gestures, forms and gestures from ancient cultures, scales and intervals. In high school, they go on to work with dramatic poems, the difference between major and minor intervals, geometric forms, humoristic poems, rhymes, pieces of music. Poetry from romanticism and modernism are elaborated and often performed. Through doing this together, we aim to heighten the skills and levels of self-awareness within the group.

Class and high school graduation

At the end of the 12th year students work together on the development of a modern theatre play, the presentation of their annual individual work, the production of their individual artistic statements and a jointly prepared art journey. By the end of the following year many of the students then have spent 13 years together in one classroom, often with the same teacher for the first eight years. Many ex-students describe this time of life as the happiest ever. Most Waldorf teachers experienced Waldorf school as students themselves. Some decide to enrol their children in the school once they have their own families, while others become very active parent supporters in the school.

Waldorf teacher training

Steiner said:

> *Jede Erziehung ist Selbsterziehung und wir sind eigentlich als Lehrer und Erzieher nur die Umgebung des sich selbst erziehenden Kindes. Wir müssen die günstigste Umgebung abgeben, damit an uns das Kind sich so erzieht, wie es sich durch sein inneres Schicksal erziehen muss.*

> Any education is self-education, and we as teachers and educators are simply providing the environment for the 'self-parenting' child. We should provide the most favorable environment for the child so it educates itself with us, as it should be educated through its inner destiny. (Steiner, 1996: 131)

Prospective Waldorf teachers must have graduated from high school, the technical university or have an equivalent degree. Trained teachers who are interested in Waldorf education and graduates of colleges of education and teacher training courses at university are also welcome as newcomers who have had no contact with Waldorf education before, but who are professionally, personally and educationally suited to being a Waldorf teacher. Each school is self-managed and has a staff council, which posts vacancies, conducts job interviews and makes personnel decisions. The staff council is elected by the staff and responsible for their work. Teacher education based on the Waldorf approach is concerned with the theoretical and practical foundations of general education and with learning about Waldorf's philosophical, anthropological, methodological and historical backgrounds. Wide educational horizons offer many different subjects for teaching in Waldorf schools: foreign languages and sciences, visual arts, drama and music, sports, eurhythmy, gardening, needlework and crafts are welcome. To provide students with a breadth of knowledge, Waldorf schools have a large variety in their choice of teachers. The guiding principle is to encourage the notion of the child as the inspiration for the teacher.

Administration and leadership in Waldorf schools

Selbstverwaltung or self-management is an important feature of Waldorf schools, substituting the hierarchical organizational structures more typical of public schools in Germany. In practice, this means the kindergarten and the main school work closely together and every Waldorf school relies on strong teamwork between kindergarten, parents and teacher. There is no school principal. Each school has a manager responsible for finance, but this is kept strictly separate from the decisions made by us as teachers about the school and our educational tasks. Educational management is organized through a weekly staff meeting or conference, in which all teachers participate. The meeting works on the principles of freedom of culture, equality in the political community and fraternity in economic life, which, as I described earlier, inform all aspects of the Waldorf school life. This teamwork is not always easy and there are times when I have longed for someone to lead us in decision-making. However, the way we work and organize this keeps me alive and always aware of my responsibilities to my school. It is also supported by the key role of parents in the school. They also have a weekly meeting and are encouraged to participate in the school at all levels, to take responsibility as much as possible and to contribute according to their social and professional abilities. This can include, for example, help with simple tasks such as gardening, running the school library and housekeeping but may also draw on their skills to help in dealing with conflict, organizing festivals and celebrations, as well as financial support and consultations about changes and developments around the school building and environment.

Challenges for Waldorf schools today

Waldorf schools are highly successful. The PISA 2006 survey in Austria, in which results for all Waldorf schools were included and analysed separately, investigated the scientific knowledge of students. The Waldorf students had very good results in terms of their interest in the natural sciences, not only far above the state average, but also significantly higher than the OECD average. In Germany, Waldorf schools' student achievement levels compare favourably with state-supported schools and, for example, the Frankfurt Waldorf School is always among the three best schools in the city.

However, the Waldorf schools also face some significant challenges today, and these range from finance, to teacher recruitment, to issues about student qualifications and accreditation. It requires constant work to keep the Waldorf schools on a sound financial footing. The Waldorf schools in Germany receive government subsidies to cover some operating costs, receiving about 60 per cent of the costs per pupil received by state schools. Parental contributions are part of the commitment expected to the school and are always needed to make up the shortfall. On average, this is currently around €300 per child per month. Theoretically our school is open to all children and parents, but this parental contribution is not possible for all families. To address this it is possible to seek a reduction in the expected financial contribution. Some parents choose to pay more than the expected contribution and some others make substantial contributions to resources in other ways.

Being a Waldorf teacher is an idealistic occupation. Teachers' pay is low compared to that offered in state schools. Many Waldorf teachers accept this because they value the emphasis on inner freedom and autonomy, but perhaps more would be able to join us if pay levels were higher.

In respect of student qualifications, a challenge arises because of the very different approach we take to assessment of learning. Waldorf schools have no exams until Class 10, when the students are about 16 years old. School reports generally consist of a detailed account of the progress of each student in all subjects. However, in Germany, the last three years of Waldorf education are a compromise between the expectations of the German Department of Education on one side and the wishes of Waldorf teachers, students and parents on the other. We want students to be qualified to participate in all kinds of vocational training and to be able to enter any university. The curriculum for senior students is therefore designed to meet the requirements for different kinds of school graduation in accordance with the national Education Act. For this to happen we have introduced the use of grading and marks from Grade 11 onwards. Parallel to these assessments, students continue to receive detailed reports and feedback on their individual learning, as we still believe that the diversity of learning styles and the individuality of the pupil are better understood in dialogue than in numbers and rankings.

For those of us working in a Waldorf system, school is primarily about working with people. We take the view that everyone is different and that we all learn at our own speed and in our own way. A grading system does not meet this requirement. I feel that the introduction of the assessments makes for a sad contradiction with the methods used in the teaching of younger students, where assessments are avoided as a matter of principle. The students themselves admit that under the pressure of grades, they begin to change. Greed, envy and competition emerge. And even if the students and teacher don't want or like it, it is hard to avoid. However, we are hopeful that a new kind of recognition of achievement will soon resolve this contradiction: the Steiner School Certificate (SSC), based on recognizing acquired skills and competencies. Working towards gaining this certificate will allow pupils to learn to assess themselves and help ensure that teachers are learners who show the way. The first graduations with the SSC will be in 2019. We are keen to see if this can improve the curriculum for senior students and re-align it more closely with Steiner's own principles.

Finally, I would want to recognize that Waldorf education has been criticized for being self-referential, seeing itself as a kind of 'guardian of the truth' and not moving with the times. The relationship between Waldorf education and academic educational science has often been characterized by mutual distrust, but I am convinced that initiating dialogue and exchange rather than cultivating differences could bring more mutual understanding and appreciation.

There are many such questions which now need to be addressed honestly if we are to continue to flourish. The pedagogy itself is almost 100 years old and needs to continue to develop and remain up-to-date. This requires new thinking from teachers, and it is not clear that there are enough qualified new teachers for the future. Germany alone needs to ensure stable staffing for its 230 schools. Another dilemma now occupying our minds is the potential challenge of ensuring that consistency with Steiner principles stays strong as global expansion continues, for example in China. There is also the vexed question of how best to ensure that the Waldorf curriculum content can meet ever-changing societal challenges in ways that allow children to do well in the world. An open mind, respect and willingness to communicate will always be needed to meet these challenges.

Conclusion

There are around 1,080 Waldorf Schools worldwide, across 64 countries, with 712 in Europe and around 120 in USA. At the time that Waldorf education first emerged, it was part of a wave of education reform in Europe that emphasized new, more human-scale education methods. In times of globalized turmoil and anxiety and amid recent political change, often led by authoritarian populists, we believe that Waldorf schools can provide a clear, alternative idea of education and emphasize the value of fundamental principles of creativity, personal development, social connectedness and a view of the self as always a learner. We need students to leave school confident and ready to play a role in society and make a healthy contribution to the evolving future. Waldorf education wants to be one part of this answer, and to help people learn to 'dance their name'.

Reference

Steiner, R. (1996) *The Child's Changing Consciousness as the Basis of Pedagogical Practice: Eight lectures*. Hudson, NY: Anthroposophic Press.

Chapter 14

Holistic Community College in Australia

Richard Waters

Introduction

Alternative education and alternative schooling in its many forms represent responses to elements of the mainstream education systems of schooling that, in various ways, fail to meet the needs of *all students*, particularly those who are marginalized due to their difference, in terms of socio-economic status, ethnicity, or learning needs, but also which often fail to meet *all the needs* of students, particularly looking beyond specifically academic needs, especially literacy and numeracy. This is not to label all mainstream schools, or alternative schools, the same, or to demonize mainstream schooling, but to simply observe the origins of the wide variety of alternative schools and alternative education provision as critical and active responses to problematic core elements in the mainstream system.

In the more recent forms of mainstream education there has been an emphasis on what have been described as neoliberal policy settings (Harvey, 2005), which have come from a more instrumentalist view of education as being to largely serve the economic needs of society. This view has also emphasized the importance of competition in education as supporting a nation-state's comparative advantage in the international economic environment (Sahlberg, 2006). This is not all that mainstream schools are about:

> while 'mainstream' may look very different in different places, it is characterized by a set of increasingly homogenous tendencies that are becoming globalized – neoliberal governance and financing, responsibilisation, flexibility, standardized testing, and so on. (Kraftl, 2013: 5)

Alternative education and schooling systems tend to have a more holistic view of education (Nagata, 2006), which sees students as multi-dimensional and has a broader view of health and physical education, an emphasis on social-emotional development and, in some cases, a broadly defined spiritual dimension (Woods and Woods, 2009). This spiritual dimension is a non-religious interpretation, part of the 'inner life' of the student: 'intimately bound up with matters of meaning, purpose and connection, with creative expression and moments of joy and transcendence' (Kessler, 2000: xvii). Alternative schooling practices have also often sought to respect, recognize and include parents more in schooling. Different alternative schools have emphasized some or all of these elements and there is a huge variety among and between them (te Riele, 2012), but there are also elements in common and this emerged in my study of alternative schooling in rural areas of Queensland, Australia.

This chapter examines the case of an alternative school in rural Queensland that I have anonymized as Holistic Community College (HCC). Names of individuals have also been replaced with pseudonyms. HCC is an example of alternative schooling following practices that challenge the competitive logics of the mainstream education system both as it is implemented in the mass Western education of the twenty-first century, and also as it has come to be constructed as a reflection of neoliberal policy settings. This is true both of HCC's ethos and aims, but more particularly through its alternative teaching and learning practices. The data from HCC indicated that its history has not been without the tensions and challenges that are a common experience of schools attempting to create an alternative to a dominant mainstream. However, despite compromises, it appeared to have maintained core practices that represent a viable and coherent alternative to the logics and practice of contemporary mainstream schooling.

Holistic education: Beyond a view of education for human capital formation

The core elements of the alternative ethos and practice of HCC represented a challenge to the instrumentalist view of education influenced by neoliberal policy perspectives as well as the traditional emphases of mass schooling. This starts from a more holistic view of the purposes of education and was supported by core practices that included a smaller scale school (Tasker, 2010), smaller class sizes (Schanzenbach, 2014; Zyngier, 2014), emphasis on a more personalized relationship between teacher and students (Mills and McGregor, 2014), greater focus on the social-emotional dimension of education (Noddings, 2002) and a concern for a non-coercive and non-violent approach to schooling (Harber and Sakade, 2009).

The neoliberal influence on education policy and practice privileges an economic perspective on the purposes of education (Ball, 2008; Rizvi and Lingard, 2010) as a key source of improvement in productivity, to make the nation more economically competitive internationally. Harvey suggests that neoliberalism has become the dominant discourse of the contemporary world and that the market-orientation is pervasive in its influence on many segments of society, beyond the economy: 'It holds that the social good will be maximized by maximizing the reach and frequency of market transactions, and seeks to bring all human action [including education] into the domain of the market' (2005: 3). Central to this world view is that the optimal way of advancing the objective of greater productivity is through competition forming the basis for economic and social systems, including education. This chapter suggests that what could be called the 'productivity paradigm' may be challenged through positing that non-competition and co-operation instead can be the basis of a more holistic view of schooling, as practised in this case by Holistic Community College.

The data on HCC utilized in this chapter was gathered as part of my PhD studies, which were attached to a larger research project, Pursuing Equity Through Rich Accountabilities (PETRA), which seeks to conceptualize 'richer' forms of accountability contrasted with the one-dimensional, top-down accountability regime that has been a feature of neoliberal policy settings in education (Rizvi and Lingard, 2010). Research methods utilized in the study included document analysis, quasi-ethnographic observation and semi-structured interviews with leaders, teachers, students, parents and other community members (62 participants) to gain insight into their lived experience of the nature and effects of alternative education practices. Ethical procedures were approved by both The University of Queensland and the Queensland Department of Education and Training. The author's PhD studies were attached to the ARC Linkage project Pursuing Equity Through Rich Accountabilities (PETRA) involving a partnership between The University of Queensland, Victoria University, and the Queensland Department of Education, Training and Employment. These 'rich' accountabilities could involve a broader-based, multi-dimensional and multi-directional view of accountability that would expect schools to be accountable, not only to education authorities, but also to their communities (and vice versa) and that schools should also be able to hold educational authorities to account in providing the resources schools need to meet the expectations of the system.

HCC is a low-fee, non-state independent school based on the concept of holistic education, which involves an equal emphasis on academic, health and physical, and character (social-emotional, spiritual) education. The school catered for 140 students from pre-Year 1 to Year 12, from a wide range of socio-economic status (SES) backgrounds, in a low SES rural community. The current HCC principal, Samuel, expressed the school's aims this way:

> We're trying to do more than just create an environment where the children can learn academically. We're trying to create an environment where they can learn to be good citizens as well.... You're trying to help them know and believe in themselves and have an attitude of caring for others rather than just looking out for themselves.

Figure 14.1: School buildings at Holistic Community College

This holistic view of the aims of education is derived from the educational philosophy of the founder of HCC, Dayadev, who came to Australia from Mumbai in India in the 1960s. His influences included his traditional Indian upbringing, his training in classical yoga, the schools established by Tagore and Aurobindo in India and his exposure to Gandhi's non-violent campaign for independence from British colonial rule. Dayadev's philosophy reflected his appreciation of the need to accommodate the modern world along with those aspects of traditional Indian culture that could balance the more instrumentalist-oriented nature of modern Western education.

In this holistic view of education, students were seen as whole people whose lives can and do involve much more than contribute to the 'productivity paradigm' of economic competitiveness. For example:

> Our education system today is geared to accommodate ideas and values designed to serve the commercial, industrial and technical needs of the community – in fact the mundane and materialistic needs of man[kind]. The real need of society – emotional integrity and spiritual understanding – is overlooked. (Dayadev, 1983: 12–13)

Further, in arguing for a more holistic education, Dayadev expressed the view that education should foster 'individual growth, moral living and spiritual progress' (1983: 22) rather than just providing 'spare parts for industry and commerce' (12).

The purpose of education at HCC was to engage students in learning, to make learning fun, to enable students to learn self-motivation and to prepare them for life-long learning. Specifically, HCC aimed to nurture the spirit of each person as a contributing member of the community, with a capacity for quietness and reflection and the opportunity for the creative expression of their talents in a non-competitive environment, which nevertheless produced excellence and an orientation to service. In Raywid's terms, this school could also be seen as a Type 2 alternative school. These 'are often highly innovative schools with novel curricular and instructional approaches and atypical positive school climates' (1999: 49).

The emphasis in holistic education on the importance of nurturing each individual student implies a sense of social justice, in that no young person is considered dispensable and excluded and not worthy of education. However, this is not about 'individualism' with a focus on self-interest, but about relationship to others:

> It [holistic education] seeks to develop the full potential of the person in a humanistic fashion that recognizes and honors each individual's unique talents and capacities. Holistic education sees

active positive engagement in relationships with the world and others as one of the most powerful means of authentic education. (Clarken, 2009: 3)

These broader purposes of education were reflected in the alternative practices put into place at HCC and are in common with those at many alternative schools. These practices include smaller school and class sizes compared with mass schooling, a focus on social-emotional elements of student development, a concern to cultivate more personalized relationships between teachers and students and practices of non-coercion and non-violence.

Challenging the logics of competition

The holistic approach to education and schooling modelled at HCC challenged the competitive, meritocratic, human capital logics of the currently constructed mainstream. The central place of competition in education is so pervasive it is hard to conceive of an education system without it. As Kohn suggests: 'most of us fail to consider the alternatives to competition [and this] is a testament to the effectiveness of our socialisation. We have been trained not only to compete, but also to believe in competition' (1992: 7). Nevertheless, HCC challenged the logics of competition through its school ethos and practices. It emphasized that a non-competitive approach to education was not about winning and losing as about excellence.

At HCC, the ethos, explained on its website, identified 'Five Key Features of Holistic Education', articulated in terms of how they could be identified in the school and especially the practices that would be involved in their application. These features foregrounded notions of care and compassion, valuing the individual, non-competition and co-operation, holistic development and including and engaging parents.

One of these key features, 'modelling a non-competitive ethos', is an important focus in the current discussion. This feature was articulated to pupils in the student diary as illustrated in Figure 14.2.

Competition can be self-defeating

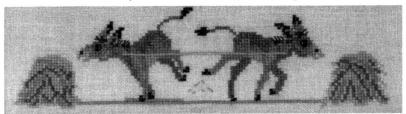

Co-operation leads to win-win

Figure 14.2: Holistic Community College student diary extract on non-competitive ethos

> ### HCC's NON-COMPETITIVE ETHOS
> Synergy refers to the principle that 'the whole is greater than the sum of the parts'. In other words, more can be achieved by a group working together than could have been achieved by each person working away on their own. If each person takes a segment of work, it can reduce the amount of work needing to be done, provided of course that they fulfil their part of the task in the appropriate time.

This explanation and these illustrations, from the HCC student diary, are an example of the discursive practices deployed by the school in promoting its ethos within its school community – of the school 'speaking' to itself (and its community) about what it values – in this case co-operation. Other discursive practices included providing explanations in the school's annual report and through the Parents' Program (see below).

The school implemented its ethos through the enactment, and omission, of various practices. For example, schooling without competition at HCC involved doing away with awards common to most mainstream schools. There were no prizes, no honour boards, no sports ribbons, dux of the school, no speech night, no stars or stamps, no awards of any kind. For one Year 6 student, Jaden, coming from a culture of competitive awards at a mainstream school, this was a great relief compared to his prior experience:

> When there's prizes, it makes you rush your work and then you don't think, and then you get stuff wrong. And then if you get stuff wrong in state schools, they won't give you a prize. And then that just builds up anger in your body, and then you just get really angry and then you bring it home and then you get told off by your Mum, and it's a whole big kerfuffle!

In mainstream education, as the quote above suggests, competition is often an important element in extrinsic forms of motivation in the provision of awards and incentives. Part of the way HCC framed non-competition was to encourage intrinsic forms of motivation that did not use comparison with other students or motivation from teachers in the form of incentives or fear of failure. Instead, students were taught to draw on their personal interest in a subject, to find enjoyment in the learning activity, to follow their curiosity, to enjoy the challenge of doing something to the best of their ability, and to strive for personal excellence, often modelled by older students. This was achieved through the teacher identifying students' interests and by adjusting the curriculum, through providing choices and opportunities that catered to those interests. This approach was supplemented by a weekly special interest programme, where students selected elective activities offered by teachers. Of course, small class sizes facilitated this flexibility.

HCC school documents, such as the website, highlighted the idea of recognizing the 'innateness' of each student, which worked against the standardization inherent in the tendency to narrow the curriculum through over-emphasis on testing and a common core curriculum, both of which have been a consequence of neoliberal policy settings in education. Innateness is similar to what others might refer to as individual talent, or what Robinson and Aronica (2009) call 'The Element' in their book, which carries the subtitle, 'How following your passion changes everything'. This is not about self-indulgence or self-interest but about self-expression within the group.

In Australia, the standardization of the curriculum is represented by the implementation of the Australian Curriculum in Years 1–10, the National Assessment Program in Literacy and Numeracy (NAPLAN) in Years 3, 5, 7 and 9 and the reporting of school performance in these tests on the government's My School website (AKARA, 2016). Accommodating these government requirements while maintaining its emphasis on non-competition and innateness, was one of the tensions faced by HCC in the current education policy environment.

At HCC, emphasis on co-operation and service took the focus off the self-interest of the individual and placed it instead on consideration of the group. For example, the students contributed to the community of the school through daily cleaning of classrooms and courtyards, laying the tables for school meals and clearing up afterwards. School meals were also supplemented from a school vegetable garden and eggs from chickens looked after by students. These practices all helped cultivate forms of cultural capital amongst these students that were based on co-operative principles, rather than competition. Jackie, a senior teacher at HCC, expressed the idea this way:

> [In competition] you're working against each other and it encourages the ego a lot. Whereas, I think … you can minimize that focus and encourage students – obviously, in this case – but all people to get a larger sense of who they are as part of a group or part of humanity or part of the class, and wishing the best for other people or for a group to progress, as opposed to just yourself, at the expense of someone else.

Tensions inevitably arose with some parents, who had grown up in and were working in a highly competitive society and fixated on a need to be competitive to survive and achieve. They worried about how their children, educated in a non-competitive atmosphere, would survive and thrive in the wider world of a capitalist society where competition was normalized. Over time, however, as they saw how their children achieved success and built confidence without competition, and heard about the experiences of graduates who thrived in the 'real' world, parents overcame their reservations. Working and achieving success and excellence was supported by the school, but in an environment of *working with* rather than *working against* others. Parents were able to see this applied to everyone at the school so that there was a social equity dimension to non-competition.

These more co-operative logics express quite a different 'structure of feeling' (Williams, 1977) in relation to how learning was experienced by these HCC students. Williams refers to 'specifically affective elements of consciousness and relationships' (132). This is not just about different structures and practices but about relationships and emotional responses where students are not in a constantly competitive and comparative mode of teaching and learning. In the environment of HCC, there was a contribution of fellow feeling and working together. As expressed by Fielding (2015), '[t]he sociality of human endeavour [in a non-competitive environment] has a less instrumental feel to it. Differences are companionable and productive rather than antagonistic and destructive of other's intentions and aspirations' (21). In the co-operative model of HCC, the basis of interaction took on a different character and spirit to one where the basis is competition. This approach was further reinforced by specific schooling practices such as the Quietness Program for students and the Parents' Program, which were a particular focus of my study.

Alternative practices challenge the instrumentalist view of education

HCC's Quietness Program and the Parents' Program demonstrated alternative schooling approaches that challenged the dominant logic of an instrumentalist education. The Quietness Program illustrated a view of education that went beyond preparing students to fit into a competitive society as appropriately prepared human capital. The Parents' Program illustrated HCC's perception of parents as worthy of respect, recognition and inclusion in education schooling as partners, colleagues and sources of knowledge about child development, rather than in the neoliberal construction of informed clients, consumers and sources of extra resources to limit the need for government input. These programmes also promoted the practice of reflection as a means for personal growth and development, not irrelevant to academic learning, but potentially contributing to much more than this.

The Quietness Program

The Quietness Program at HCC, which has similarities with the Buddhist-based mindfulness system, started with primary children through twice weekly 'quiet time', when the primary children listened to a story told by a teacher followed by quiet music or ambient sounds in the environment. The programme was further developed in the subsequent primary and secondary years (Year 5 to Year 12) through the daily listening and breathing exercises. This practice was described in school documents: 'Each day, students spend five to ten minutes in practices, derived from yoga, to help still their mind through listening to ambient sounds and watching their inward and outward breathing'. These programmes were complemented by non-compulsory yoga classes in secondary school and quiet reflection as an integral part of the Outdoor Education Program.

Figure 14.3: Year 10 students doing the breathing and listening exercises

The effectiveness of the quietness practices depended on the application of students to the practice. As one teacher explained, 'You don't know what's going on behind their eyes!' For example, some students in the early developmental stages of adolescence found it harder to focus or sit quietly, as did students coming from other educational environments where quietness or reflection was not emphasized. The extent of a longer-term benefit, in terms of focus and concentration for students, also varied between groups, as a consequence of variations in teacher awareness and understanding of and commitment to the practices. Creativity, consistency and understanding by teachers of the practice was important. Teachers varied the practices, including more active listening to music and taking students into an outdoor environment where they had the space to settle more easily. Whole school practice at same time also helped create a quiet environment and support the expectation that everyone would be involved for a short time each day. The quietness practice resulted in more settled classrooms and playground activity.

According to students, teachers and parents, the effects of the quietness practices were evident in the students' application to their academic studies. For example, Year 5 students, Kyle and James made the link between the quietness practice and their ability to concentrate and complete their academic work: 'It empties our minds, so it's easy to start thinking.... It helps us relax and clear our minds and helps us get through the work much quicker.'

The quietness practices at HCC also contributed to the social-emotional development of students through a greater capacity for stress management, conflict resolution, and detachment in times of provocation and resilience. These capacities were demonstrated in the data by students and teachers commenting, for example, that students developed a sense of emotional equanimity and more balanced social-emotional development. A Year 12 student, Inez, articulated it as, 'I think it lowers stress levels and I think that affects especially the relationship – like my relationship with all the other kids'. Quietness, in this respect, was associated with self-acceptance and as a reference independent of the peer group's influence but also influencing relationships with others. That this was a valued form of cultural capital was also evident in how the programme was seen as an effective vehicle for calming students in that, '[a]ll you can say is that we get agitated children come to the school and in a very short space of time they start to settle and their parents let us know that' (Samuel, principal, HCC).

These quietness practices at HCC focused on settling the mind to allow it to function more freely and were therefore framed as a contrast to competitive striving for individual achievement. Understood in this way, the quietness practices at HCC had the potential, through the experience of stillness and reflection, to influence the student's mind towards becoming less emotional and mentally more peaceful. There is something fundamental here in shifting the consciousness of young people even further in terms of a spiritual dimension, as defined earlier, which contributes to challenging the dominant logics of the mainstream which privileges competition and a primarily economic perspective.

Students commented that the quietness practice was quite a different experience from that in their mainstream school experience. Further to this, students were aware that the inclusion of such practices indicated a different priority in terms of the valuing of the purposes of education (Noddings, 2005: 10). One Year 12 student, Cooper, reflected:

> I didn't experience anything like it in my other school. I think a lot of schools, like highly value the grades and that sort of thing as the highest priority, as probably a lot of people would expect in a learning environment. I think this school has … a different approach to the kid actually, and their emotional and mental development comes first over the actual grades of the kid.

The Parents' Program

Negative effects can arise from the intrusion of economic imperatives into the education field, as is evident in English and Australian education policy, which promotes a competitive market in schooling. Trust can be severely eroded as part of this process. When 'parents saw themselves as "customers" rather than partners in their children's education, the level of trust and the child's education was severely disrupted' (Collins, 2012: 3). Ball (2010) in the UK and Demerath (2009) in the USA, in writing about parents as consumers in an education market, demonstrated the lengths to which parents were willing to go to obtain a competitive advantage for their children.

Even though HCC is an independent, low fee-paying school, supplemented by government grants, the school worked at trying to avoid the fee-for-service relationship with parents that tends to be promoted by the 'education as market' policy. While parents are paying fees, there could well be consumer-like thinking, which potentially undermines the 'relational trust' (Bryk and Schneider, 2002) between the school and the family. In the case of HCC, the school actively encouraged more productive and substantive relationships between parents and school through initiatives like its Parents' Program, rather than more economistic/exchange value relations:

> When you drop the children off, you come in with them. You bring them to the classroom and then on Friday nights or Sunday morning, you have time for the Parent Program. You come into the school and you talk with us and with other parents about how things are going with you as a parent, the issues and challenges that you might be facing and the things that you've learnt and can share with other parents. With the school, it changes their relationship from one of a contractor to one of a participant. (Samuel, principal, HCC)

This comment indicated the school was seeking a relationship with parents beyond economic relations: a social and educational partnership. Of course, such economic relations are a feature of non-state schools, where parents pay tuition fees, but HCC tried to ensure that the economic field served the education field, rather than dominating it through economic relations. This reframing involved a collaborative approach rather than being based on more competitive or transactional logics.

The HCC Parents' Program, explained and emphasized at enrolment interviews as an essential part of the important school–teacher–parent relationship, was based around weekly discussion groups led by group leaders selected from the parent body, bi-monthly seminars and parent forums. Attendance at the Parents' Program was a condition of enrolment at HCC. This is an example of reciprocal parent–school accountability, through participation, to balance the expectations parents may have of schools. It could be likened to the requirement of compulsory voting in Australia, where participation is a legislated expectation of citizenship.

Schools have tended to perceive parents as passive participants in the schooling process and as subordinate to the school rather than as equal and knowledgeable partners in education. It has been challenging, therefore, for schools (and families) to change the way they relate, as part of the broader community, despite recent government policy encouraging schools to include parents more in schooling.

The data from HCC, which involved semi-structured interviews with 13 parents with children of primary and secondary age out of around 100 parents, suggested that parents wanted to be involved in schooling and that more personalized relationships and connections were possible with schools. One parent group leader described the impact of hearing about how other people went about their parenting and the connection between that and what kind of people their children became:

> I'd grown up in a fairly traditional, probably autocratic, behaviour-managed, punishment/reinforcement kind of home and I saw people doing it quite differently. I would have thought it was probably a little relaxed, but what I also observed was their children, when they were older, were really great kids. That really made me think differently about the way I parented.... That spoke very loudly to me. (Leanne, parent group leader, HCC)

The Parents' Program at HCC facilitated the growth of a sense of togetherness, and ongoing learning. This is part of what Lynch (2007) refers to as 'love labour'. This was evident in the way an Indigenous parent at HCC shared the sense of developing community as being very important and valuable to her experience of the school:

> It helps because it's a deep ... I think it's philosophical. I think it steps into a community kind of group, opening yourself to others and I think it's that deeper understanding, that awareness of others' journeys in the community and peoples' struggles.

> Voicing those things and it's very respected and it creates that
> respect for each other. (Serena, parent, HCC)

At HCC, this sense of a family and community was actively nurtured.
Relationships with other parents and teachers developed over many years
through the Parents' Program; friendships formed and trust developed, so
that discussions often had a very personal character. A valuing of social
capital forged through this programme was evident in the positive way
parents shared their experiences with other parents, so there was a sense of
mutual benefit and collaboration:

> It definitely ... puts you into the thing of like, even like a big family
> sort of thing. A big community, supportive, that you know.... But
> it's definitely that feeling of being part of something, and even
> just knowing that ... if I do have something I would like to share
> or would like to some support, I guess it would be always there.
> (Marie, parent, HCC)

There were challenges at times in maintaining parents' attendance and
interest in the Parents' Program, especially where one parent might be
more committed and interested. For others, it was hard to overcome a
fee-for-service mentality and the notion that education was the school's
responsibility. Also, other parents found the idea of group discussion about
parenting challenging, including some Indigenous parents who sometimes
felt uncomfortable in a discussion group of largely non-Indigenous parents.

To reinforce the reciprocal nature of the home–school relationship,
parents were asked to write a confidential report at end of the year, both on
the perceived progress of their children at school and also to give feedback
on the Parents' Program. It took time and patience for parents to understand
and trust each other, to think of the school as a community, to work on
things together.

The Parents' Program at HCC played a role in building social
connection between families and this led to friendships and mutual support
in times of need. Parent groups included meeting for coffee or dinner at
someone's home. Families organized group camping trips or excursions to
films, plays or festivals. These practices were particularly beneficial where
parents had previously felt left out or where children had experienced
difficulties with others. A sense of connection was evident that was
family-like:

> I just love the support it gives. The parents really knowing each
> other and knowing each other's children and they can discuss.

> You often find at the end of a meeting, parents will be saying we've got this coming up, is that okay, do you want your child to come? How can we help out? It sort of you know, fosters this, it's a kindness isn't it, looking after each other. (Kerry, parent group leader, HCC)

This conception of community as family is similarly reflected in Lynch's idea of 'nurturing capital' (2007: 565) and the role of affective relations in the dimensions of love, care and solidarity in the alternative practices of the kind described above. What Lynch points out is that the neoliberal policy framework is based around a conception of human beings working towards their own self-interest, through the market place, whereas caring is actually based primarily on 'other-centredness', expressed in the classroom, in real-world experience and in the care and support of teachers and other parents. There is a different character to these more co-operative logics.

Both these examples of particular alternative practices at HCC represent challenges to instrumentalist views of education involving the nurturing of deeper reflection on experience, valuing quietness and parent interaction. Practices involving the experience of stillness and reflection on the part of students, the sharing of experience between parents, encouraging mutual support and welcoming parents in schools as sources of knowledge were a balance to the pressures of neoliberal policy imperatives and competitive logics in schooling.

Conclusion

Anyone involved in alternative schooling will recognize the tensions and challenges faced by HCC in the difficult 'dance' of negotiation with the dominant education system, which has the tendency to try to bring alternatives back into line with mainstream settings so they can be absorbed and no longer represent an 'oppositional' position (Williams, 1977). What can be surrendered? What should be maintained? HCC, for example, participated in the national curriculum, nation-wide testing and the university-entrance system, but sought to balance these accommodations to the mainstream with the distinctive elements of its alternative practice such as the Quietness Program, the Parents' Program and its non-competitive ethos and practices.

Other elements of alternative schooling such as small school size, smaller classes, more personalized relationships, emphasis on social-emotional and spiritual elements of learning, non-coercive and 'non-violent structures, practices and relationships' (Waters, 2017: 40), are also important features that maintain key points of difference with mainstream, both public and private, schooling systems. These elements underline the desirability of maintaining 'edu-diversity' at a time of standardization and the imposition of a monoculture in education. Alternative schooling systems also represent the preservation of what te Riele (2008) has called 'incubators for change'.

What HCC adds to this 'edu-diversity' is the modeling of an alternative based around an ethos and practices that demonstrate the viability of a non-competitive, co-operative and collaborative school culture. This example provides an alternative and a 'challenge', in Woods' (2015) terms, to the dominant neoliberal view that for optimal outcomes in education, and national productivity, a competition-based schooling system of teaching and learning is the only workable option.

References

Ball, S.J. (2008) *The Education Debate*. Bristol: Policy Press.

Ball, S.J. (2010) 'New class inequalities in education: Why education policy may be looking in the wrong place! Education policy, civil society and social class'. *International Journal of Sociology and Social Policy*, 30 (3–4), 155–66.

Bryk, A.S. and Schneider, B. (2002) *Trust in Schools: A core resource for improvement*. New York: Russell Sage Foundation.

Clarken, R.H. (2009) 'Holistic education'. In Provenzo, E.F., Renaud, J.P. and Provenzo, A.B. (eds) *Encyclopedia of the Social and Cultural Foundations of Education* (Vol. 1). Thousand Oaks, CA: SAGE Publications, 416–17.

Dayadev, V. (1983) *Holistic Education*. Melbourne: Centre Publications.

Demerath, P. (2009) *Producing Success: The culture of personal advancement in an American high school*. Chicago: University of Chicago Press.

Fielding, M. (2015) 'Why co-operative schools should oppose competition and what they might do instead'. In Woodin, T. (ed.) *Co-operation, Learning and Co-operative Values: Contemporary issues in education*. London: Routledge, 17–30.

Harber, C. and Sakade, N. (2009) 'Schooling for violence and peace: How does peace education differ from "normal" schooling?'. *Journal of Peace Education*, 6 (2), 171–87.

Harvey, D. (2005) *A Brief History of Neoliberalism*. Oxford: Oxford University Press.

Kessler, R. (2000) *The Soul of Education: Helping students find connection, compassion, and character at school*. Alexandria, VA: Association for Supervision and Curriculum Development.

Kohn, A. (1992) *No Contest: The case against competition*. Boston: Houghton Mifflin.

Kraftl, P. (2013) *Geographies of Alternative Education: Diverse learning spaces for children and young people*. Bristol: Policy Press.

Lynch, K. (2007) 'Love labour as a distinct and non-commodifiable form of care labour'. *Sociological Review*, 55 (3), 550–70.

Mills, M. and McGregor, G. (2014) *Re-engaging Young People in Education: Learning from alternative schools*. London: Routledge.

Nagata, Y. (2006) *Alternative Education: Global perspectives relevant to the Asia-Pacific region*. Dordrecht: Springer.

Noddings, N. (2002) *Educating Moral People: A caring alternative to character education*. New York: Teachers College Press.

Raywid, M.A. (1999) 'History and issues of alternative schools'. *Education Digest*, 64 (9), 47–51.

Rizvi, F. and Lingard, B. (2010) *Globalizing Education Policy*. London: Routledge.

Robinson, K. and Aronica, L. (2009) *The Element: How finding your passion changes everything*. New York: Penguin.

Sahlberg, P. (2006) 'Education reform for raising economic competitiveness'. *Journal of Educational Change*, 7 (4), 259–87.

Schanzenbach, D.W. (2014) *Does Class Size Matter?* Boulder, CO: National Education Policy Center.

Tasker, M. (no date) *Human Scale Education: History, values and practice*. Bristol: Human Scale Education. Accessed: www.hse.org.uk/downloads/HistoryValuesandPracticebyMaryTasker.pdf

Te Riele, K. (2008) 'Are alternative schools the answer?'. *New Transitions: Re-engagement Edition*, April, 1–6.

Te Riele, K. (2012) *Learning Choices: A map for the future*. Bondi Junction, NSW: Dusseldorp Skills Forum.

Waters, R. (2017) 'Symbolic non-violence in the work of teachers in alternative education settings'. *Teaching Education*, 28 (1), 27–40.

Williams, R. (1977) *Marxism and Literature*. Oxford: Oxford University Press.

Woods, P.A. (2015) 'Co-operativism as an alternative: Choice, assimilation and challenge'. In Woodin, T. (ed.) *Co-operation, Learning and Co-operative Values: Contemporary issues in education*. London: Routledge, 42–54.

Woods, P.A. and Woods, G.J. (eds) (2009) *Alternative Education for the 21st Century: Philosophies, approaches, visions*. New York: Palgrave Macmillan.

Zyngier, D. (2014) 'Class size and academic results, with a focus on children from culturally, linguistically and economically disenfranchised communities'. *Evidence Base*, 1, 1–23.

Chapter 15

Den fri Hestehaveskole in Denmark

Annegrete Zobbe, Vibeke Helms,
Trine Martens and Thilde Graulund
with contributions by Rikke Rasmussen and
Niels Nielsen

In this chapter, we, Annegrete Zobbe and Vibeke Helms, with the help of other teachers and students in our school, describe one example from among more than 500 Danish free schools. Each school has its own set of values, and each school has the power to define these values in its own way within its curriculum, as long as this meets expectations for all state schools. Each independent school has a story to tell, and here we tell the story of Den fri Hestehaveskole (DfH).

Private primary schools in Denmark are often 'free schools', founded on the ideas of N.F.S. Grundtvig and Christen Kold developed in the nineteenth century. Being rooted in the principles of freedom, these schools are, as would be expected, very different from each other in their curricula, their traditions and how they organize the daily education. Despite this, they have many common characteristics, which can be traced back to shared views about humankind, nature, society and education. Drawing our inspiration from them, we are committed to ensuring the best possible framework to help develop robust children and youngsters – ready for the future. Our aim is that each child should have the opportunity to gain genuine and practical experiences, have academic challenges at all levels, and develop the skills to meet those academic and social challenges, all within a safe environment. Our motto is 'Robust children and youngsters; ready for the future'.

This chapter will describe the main principles of our school: togetherness, the development of personal goals and, most important of all, to give our pupils the opportunity to learn to be responsible for real issues. First, we outline our educational approach and then describe this as it works for our oldest pupils. In the conclusion we draw attention to a number of challenges we face in our school practice.

Den fri Hestehaveskole

Den fri Hestehaveskole (DfH) has 206 pupils aged 6–16. The school has 10 grades, and there are approximately 20 pupils in each class. Until 1992 the school was a state school, but the town council decided to close the school at that point, and it was expected that the pupils would enrol in a large school in a nearby town. The parents, however, thought otherwise. They wanted the school to remain part of the local community and so they formed a 'school circle', elected a chair for a board of governors, and managed to raise enough money to buy the school building. The school was then and remains the centre for many local activities. In rural areas schools often offer a place for local people to meet, and families with school-age children will rarely move to an area that does not have a school. Our kind of school was known as a 'protest school', a protest against the decision of the town council, not against the idea of state schooling. A large number of our pupils come from the old school district, but we have still more parents who seek out the school for ideological reasons. Parents choosing the school agree with our principles for teaching, they welcome the possibility of having an input, and they value the fact that their children are not focused on sitting tests all the time.

Our school aims to provide a flexible and secure framework that helps create the best opportunities for children to learn and thrive. The youngest pupils, from preschool to 4th grade, can attend after-school care called *Skole Fritids Ordning* (SFO) or 'School Free Scheme'. The SFO is open from 6 to 8 a.m. and then again from 1 to 5 p.m. The SFO and the kindergarten (for children aged 3–6) have their own brand-new building, which is connected to the school, both physically and in terms of philosophy and values. Both SFO and the kindergarten can use the school facilities. Most of the children in the kindergarten continue on into our school once they leave kindergarten stage.

Kindergarten, SFO and the school have a joint board of governors, principals, and staff. We share fundamental values and everyday life. There are approximately 35 employees altogether at DfH. Below we explain how some of these structures work in the everyday life of DfH.

Figure 15.1: Children in kindergarten

School life

Each day begins with morning assembly. In assembly, the whole school meets for singing and storytelling. The assembly is focused on building a positive ethos in the whole school community and building connectedness. The pupils sit close together, sing together and sometimes do presentations for the whole school. The teachers take turns at being responsible for our morning assemblies.

All pupils up to 6th grade have weekly story time. During these sessions, pupils are presented with the key stories from Norse mythology, stories from the Bible and Greek myths, as well as stories from everyday life and general ethical and moral dilemmas. Storytelling encourages engagement with ideas, development of the imagination and also strengthens pupils' perspectives on their own lives.

The curriculum also includes sports, PE, music, workshop subjects, art, elective subjects and research. These subjects promote students' general education but also deepen understanding of the connections between school and life outside school. They teach students specific practical skills but also help them develop understanding of their strengths and capabilities.

Figure 15.2: School assembly

In DfH we give high priority to this, but they also learn Danish, mathematics, English, German, physics, biology, social studies, religion, history and geography – the traditional academic subjects. We often work across subjects and classes. For approximately eight weeks per year we set aside our regular schedules. During this time, we focus on professional and social issues. For example, we may have a focus on music, school camps, mini societies, history, Danish, mathematics, science, projects or research. In Figure 15.3, students are working on a maths project in the outdoors.

We expect all pupils, parents and staff to contribute actively to building the school community. We see this as a prerequisite for a well-functioning community. So we work hard to build a common structure that works for all pupils but has enough flexibility that we can make and adapt it as needed during the school day. This might mean, for example, giving a short extra break for some pupils one day or letting some children have a small snack before lunchtime another day.

Building the school community requires openness and targeted work to get parents, pupils and teachers to maintain our common goal: that every student in the school should have a safe and learning-filled education. Parents are required to participate as fully as possible in the life of the school and within the classes. To a large extent parents contribute to creating the framework of their own child's schooling. They help by offering financial support, by helping run events and helping with the general upkeep of the school. We also involve them in dealing with and resolving conflicts. We see many ways in which parental support strengthens student engagement in their own learning.

Figure 15.3: Maths in the outdoors

There is a tradition of close relationships between students and teachers in free schools. We are a family school, and many families are part of the school for many years. We have a small number of staff, each with many different roles, so the pupils know us as teachers, as storytellers, as the person who comforts you after a fall in the schoolyard, and as the person who requires academic results. These different roles strengthen relationships and enhance students' confidence in adults. We find that when we have close relationships we see students make strong academic progress. Our students take the same exams as students in public schools (this is explained in detail below) but in addition we also give them our 'free school testimony' in which we describe their personal achievements in their time in school.

The role of the teacher

When we are brave and outspoken, when we show the students a good example, they too become more courageous and bold – and dare to set themselves greater and greater academic challenges. Our teachers are very dedicated. We make a strong commitment to students, parents, school, our peers and to the subjects we teach. All teachers strive to continually make things a little better, and this provides a very high level of energy in the school. Teachers are largely free to plan and carry out the teaching and training that they consider best aligns with the school's goals, and this gives tremendous scope for the individual teacher. Teachers decide how the part of the budget for teaching materials is spent. When given time and room to think, it is possible for the teacher to create a setting where the gap between school and real lived life becomes blurred – at least in some ways. When we do school in experimental ways, for example when we step out of the normal timetable, we create possibilities for both students and teachers to ask new questions and develop new ways of thinking. An example of this is given below.

Monday morning begins a full week of mathematics for the school's three senior classes. All tasks will revolve around the same problem. In groups of four across all three classes they are to move out of home and have to find an apartment, organize a budget for rent and other expenses connected with moving out. They have to balance their own accounts and work out interest rates and payments due. These questions and decisions are often very new for most of the students. Though it is a game, the students get involved with great enthusiasm, both because it is fun and because they know it will be reality in the near future. At random, each student is allocated a personal budget. All students receive the same financial help through State Education as would be given in real life. Some find they are wealthier than others because they have a bank account from their parents, others have part-time jobs to manage alongside studying, and yet others find they have responsibility for a loan. The information on their different economic situations of course, influences their choice of apartment and the living standards they can afford. These issues can be solved in various ways, but mathematical skills are needed at every stage. Throughout the week a set of unexpected situations occur; they may find they need to buy new furniture or kitchenware, they may have to throw a party for friends, and one day the Red Cross unexpectedly comes by and one of the flatmates decides to donate money to them from the collective food account. These moral dilemmas are part of everyday life, and by presenting the students with both small and large dilemmas, we give them opportunities for debating and practising skills of negotiation, all of which help to form moral character in ways that give life to all school subjects but, importantly, also reach far beyond the what can be taught by looking at a spreadsheet.

Pupil achievement

Our 9th graders (16-year-olds) sit the same exams as those in the state schools, and an external examiner from the state system or the Ministry of Education assesses both oral and written exams. These exam results for each year must be published on the school's homepage. However, when we evaluate the results of our students as they leave school, we do not regard it as adequate simply to look at the grades they get. At DfH we find it much more interesting to ask what kind of young people our school leavers have turned out to be. What kind of 'extras' have they gained by being pupils at DfH? Are they confident in themselves? Do they know how a democracy works and are they ready to play their part? Are they confident enough to speak in front of a lot of people and express their personal thoughts and beliefs?

We will exemplify this by describing a recent multi-disciplinary challenge undertaken by our students in 8th and 9th grade (15–16-year-olds). It was a project that included Danish, English, German, geography, history and social sciences as well as a six-day visit to Berlin. For a lot of young Danish pupils our neighbouring country, Germany, is somewhere you go to buy cheap candy, cheap beer and cheap soda pops. You can pay with Danish Kroner, and the people in the shops speak Danish, so you do not need to step out of your comfort zone. The teachers therefore decided it would be a good idea to present the pupils with another view of the country. The specific areas of study in what we called the 'Learning Zone' included:

- History: Germany from World War I to present day, 'A divided country, a divided city', the Cold War.
- Geography: Germany between East and West.
- German and English: scaffolding languages. This involved asking and giving information, describing events, objects and people, expressing agreement and disagreement, expressing likes and dislikes, expressing an opinion, greeting someone and introducing yourself and telling a story. The pupils also had to make a tourist brochure about sights in Berlin in both English and German.
- Social studies topics: to investigate how ordinary people live/survive in a communist regime; what life was like in East Berlin.
- Danish: Scaffolding the trip, preparations, expectations…
- The pupils also watched and discussed several films including: *Napola*, *The Boy in the Striped Pyjamas*, *Der Fälschner*, *The Wave* and *Das Leben der Anderen*.

A daily task on the trip was for each pupil to document with photos/film what we had seen, and keep a logbook in English (Figure 15.4).

Figure 15.4: Berlin logbooks

The main items on our programme were as follows:

> Getting to know Alexanderplatz, Visit Alexa, Visit to the Reichstag (remember your passport), The Holocaust Memorial, Brandenburg Gate, Friedrichstrasse, Dussmann (everybody had to buy a book), Ritter Sport Museum, Berlin Underworld, Berlin Wall Memorial, Kaiser Wilhelm Memorial Church, Ku'dam, KaDeWe (department store), East Side Gallery, Hohenschönhausen (the former Stasi prison), Hamburger Bahnhof Museum, Mauer Markt, Berlin Cathedral, DDR Museum, Otto Weidt Workshop for the Blind, Chameleon Theatre, Märchen Brunnen im Volkpark, the Jewish Museum, the Olympic Stadium, and dinner at the Münchener Hofbräuhaus. Although it was an intensive programme, there was still time for some unplanned activities. Breakfast was at 6:30 AM – and we were back at the hostel around 10 PM each day.

Berlin was a very good choice of destination for our group of 40 students. Although it is the capital city of Germany, they did not find it too large and frightening. Working in small groups they soon found their way round the U-Bahn, the trams and the buses, and each group felt confident about finding their way to meeting points and being there (almost!) on time. It was a good lesson for them to learn and master, and their experience will prepare them well for when they need to use public transport in another major city. The visit to Dussmann bookstore was a hit! Everybody had to find at least one book in either German or English. To begin with a few of the students were a bit grumpy, but very soon the booklovers managed to convince them that it wasn't hard to find books they actually would like to read. We urged the pupils to speak as much German as they could. Some of them were quite disappointed when the people they were talking to switched to English. On our last night in Berlin we all had dinner together at the Münchener Hofbräuhaus, which was a huge success. The waiters and waitresses were wearing *Lederhosen* and *Dirndl*. Everybody was enjoying himself or herself, there was live music, the pupils were on the dance floor as much as possible – and they carried a song home with them. They had heard this song the first time after skiing in Austria, and they taught it to the whole school at morning assembly. The song was also used when the boys from 9th grade were in charge of the warm-up before running on our annual sports day (Figure 15.5).

Figure 15.5: Warm-up for the sports day

As part of their evaluation of the trip, the students shared their experiences with the whole school at the morning assembly. The speakers were divided into small groups, and each group had to talk about a topic from the trip. These speeches at the assembly served a double purpose. It is a genuine task to stand in front of a group of more than 200 people and tell them about your personal experiences in another country. It causes sweaty palms and lots of anxiety, but once they try it, the students become very confident. The younger pupils are a very good audience for these speeches. They admire their elders, and they learn from them and know what will be expected of them later on. At a later date, the parents of 8th- and 9th-grade students were invited to come in to school and hear about the trip. There was a remarkable improvement in the speeches by then and the pupils were able to give a really strong performance rather than simply give a speech.

Open School 2016

Another example of how we build community spirit and confidence among our pupils is the open school event. This is an annual event under the theme 'No two schools are the same'. State schools and independent schools are part of the event. At DfH the oldest students are the hosts. It is an evening for parents from the whole school as well as for anybody else who wants to know more about the school. In 2016, Rikke Rasmussen and Niels Nielsen from 9th grade in DfH assisted in arranging the open school event. They gave presentations and showed photos from their school trips to an audience of about 100 people, most of them parents of the younger pupils. The teachers gave Rikke and Niels the task of choosing which aspects of school life they wanted to talk about. They wrote their presentations themselves and decided what they wanted to say. The teachers were as curious as the guests. In our school we believe it is important to give pupils appropriate challenges and gain real experiences.

Part of Rikke's presentation for the open event is below:

A very warm welcome to you all!

We would like to tell you something about what you gain by going to this school – apart from learning how to spell, do maths, and all the other things you are supposed to learn when you go to school. Of course we learn all these things at our school, but we learn a lot of other stuff as well! When we go on trips and travels, we learn how to fill our role in a different place, we get real life experience that we can use in later life – we learn to take turns and that the person next to you is as important as yourself – it is not always 'I' who comes first. We also learn to fend for ourselves. Some of the most valuable lessons we learn stem from the travels abroad. During our time at DfH we have been on two trips abroad. One of the trips involved sports and physical challenges; the other, culture and language. Our class went skiing in Austria, and the culture trip was to Berlin.

I was so nervous and anxious about this skiing trip! I had never been skiing before, and I was certain I would be terrible on a pair of skis! Going down a mountain with long wooden planks on my feet? I was sure I would break arms and legs! Luckily nothing like that happened. I found it really hard to learn to ski, but after three lessons at the ski training centre, I was no longer Bambi on ice. I was not good, and I spent a day and a half on the hill for beginners. I managed to go on some of the blue slopes, and a few of the red ones. It was really beyond my limits, but also something I learnt from and never will forget. One of the most fantastic things about this school is that the teachers trust us, so we do not need to be accompanied by a teacher all the time. We have so much freedom, but we are expected to turn up for meetings at the appointed time – not shuffling in five minutes late. Our freedom allowed us to stay on the slopes for a whole day of skiing, or have hot cocoa in the restaurant if we so desired.

When we go on the trips abroad we are put together with the class below or above us. It may be a bit awkward at the start, but after the first few hours it is super. You get to know the other class much better; perhaps you have not been talking a lot together before, but then you begin to bond, and when you are home again you have a set of new friends to talk to and you have a common experience to build on. It really is great being together. We have seen each other's anxiety and weaknesses, and we have gained a greater acceptance of ourselves and the others (Rikke Rasmussen).

Niels Nielsen also presented at the open event. Some of what he said included the following:

This year we went on a language/culture trip to Berlin. I was not nervous about this trip. Unlike the ski trip, the possibility of breaking something was not likely, and the worst thing to happen would be to miss a train. It was not that easy to travel on the U-Bahn. In our part of Denmark the bus is the means of public transport, with one scheduled departure every other hour! Most of the time, we were travelling with the teachers. We were divided into groups and travelled on group tickets. Each group had to have one person who was 15 years old – and s/he could travel with three persons below 15 on his ticket. That meant that the travel groups consisted of persons from both 8th and 9th grade. We had to stick together all the time – if one person from the group was late, we had to wait, and take the next train. All of us had breakfast together at the hostel. We had lunch in free groups, and also dinner some of the nights. On two nights we had dinner together all of us. Each person had 10 Euros a day for lunch and dinner. If we wanted more, we had to pay ourselves. It was quite challenging for us to stay at a hostel and have to be in charge of everything ourselves, some of us realized. If we were not ready at the appointed time it was bad luck! We risked missing some of the things we were going to do that day! One of the teachers would stay behind and wait for the latecomers and their groups while the other two teachers went ahead with the groups who were on time! I think you can definitely say that at our school we learn that our actions have consequences.

Niels also talked at the open event about the importance of friendships at our school:

We like to get to know each other in this school, not just the pupils in our own class but also across classes. When you begin in preschool you will be matched up with a 'buddy' who is in 9th grade. Then you sit with your senior buddy at the assembly for the first six weeks. As a preschooler, this helps you learn not to be afraid of the 'big ones'. You get to know them and you can always ask them for help. As a 9th-grader you learn about being responsible. It is your task to take care of a small girl or boy, and you must see to it that your school friend feels at ease. It is a big responsibility! The little ones often come to us if they have problems. We learn how to take care of others, and we also learn how to say 'no' so people can understand it without being cross. It is a unique experience to be a buddy.

As a pupil in this school you build up a lot of skills in your 'backpack'; not only about school subjects, but also vital skills that we can use later on in life. One of the skills is being able to speak to a large group of people like here today. We get the chance to practise and learn how to do it. It gives us a sense of confidence. Another thing we learn from is having arranged this Open School event (with a little help from Vibeke). It is a quality in itself to take the initiative for an event and see it through. That is why we love DfH (Niels Nielsen).

Figure 15.6: Annual open day for parents and families

These words from Rikke and Niels mirror the feelings and thoughts of most of our former pupils.

The challenges for free schools

It may sound as if we are trying to promote our own school. Of course we are proud of our school, and we focus on the things we think are important for our pupils. We are sure that if you ask any alternative school the same question you will get an answer where the focus is on the things they do well! However, alternative schools also have many challenges in common. We now turn to discuss these challenges and the ways we try to meet them, while always bearing in mind a common saying these days: 'Teach children for their future – not for their teacher's past!' We cannot foresee which skills our pupils will need, but we can teach them the virtues that go with being a decent human being.

In many ways our school is old-fashioned. We think hard about the key virtues we want to instil, which need to be imparted and worked on every single day. We employ a framework based on values, which can be challenging for some modern families. Not everything at school is a labour of love and not only for pleasure. Things need to be trained and practised even when you don't feel motivated or entertained!

Some children and parents ask for more traditional education than we offer in our schedules. We believe that movement, music, singing, creative skills and art experiences play a decisive role for the overall high quality of skills, knowledge and viability of the children but we often have to remind parents about this.

The Danish state school system has introduced very extensive reforms during the last five years. The reforms are focused on targeted learning, evaluation culture and a great number of tests. As an independent school we have the opportunity to find our own way to meet the expectation that the pupils must be at least as skilled as the pupils who have been in state schools. In the free schools we must be very attentive towards adhering to our own values and developing our educational practice on our own terms. To a large extent both teachers and kindergarten teachers take part in the same seminars as teachers in the state school. Teachers also find inspiration in and have access to the same teaching materials in both school systems. Thus, it is a big challenge to hold on to the freedom of educational content and organization. We have to continue to develop the independent school and at the same time take a critical look at the very centrally directed development in the state school.

Finance for free schools is always a challenge. Small schools in sparsely populated areas in Denmark face considerable challenges in ensuring they have enough pupils to maintain financial stability. In the cities the intake of pupils is large, but the cost of the school buildings is high. DfH is in a rural area but close to town settlements. Our pupils come from a very large area, and the school offers a meeting place for the families, which helps the school stay financially viable. Most schools need at least 140 pupils for this to happen.

Including pupils with special needs can be a challenge. In DfH we have had some good success regarding inclusion of pupils with special needs. We are able to provide appropriate individual solutions in certain respects. If, however, a pupil has very extensive special needs, physical, psychological or cognitive, we may find that our professional skills and resources are not enough to meet the pupil's needs. The whole approach to learning in our school may also be a barrier for some children. We place strong emphasis on unstructured play, for example, and give a large amount of autonomy to pupils. Therefore we may not be able to enrol a child who needs individual support and constant monitoring. These factors must be taken into consideration before a pupil is accepted in the school, and again if extensive special needs become obvious later on.

Conclusion

When we plan and build ideas for how we want our school to be, and what we want our pupils to achieve, we always strive to find the right balance between the ideal and the possible. There are many challenges in running a free school but we also know there are many challenges ahead for our pupils in their adult lives and this is why we feel so committed to our mission to help nurture – as our motto says – 'Robust children and youngsters: ready for the future'.

Figure 15.7: Joy

Part Three

Alternative education and
the mainstream

3

Chapter 16

Alternative education in Germany: Influencing the mainstream?

Anne Sliwka and Britta Klopsch

History of alternative education in Germany

In Germany, the first traces of an alternative pedagogy can be found as early as the nineteenth century (Benner and Kemper, 2003). The term *Reformpädagogik* (literally: 'reformist pedagogy'), the German language equivalent to 'alternative education', first appeared in 1863 in relation to the pedagogical ideas of Friedrich Fröbel, widely seen as the father of the modern kindergarten.

Since then, the term *Reformpädagogik* has been used to describe attempts to reform education with the aim of moving from teacher-centred instruction to pedagogies that enable students' profound engagement in their learning process through rich and multi-faceted educational experiences. During the first three decades of the twentieth century, which are often seen as a particularly fruitful period in the development of alternative forms of education (Keim and Schwerdt, 2013), multiple ideas were developed and tested to counter the authoritarianism of schools perceived as mere places of cramming and drilling. Through an alternative understanding of education and learning, reformers aimed at focusing on learning instead of teaching to enhance student agency in the learning process.

Many of the reformers, like Georg Kerschensteiner, Herrman Lietz, Bertold Otto or Peter Peterson met in the *Bund für Schulreform* (Association for School Reform) founded in 1908, which in 1915 became the influential *Deutscher Ausschuss für Erziehung und Unterricht* (German Committee for Education and Instruction) and later in the interwar years the *Bund entschiedener Schulreformer* (Association of Determined School Reformers). Their reformist agenda gained significant influence in the academic and political sphere (Amlung *et al.*, 1993). They held a number of influential conferences, published books and instituted the journal *Neue Erziehung* (*New Education*), in which they argued for increased student agency and democratic participation. According to the Weimar constitution, 'talent and interest' instead of social background were to decide the course of a child's schooling. In those years, the German reformers began to network with international reformers like the Italian physician Maria Montessori, the French teacher Célestin Freinet and the Austrian philosopher Rudolf Steiner, whose educational ideas were part of a student-centred anthropology and world view (Röhrs, 2001).

When Adolf Hitler came to power in 1933, almost all of these activities ceased. Reformist associations were disbanded and most alternative schools had to close (Knoll, 1998). After 1945, the ideas associated with alternative education were slow to take root again in Germany. In the 1960s, the term *Alternativpädagogik* (alternative pedagogy) was imported from the English language and used synonymously with *Reformpädagogik*. As a response to the 1968 student movement in particular, alternative ideas and schools began to blossom again in West Germany. Montessori and Steiner pedagogy were the first movements to regain a broader influence in the second half of the twentieth century. Between 1960 and 1989, hundreds of Steiner schools (called Waldorf schools in Germany) and Montessori schools were founded in West Germany. After the fall of the Berlin Wall, the development of alternative schools extended to the former German Democratic Republic. All 16 German states now have legal provisions in place for the founding of alternative schools, which are most commonly called *Freie Schulen* (free schools) (Hofmann, 2013). In this chapter we will argue that many of the pedagogical ideas developed in alternative settings have become part of mainstream schooling in Germany. We will start by examining some of the core educational concepts developed in alternative education settings.

Core concepts of alternative education in Germany

Alternative schools and education settings have in the German context always drawn on concepts of student choice and agency, active engagement in learning, authentic learning environments and diversity as a resource for learning. Based on these understandings, a whole range of innovations in learning have emerged over the past century of schooling in the German context.

Student agency and self-determination

According to alternative educational philosophies in Germany, students are to be seen as the core agents of their own learning process. Motivation to learn is seen as a precondition for sustainable learning and achievement. It can only develop if student talent and interests are seen as a starting point of a learning process. Alternative pedagogies in Germany have thus been applying a range of methods to enhance student agency and self-determination. A good example of this is *Wochenplanarbeit* (weekly work plans). Weekly work plans have been widely used in German alternative settings and have their roots in the pedagogy of Peter Petersen and Célestin Freinet. Students are given learning plans for an entire week consisting of compulsory tasks that students have to work on over the course of the week, typically in core subjects such as German, English or mathematics, and optional tasks from which students can choose according to their talents and interests. Often these weekly plans also create a structure for self-chosen projects. Within the given time frame of one week, students can choose when to work on a particular task and where to do the work. That way, self-organizational skills are being strengthened and individual learning needs are taken into account. The freedom typically goes along with some level of accountability, typically a structured conversation and feedback between the student and the teacher.

Active engagement in learning

Project-based learning, problem-based learning and inquiry-based learning are typical processes in alternative settings in Germany. In Peter Petersen's Jenaplan school, school projects were a core part of learning and the results of these were presented at the end of each week in a public celebration to which all students were invited, and often their parents too. The scientist Martin Wagenschein (2009) was a pioneer in applying problem-based learning in science education and developed his own theory, 'genetic teaching', as a hands-on exploratory form of science teaching. While John Dewey's educational thinking has never been widely received by mainstream schools in Germany, reformist teachers have been using Dewey's ideas extensively in the German context (Knoll, 2011). The reformist educationist Hartmut von Hentig, who familiarized himself with Deweyan pragmatism during his studies at the University of Chicago in the 1950s, set up a German version of Dewey's Chicago Laboratory School, the *Laborschule* at the newly founded University of Bielefeld in 1974. The teachers and researchers affiliated to this school were mainly responsible for popularizing the idea of project-based learning in its various formats. More recently, another alternative school, Evangelische Schule Berlin-Zentrum, gained a lot of public attention for its bold move to include two full three-week periods for project-based learning in the curriculum for Grades 7 and 8. 'Project Responsibility' requires students to find a community-based project to work on in teams.

In 'Project Challenge' students are asked to define a group challenge for themselves and work on it for three weeks.

Since the 1970s, 'learning through teaching' has been popularized in alternative settings in Germany. Jean-Pol Martin (1996), an expert on teaching foreign languages, applied this concept to French teaching with significant success. Martin engaged with students by letting them teach French to each other. He distinguished learning phases and assessment phases. During the learning phases his students taught each other French, while he only intervened when significant mistakes were made. In this stage, Martin also encouraged students to correct each other to jointly improve their language skills. It was only in the assessment phase at the end of a learning unit that Martin assessed students and graded them. By that time the students had learnt so much through their active use of the language and through correcting each other's mistakes that learning outcomes were impressive (Martin, 1996).

Authentic learning environments

The characteristics of the spaces and places in which learning takes place influence learning opportunities in significant ways. Maria Montessori was among the first educators to describe the learning environment as a core feature of any learning process. In alternative education traditions in the German context, the learning space has been called the 'third educator' after a statement by the Italian educator Loris Malaguzzi (1920–94), who considered peers to be the first educator, teachers the second educator and the space the third educator. According to this view spaces determine the structure of learning opportunities. Alternative educators in Germany have always looked for rich learning environments, such as rural areas with a variety of landscapes, inner-city environments with dense infrastructure or cultural spaces with a diverse body of human talent at hand. These environments do not only stimulate and create natural incentives for student agency; they also offer authentic choices that allow learners to explore their personality and talents by choosing tasks seen as personally meaningful.

Diversity as a resource in learning

While traditional education settings in the German context have been structured by concepts of homogeneity and streaming, alternative settings tend to embrace the idea of diversity in education. To this day, traditional German schools group students by age (in primary education) and by age and ability level (in secondary education). In the German tradition, homogeneity of learning groups has often been seen as a precondition for effective learning. Alternative schools tend to embrace the opposite concept.

The diversity of human talent and interest is seen as the very foundation of learning. In his Jenaplan school in Jena, Peter Petersen introduced mixed-aged groupings as early as 1927 (Koerrenz, 2011, 2014). In these multigrade classes, students in Grades 1, 2 and 3 would learn together in the *Untergruppe* (lower group), Grades 4, 5 and 6 in the *Mittelgruppe* (middle group) and Grades 7, 8 and 9 in the *Obergruppe* (upper group). These groupings would enable teachers to perceive each child as an individual with unique talents and interests. Because of their obvious diversity children would help each other in their learning process and grow in maturity. Today, mixed-age classes are frequently used in alternative education settings in Germany. In some German states, mainstream primary schools have adapted the idea for Grades 1 and 2 to account for the diversity in learning abilities when students first start their schooling. Older students help younger students in their learning. Multigrade classes make it possible for students to stay for one year, two years or up to three years in this first learning group, according to their developmental level and progress.

Alternative forms of assessment

Innovative assessment practices have also been a distinctive feature of alternative schools in Germany. Whereas mainstream schools still tend to use norm-referenced testing based on the comparison of students in a class or school, reformist pedagogy has focused on the diversity of learners and the dignity of the individual child. Alternative schools have used individual progress as a reference in assessment since the beginning of last century. As a consequence, alternative forms of assessment, such as individual learning reports and student–teacher feedback conferences have dominated in these settings. Steiner schools in Germany do not compare different learners but provide them with detailed learning reports in which the teacher describes the individual student and his or her progress in learning. In the Jenaplan school, which is based on the 1920s model started by Peter Petersen and refounded by parents after the fall of the Berlin Wall in the early 1990s, students receive detailed written comments of their work that are then discussed in a student–teacher–parent conference taking place at the end of each semester in school.

More recently, free schools and some state schools have been combining the individual reference norm with the criterion reference norm, using various methods such as rubrics and checklists, student self-evaluation, peer evaluations and portfolios, which students use to showcase and comment on their work and their learning process. While the practice of low-achieving students having to repeat an entire year still exists in traditional German schools, alternative schools have successfully fought for their right to go a different route. Instead of having students repeat an entire year of schooling, they typically offer alternative forms of support to overcome deficits in core knowledge areas. Alternative schools in Germany were among the first to establish tutoring and mentoring structures and to offer extra courses and summer programmes for students with remedial needs.

From alternative education to mainstream schooling: How concepts from alternative education are impacting mainstream German schools

The first PISA study published by the OECD in 2000 triggered an enormous debate on the state of the German education system. The study revealed that the German system had failed to support the most underprivileged learners: those from families with low socio-economic status as well as recent immigrants (Sliwka, 2010). Features of the country's education system that had always been taken for granted were now being re-examined and across Germany policies were changed to allow for more experimentation and innovation. The rigorous sorting and sifting of students as young as 9 or 10 years old began to be questioned once it was realized that streaming obviously played a big part in cementing the social structure of German society.

Factors encouraging students' intrinsic motivation to learn and their active engagement as learners gained a lot more public attention. The detailed analysis of German PISA data at the level of individual schools showed that some alternative schools had had positive effects on students' motivation to learn, which was reflected in their good results. It also led to an increasing number of parents opting out of the state school system to look for alternative education in private and free schools. These were often Steiner schools and schools run by the Protestant or the Catholic church. In the first decade of the twenty-first century, Germany saw the emergence of a public discourse on what constitutes a good school. Even if this discourse is quite controversial, with hotly contested areas like early streaming and equity, the national debate has had some fruitful results. There have been a number of policy initiatives aimed at increasing the quality of German schools, and private foundations and NGOs are increasingly active in supporting the dissemination of innovative ideas in education.

Anne Sliwka and Britta Klopsch

Policy initiatives

The debate on school quality has led to the development of frameworks to define school quality (Klopsch, 2009) and help schools in assessing their own work. It is interesting that these mainstream policy tools nowadays draw on and reflect ideas and concepts from alternative education. Students are now seen at the centre of learning, and there is a focus on the individual student and his or her learning progress. This new focus on individual learning needs, emotions and motivation has led to a new perspective within the German school system. Diversity is now officially seen as a resource in learning and requires personalization of learning to meet the needs of different children and adolescents. Planning learning and teaching with the individual in mind requires new forms of professionalism. Professional co-operation in learning communities and ongoing professional development along the career path are highly valued in the new framework. Whereas teachers in alternative schools have always collaborated very closely, German state schools until very recently were dominated by a culture of isolation and fragmentation of the teaching profession. These alternative cultures of close professional collaboration have had a clear impact on the notion of professionalism in mainstream education. Close professional collaboration is now seen as a necessary prerequisite for supporting students well, and teachers are asked to come up with new ways of learning together and of assessing their own work.

This concept of working together, of professionals being not only teachers but also learners, is also relevant for school leadership. School leaders are expected to enable teachers to develop their individual strengths and to facilitate democratic decision-making in the teaching teams. This can be seen as a paradigm shift within a school system that has been guided by bureaucratic rules and top-down decision-making for more than a century. That both school climate and class climate are now being taken into account in both self-evaluation and external evaluation of schools can also be traced back to the impact of alternative education. In alternative schools a positive learning atmosphere has traditionally been seen as an asset to learning. A similar idea rooted in alternative schools is the fact that all schools are now expected to form partnerships with agencies such as theatres, museums, nature parks, etc., to allow for authentic learning environments.

It is clear that multiple ideas from alternative education settings have now found their way into regular German schooling and discussions about school quality and excellent schooling, although most of today's teachers wouldn't recognize these as alternative pedagogies. These ideas constitute

224

what has come to be seen as a contemporary student-centred way of teaching in the twenty-first century. In that sense, alternative ideas have come a long way and moved from the margins to the mainstream.

German School Award: The impact of alternative pedagogies

Schools explicitly using and further developing alternative pedagogies have formed a national network called *Blick über den Zaun* (Learning from others) (www.blickueberdenzaun.de). Members organize mutual school visits, do peer reviews, share their knowledge in conferences and publish ideas and practices. In 2006, a group of influential foundations under the leadership of the Bosch Foundation awarded the *Deutscher Schulpreis* (German School Award) (www.deutscher-schulpreis.de) for the first time. Six schools from all over Germany are selected every year by a jury of experts for their potential to motivate students to learn and achieve results on a high level. The award receives a lot of media attention and is presented to the schools by either the President or the Chancellor of Germany. So far, an impressive number of schools which have shown that they can enhance students' learning through innovative pedagogy – some of them in deprived areas – have won the award. A look at the criteria underlying the selection of schools reveals that many of the educational philosophies first developed in alternative schools over the course of the twentieth century have now moved centre-stage and are increasingly shaping our understanding of what constitutes a good school in the mainstream state-funded system of education.

CRITERIA UNDERLYING SELECTION FOR THE GERMAN SCHOOL AWARD

Achievement: Students need to achieve outstanding learning results (in relation to their base line) in the core subjects (mathematics, languages and sciences), in the arts (e.g. drama, fine arts, music or dance), in sports or in other areas (such as national student contests).

Diversity: The schools need to have found effective ways and means to work productively with educational disparities, different student interests and talents, diverse cultural and national backgrounds, diverse educational backgrounds of families, and the gender of their students. They need to contribute to the compensation of educational disparities and support individuals in their learning systematically and continuously.

Quality of teaching: The schools need to stimulate students to take charge of their own learning process. They enable their students to learn in hands-on ways that focus on deep understanding and let students experience learning in authentic learning environments outside the classroom. The schools continuously digest new knowledge to improve the quality of teaching and learning.

Responsibility: The schools must not only advocate but actually find ways to enhance respectful behaviour, violence-free conflict resolution and care for the school and its environment. They support and request active participation and democratic engagement, citizenship and community in the classroom, the school and beyond.

School climate, school life and partners in the community: The schools need to demonstrate that they have a positive climate and an active and stimulating school life. They are schools that students and teachers like to attend and parents enjoy visiting. They maintain meaningful relationships with their partners outside the school and with the public at large.

Schools as learning organizations: The schools need to practise innovative and results-driven forms of collaboration within the school team, the leadership practice and the democratic management and enhance the motivation and professionalism of their teachers effectively. They perceive the creative use of the curriculum and the organization and evaluation of learning as a core task and commit to it in a sustainable manner. (www.deutscher-schulpreis.de).

Many of the schools that won the award in recent years have been shaped by ideas and concepts developed in alternative schools. Among the winners are a range of schools applying the Jenaplan methodology; others refer to ideas by Dalton, Dewey or Montessori. One of the core features of these schools is the shift towards student self-regulation, with teachers being supporters in the learning process. To provide an insight into the practice of the winning schools we give a glimpse here into two different schools.

GYMNASIUM ALSDORF
Gymnasium Alsdorf (www.daltongymnasium-alsdorf.de) is a state high school that won the award in 2013. It has a strong focus on developing skills for self-regulation and offers its students training in self-regulation skills and flexible work time twice a day. Students get to choose what to work on.

The students decide on weekly learning aims and write these down in their week plans. If a teacher identifies clear learning needs within one subject in regular lessons they advise the students to work on those needs during flexible work time. This might be the need to practise past tenses in English or multiplication in maths. Students are encouraged to be fully responsible for their own learning and to use teachers or peers as a form of scaffold and support in their own process of cognitive development.

STÄDTISCHE ANNE-FRANK-REALSCHULE
Städtische Anne-Frank-Realschule (www.afr.musin.de), a girls high school, won the award in 2014. Learning takes place in traditional teacher-led classes as well as in so-called *Lernbüros* (learning offices). Within four lessons (two blocks) per week students have to work independently in small mixed-age teams on specific projects. The students get to choose what projects they work on, but they have to have completed projects in maths, German and English by mid-term. The programme is now being extended to physics, geography and French. Every student has a logbook to document her individual growth. Students not only outline what they did and how they succeeded but also self-assess how to improve their learning in the future. Every other week, students present their logbooks to a teacher, review their work and set goals for their development until the next project presentation. All tasks that have to be fulfilled in these *Lernbüros* have been designed by teachers themselves to meet the needs of their students best, a feature that goes back to the strong ethos of collaboration in alternative schools.

The teacher in alternative educational settings
Changing the learning setting leads to changes in teacher roles. As teachers and students operate in an interdependent and synergistic relationship it is expected that teachers act differently according to the settings they work in. Alternative schools have always described the role of their teachers as multifold: providing learning opportunities, diagnosing, coaching, scaffolding, accompanying learning processes, reviewing learning outcomes, providing formative feedback and encouraging students (Gudjons, 2006). Alternative education settings have valued both instruction and construction and perceive those to be highly interdependent. In instructive phases of teaching the teacher is predominantly seen as an expert, a knowledge source and a leader. During phases in which students construct their knowledge in more self-regulated ways the teacher assumes the roles of manager, organizer, facilitator and adviser. Alternative educational settings regard cognitive and social-emotional processes as intertwined in any process of learning. In this regard, a teacher can also assume the roles of a partner in a

co-constructive learning process or a therapist (Gudjons, 2006). Nowadays a much more flexible understanding of the multiple 'hats' a professional teacher wears has become part of our mainstream understanding of teacher professionalism. Teaching requires many different skills, the most important of which is perhaps the shift from a passive 'role taking' to an active 'role making' (Schratz and Schrittesser, 2006). In alternative educational settings, this active part of role making by a teacher has always been considered important. Dealing with a diversity of learners, applying different forms of assessment and encouraging student self-determination requires teachers who are flexible in their thinking and acting and who are able to question their routines. Empirical research on effective teaching shows that learning outcomes depend on a professional mix of classroom management skills, the ability to cognitively activate different learners and to support them through adequate scaffolding (Kunter and Voss, 2013), professional competences which require teachers to be flexible and adaptive. In alternative settings such as the Montessori schools, the Waldorf school and the pedagogy of the Jenaplan, the focus has been on the individual and his or her learning needs. Alternative schools and settings have played a crucial role in modelling the various professional roles teachers need to play in order to activate and support learners with different needs (Klopsch, 2016). Many of the multifold roles and strategies that are seen as a prerequisite for effective teaching have been developed and written about in the context of alternative schooling, before they have become part of the mainstream understanding of what makes a good teacher.

Conclusion: Alternative educational ideas on their way from the margins to the mainstream

After a century of attempts to reform schools in Germany, the boundaries between traditional and alternative pedagogies are finally becoming more blurred. International empirical research on learning has confirmed the efficacy of some of the innovations that have emerged from alternative pedagogy (Boekaerts, 2010; Dumont *et al.*, 2010). Cognition, meta-cognition and motivation cannot be seen as separate; they form the DNA of any learning process. Learners have socio-emotional needs, and learning itself is a social process. These and other key understandings of how we perceive the process of learning today are in line with the beliefs German reformers voiced almost a century ago. While many alternative concepts are increasingly visible in mainstream German schooling – such as flexible differentiation instead of early streaming, individual learning support instead of having to repeat an entire school year, the extension of schools to encompass other more authentic learning environments instead of students just cramming in classrooms – others have been challenged and discarded. One example is the once renowned Odenwaldschule, a now closed former paragon of alternative education in Germany, where sexual abuse was discovered to have been endemic. The school's concept called for a dual role of faculty: friend and teacher of the students. This blurring of roles was said to have facilitated a crossing of the line that led to sexual abuse. This has led some academics to question certain features of alternative educational settings. Their critical examination has made some educators consider the difference between teachers as professionals and as friends of their students and the right balance between closeness and distance (Oelkers, 2011; Miller and Oelkers, 2014).

Looking back over one century of alternative education in Germany, one thing stands out. Alternative pedagogies, developed at the margins of our society and of our school system, often politically contested and even at one stage outlawed by totalitarianism, are finally becoming part of mainstream education, while also learning important lessons about the role and position of the teacher. As state-funded mainstream schools in Germany are encouraged to develop their individual pedagogical profile, they are now using the range and diversity of alternative pedagogies to activate and motivate students and to develop school life into a rich and beneficial experience. Innovations having emerged from alternative educational settings are becoming a core part of how we see education in our society today.

References

Amlung, U., Haubfleisch, D., Link, J.-W. and Schmitt, H. (eds) (1993) *Die alte Schule überwinden: Reformpädagogische Versuchsschulen zwischen Kaiserreich und Nationalsozialismus* (Sozialhistorische Untersuchungen zur Reformpädagogik und Erwachsenenbildung 15). Frankfurt am Main: Dipa-Verlag.

Benner, D. and Kemper, H. (2003) *Theorie und Geschichte der Reformpädagogik*. Weinheim: Beltz.

Boekaerts, M. (2010) 'The crucial role of motivation and emotion in classroom learning'. In Dumont, H., Istance, D. and Benavides, F. (eds) *The Nature of Learning: Using research to inspire practice*. Paris: OECD Publishing, 91–111.

Dumont, H., Istance, D. and Benavides, F. (eds) (2010) *The Nature of Learning: Using research to inspire practice*. Paris: OECD Publishing.

Gudjons, H. (2006) *Neue Unterrichtskultur – veränderte Lehrerrolle*. Bad Heilbrunn: Klinkhardt.

Hofmann, M. (2013) *Geschichte und Gegenwart Freier Alternativschulen: Eine Einführung*. Ulm: Klemm und Oelschlaeger.

Keim, W. and Schwerdt, U. (eds) (2013) *Handbuch der Reformpädagogik in Deutschland (1890–1933)*. Frankfurt am Main: Peter Lang.

Klopsch, B. (2009) *Fremdevaluation im Rahmen der Qualitätsentwicklung und -sicherung* (Erziehungskonzeptionen und Praxis 75). Frankfurt am Main: Peter Lang.

Klopsch, B. (2016) *Die Erweiterung der Lernumgebung durch Bildungspartnerschaften: Einstellungen und Haltungen von Lehrpersonen und Schulleitungen*. Weinheim: Beltz Juventa.

Knoll, M. (ed.) (1998) *Kurt Hahn: Reform mit Augenmaß: Ausgewählte Schriften eines Politikers und Pädagogen*. Stuttgart: Klett-Cotta.

Knoll, M. (2011) *Dewey, Kilpatrick und "progressive" Erziehung: Kritische Studien zur Projektpädagogik*. Bad Heilbrunn: Klinkhardt.

Koerrenz, R. (2011) *Schulmodell: Jena-Plan: Grundlagen eines reformpädagogischen Programms*. Paderborn: Schöningh.

Koerrenz, R. (2014) *Reformpädagogik: Eine Einführung*. Paderborn: Schöningh.

Kunter, M. and Voss, T. (2013) 'The model of instructional quality in COACTIV: A multicriteria analysis'. In Kunter, M., Baumert, J., Blum, W., Klusmann, U., Krauss, S. and Neubrand, M. (eds) *Cognitive Activation in the Mathematics Classroom and Professional Competence of Teachers: Results from the COACTIV Project*. New York: Springer, 97–124.

Martin, J.-P. (1996) 'Das Projekt "Lernen durch Lehren" - eine vorläufige Bilanz'. *Fremdsprachen Lehren und Lernen (FLuL)*, 25, 70–84.

Miller, D. and Oelkers, J. (eds) (2014) *Reformpädagogik nach der Odenwaldschule – Wie weiter?* Weinheim: Beltz Juventa.

Oelkers, J. (2011) *Eros und Herrschaft: Die dunklen Seiten der Reformpädagogik*. Weinheim: Beltz.

Röhrs, H. (2001) *Die Reformpädagogik: Ursprung und Verlauf unter internationalem Aspekt*. 6th ed. Weinheim: Beltz.

Schratz, M. and Schrittesser, I. (2006) 'Was müssen Lehrerinnen und Lehrer in Zukunft wissen und können?'. In Berner, H. and Isler, R. (eds) *Lehrer-Identität, Lehrer-Rolle, Lehrer-Handeln*. Hohengehren: Schneider Verlag, 177–98.

Sliwka, A. (2010) 'From homogeneity to diversity in German education'. In *Educating Teachers for Diversity: Meeting the challenge*. Paris: OECD Publishing, 205–17.

Wagenschein, M. (2009) *Naturphänomene sehen und verstehen: Genetische Lehrgänge*. Ed. Berg, H.C. Bern: hep.

Chapter 17

What can a socially just approach to education learn from alternative schools?

Martin Mills and Gillean McCluskey

Introduction

As we indicated in the Introduction of this book, this text had its origins in the invitations we both received to present at an international forum in Seoul on alternative education in 2014. The presentations at this forum were as diverse as the collection in this book. There were presentations by people from Waldorf/Steiner schools, South Korean alternative schools, Danish Free Schools, and although not covered in this book, Big Picture, and democratic schools such as Sands in England. Presenters came from North America, Europe (Scotland, Germany, Denmark), Australia and Korea. Topics covered included: US charter schools, alternatives for those excluded from school, school organization, and alternative pedagogies and assessment. Some of the presenters were based in schools, some in universities and some in the policy spheres in their various countries.

The group was very eclectic and at the time there seemed little coherence across all of the presentations from the invited guests. We say this not to disparage the presentations or the forum programme, but rather to indicate that the term in many people's minds, as with perhaps the forum organizers, has multiple interpretations. Similarly, the reason for looking towards alternatives has multiple purposes. During the event we asked our hosts why it was that the South Korean Ministry of Education and the National Policy Youth Institute (NPYI) were so interested in alternative schooling (see also Abelmann *et al.*, 2012). The reasons given related to many that we had heard before in other contexts. They indicated that some young people in South Korea were becoming very stressed by the pressures of exams and the focus on outcomes, so much so that their parents had become worried about their welfare and were looking for schools, or wanted to set up schools, where their children would not be subject to the current performative pressures of neoliberal agendas in schooling. Many of these schools were based on philosophies grounded in student-centred learning. Fielding and Moss (2011), in their critique of the current moment in English schooling, have argued that there is no alternative but to look to alternatives. This would seem to have been the conclusion that the Ministry and the NYPI had reached in Korea.

At the forum we also heard stories about the increase in the number of alternative schools in Korea for those students who were not wanted by their regular school because of their perceived abilities or the damage that they were doing to school reputation. The development of such schools of course has resonance elsewhere (see, for example Mills *et al.,* 2013; Mills and McGregor, 2014; te Riele, 2009; Thomson and Russell, 2007). However, it was clear that the Ministry and the NYPI did not want these schools to become 'dumping grounds'. Hence in bringing the people together for the forum, the organizing group invited people who had had experience with creating schools that were democratic and/or that were underpinned by child-centred philosophies. There were those who delivered presentations on forms of pedagogical and assessment practice that challenged rote learning and direct instruction. There were also those who were concerned with how some young people, primarily those marginalized by class and race, had become the 'collateral damage' of mainstream schooling. It was very apparent that 'alternative' had multiple meanings for the organizing team and the presenters.

In bringing together the international and diverse contributors to this volume we adopted an approach somewhat like that at the forum, inviting as many different contributors with different perspectives as possible and from as wide a variety of contexts as possible (within the limitations of space). In putting these chapters together, we also did not just want to put together a snapshot of what is occurring in the alternative schooling space, but to see what we could learn about creating a more socially just form of schooling. A social worker from an alternative school for unwanted young people once said to one of us that her school's very existence was the 'canary in the mine' for mainstream schools – they were evidence that the mainstream was unsafe and not working for marginalized young people. We too have the view that the success and growing interest in alternative schools suggests that something is broken in the system and that mainstream schools as they are can be damaging to both students and teachers within them (Francis and Mills, 2012).

In putting these chapters together we wanted to represent the struggle that is evident in the use of the term 'alternative'. For some it conjures up images of radical forms of schooling that challenge the status quo in ways that A.S. Neill (1968) envisaged with Summerhill and as did many of the schooling initiatives and experiments of the late 1970s and 1980s (Australia's School without Walls comes to mind here, as does England's long-running Sands School in Devon). However, in more recent times it has come to represent those schools perceived to be 'dumping grounds' for unwanted students (see, for example, Shay and Heck, 2015).

We thus begin this last chapter with a consideration of how we understand the term 'alternative education'. We then address what we consider to be some of the issues and tensions that have surfaced in our own work with alternative education and through the chapters in this book. These include whether it is students or schools that are expected to change; a differentiated curriculum; levels of choice in school selection; school fees; teachers' work; and whether 'alternative' is a signifier for 'better'. Following on from these discussions we provide a tentative consideration of what these schools can offer to a socially just approach to education by drawing on the work of Nancy Fraser (1997; 2009), which we have used elsewhere (McCluskey *et al.*, 2016; Mills and McGregor, 2014).

Alternative to what?

What constitutes an alternative school, as indicated throughout the book, is a vexed question. As Tierney (Chapter 2, this volume) has stated: 'When saying "alternative school" one could mean everything from a juvenile detention centre, to an online school, to a wilderness focused leadership school'. While we have not provided case studies of any of these three types of school, we have covered schools that support North Korean refugee students, schools set up in bus stations, and schools that rely on affluent parents who can pay school fees. There are huge differences amongst the schools represented in this book. However, what is common amongst them is that they challenge what Tyack and Tobin (1994) call the 'grammar of schooling' – the fixed rules as to what constitutes a school – in varying degrees.

While the schools represented in this book mostly offered traditional curricula, usually had teachers and sought to award qualifications of some sort, they had a particular 'grammar' that disrupted some of the traditional ways of doing school. Some of these disruptions may seem minor, such as referring to teachers by their first names. However, they are not minor for many of the young people because they represent for them a challenge to the distinct superior–subordinate, teacher–student relationship they experienced in mainstream schools. Other features of the schools distinguish them from traditional schools, for example the presence of crèches on site, access to legal aid and accommodation services. There are also organizational features in some schools that challenge traditional grammars of schooling, for example the use of the school meeting, involving students and teachers as equal participants, to make all decisions regarding the running of the school, including the employment of teachers.[1]

While they are all very different from each other, the range of schools and learning sites covered in this book points to the possibility that school can be done differently. Very few of these schools are 'perfect' – indeed we would suggest that in social justice terms all of the schools are works in progress. However, in each instance there are pointers to the ways in which schools can be reformed or 're-imagined' (McGregor *et al.*, 2017) in more socially just ways. Before we comment on some of these pointers we will address some of the tensions that permeate considerations of alternative schooling. We begin with the purposes of alternative education, either to 'fix-up' the student or to change the school. We follow this with a consideration of differentiated education, notions of choice, cost and the mainstream/alternative dichotomy.

Changing the student or changing the school

Te Riele (2007) and Raywid (1990) draw attention to the purposes of alternative schools and distinguish between those forms that seek to change the young person and those that seek to change the school. Both forms of schooling have been considered in this book. Some forms of alternative school, often those encapsulated under the term 'alternative provision', seek in Foucault's (1977) terms to work with students in order to 'discipline' them into the school regime. These schools might employ therapies, behaviour management techniques, and various counselling services to ensure that the students can learn how to fit into school, and often into 'society' (see Hepburn and Dwyer, Chapters 11 and 12 in this volume). In many cases this is essential. There are young people in these schools whose behaviours pose a threat to both themselves and others, and the behaviour does need challenging. Furthermore, many, although certainly not all, of these behaviours have a gender dimension to them that does require problematizing (see, for example, Mills, 2001). Some students in these schools have experienced severe trauma in their lives and they no doubt benefit from some forms of counselling. However, as has been argued in many of the chapters throughout this book, this alone will not serve to meet the needs of these young people. Indeed, it can be argued that the very structures of traditional forms of schooling are the reason why many of these young people have not fitted into school. Hence, without changing the structures of schooling, little is likely to change for these young people, especially if they return to their original mainstream school.

There are many schools described in this book that have sought to change or trouble the 'grammar of schooling', in ways that facilitate young people's engagement with education: within schools aligned with a democratic tradition and within those that are of the flexi, second-chance type of school. Within the former set of schools there are schools that seek to change the world through their advocacy for democracy and student voice, as evident in the chapters by Saggau, Chapter 13, Storgaard and Skotte, Chapter 14, and Waters, Chapter 15 (see also Mills and McGregor, 2014 for discussion of democratic schools). These schools seek to embed their principles into the everyday running of the school in such a way that all of the students are able to make a meaningful contribution to the governance of the school. However, many of the latter set of schools also have a political agenda that seeks to change society and current systems of schooling (see Murray, Chapter 8, this volume).

There is a recognition within these schools that many of the students have been failed by the mainstream due to their socio-economic and/or their racial/ethnic backgrounds. Hence, many of these schools have adopted an approach focused on 'clearing the path for learning' (McGregor *et al.*, 2017). That is, they have sought to remove the obstacles that have prevented these young people from attending school and engaging with the curriculum. They have, for example, addressed transport issues, provided food, or connected students with accommodation services. Relationships between students and teachers were often enhanced through respectful engagements. There was an inbuilt flexibility in relation to, for instance, lateness, absenteeism and extensions on assignments, all grounded in a recognition of the students' personal circumstances. There were also often attempts to ensure that the curricula and approaches to pedagogy were relevant to the students' needs and interests. This latter point raises another tension: differentiation.

A differentiated curriculum

In most cases fee-paying alternative schools tend to provide similar curriculum offerings to those available in the mainstream, although the ways in which lessons are taught might differ greatly. In these schools the students often acquire what Young (2008) has referred to as 'powerful knowledges' – knowledges which facilitate entry into higher education, and which are loaded with cultural capital. There is a strong argument that all students, but particularly those students who come from marginalized backgrounds, should be provided with an opportunity to acquire such knowledges. Any form of differentiated curriculum that fails to provide students with such opportunities could be considered as perpetuating inequalities. We have some sympathy for this argument.

There is a danger that the current emphasis on basic literacy and numeracy skills can work to provide students in flexi-schools with an inferior curriculum that is formed around the completion of worksheets and workbooks. To some extent this is understandable given that the reading age of many students in these schools is well below that expected of others in their age group. However, we are of the view that such a curriculum may not only alienate students from education further, but also prevent them from benefiting from their time in school. There are ways, as some of the schools in this book have demonstrated, to ensure that a meaningful curriculum can be constructed for students, which also enhances their basic literacy and numeracy development.

This is not necessarily easy though. It is apparent that for many of the students who attend alternative schools, the traditional curriculum had appeared irrelevant to their needs and interests and they have consequently rejected it. Engaging their interest in this kind of curriculum without dramatically changing the pedagogical relationship and without taking into account students' background knowledge, or what González *et al.* (2006) call 'funds of knowledge' (see also Zipin *et al.*, 2012), is unlikely to be well received by the students. There are also some words of warning in relation to gender that need to be acknowledged in attempting to make the curriculum relevant to students. For example, Thomson and Russell (2007) have raised concerns about the ways in which some alternative provision in England perpetuates dominant constructions of masculinity and femininity. The task then is to find ways in which students' background knowledge can be linked to various disciplinary content and concepts, in ways that cause them to engage in activities that question and problematize existing knowledge, including, for example, their own views of gender. Some alternative schools, including flexi-schools, can carry this off. In the process, they recognize that students do need to be extended intellectually as a matter of social justice (see Hayes *et al.*, 2006; Darling-Hammond, 1997).

First choice or no choice

The notion of choice is central to understanding the relationship between alternative schooling and social justice. Across the schools considered in this book there are several which were chosen by students, or their parents, as an ideal school because of the school's philosophy. In such cases these first-choice schools (although in some instances they have been sought out after students have rejected the mainstream) represent an opportunity for students to access traditional curricula in a highly positive climate. However, for the vast majority of students in flexi-schools these are not their schools of choice, but the product of their alienation from one or more mainstream schools. For some students in these schools there is a desire to one day return to the mainstream sector. However, for others, their new school represents an opportunity to engage with schooling in a way that they feel would be impossible in a mainstream school.

For those students who would like to return to the mainstream, their engagement with the alternative school is not likely to be as positive as that of those who have decided to remain with the alternative school. Their resentment at being 'sent' to an alternative school is also likely to be compounded if the students feel they are heavily monitored or the curriculum is perceived as boring or divorced from their lives. Those students who appear to be most positively engaged with the alternative flexi-schools are often those who have been out of education for a little (or long) while and have found their way back to schooling through the alternative schooling sector. For these students, their 'choice' of returning to school is often accompanied by a view that suggests that had they had this type of education in the first place they may have stayed at school (see Mills and McGregor, 2014). At the same time, for some of these students any thought of returning to a mainstream school is not an option. As Rosmiliwati and her colleagues in this book (Chapter 6) indicate in relation to the Indonesian alternative schools, which equally applies to students in flexi-schools in most locations, the choice is 'this school or no school at all'.

Fee paying or non-fee paying

The schools considered in this book include those in the public school sector, those that are independent from the state system, some that are fee-paying and some that are independent but are free as a result of state funding. In our view, all schooling should be free and available to all as a matter of social justice. The fee-paying schools in this book work to ensure that students with middle-class backgrounds are able to find schools that can provide them with the kinds of (or better) achievements and outcomes that they would have acquired from a mainstream school. Many of these options would be highly suitable for those students who have been rejected from the mainstream but are unable to pay the expected fees. The non-fee-paying schools, particularly if not state owned, are often not as well resourced as the mainstream – although class sizes are often much smaller. They are often located in ex-school buildings, parks, community halls or even, as in the case of the Indonesian schools described here, in railway stations. While we are not suggesting that the education provided in the fee-paying schools is better than in all of the flexi-schools, there are some important issues around access that need to be considered in relation to alternative schools if they are to represent a challenge to the ways in which education is provided to those who have been failed by the mainstream.

Teachers' work

The issue of why teachers seek out employment in alternative schools and the types of teaching that occurs in alternative schools has not been a strong focus across the chapters in this book. However, these are clearly important topics (Golden, 2018). In other work, we have found that many of the teachers in alternative schools are also dissatisfied with the mainstream (see, for example, McGregor and Mills, 2014). This is often for the same types of reasons that are articulated by the students: they feel restricted by the school rules, they feel that relationships between students and teachers are damaged by school organization and structures, and their ability to teach in the ways they would like is hampered by school expectations. However, there is a trade-off. In many cases to work in an alternative school means giving up a degree of job security, in some locations, as indicated in other chapters in this book (see Chapters 9, 10, 13 and 16), it means lower wages, and often longer working hours. However, for some teachers this is a trade-off worth paying in order to achieve job satisfaction.

There is also an issue of teacher capabilities and dispositions. Those teachers, and other workers, who are employed in the alternative school sector need to understand the complexities associated with students' learning and with their lives. This is picked up by Shay in Chapter 9. In the schools described by her there are significant numbers of Aboriginal and Torres Strait Islander students. For many of these students their experiences of the mainstream have been culturally inappropriate. To ensure that this experience is not repeated within the alternative schools, it is important that non-Indigenous teachers in these schools have a high degree of cultural sensitivity. The same can be said about the ways in which teachers characterize students living in poverty, those who are pregnant or have children, or those involved with the juvenile justice system. A rejection of deficit constructions of young people is an imperative of teachers' work with these, and all, students.

Does alternative mean better?

While we are of the view that there is much that is problematic about mainstream education, we are not suggesting that all alternatives are better than current forms of mainstream schooling. They are not. There is no doubt that mainstream schools offer successful students particular forms of capital (Bourdieu, 1984) that go a long way to securing their future. So too, some very marginalized students have their life trajectories altered by positive experiences of mainstream schooling. Neither do we want to disparage or dismiss the work of many fine teachers in the mainstream who care for their students, encourage their students to challenge themselves intellectually and to take risks with their learning, and who make a real difference in the lives of their students. However, again, it is our view that often these teachers do this not *because* of the system but *despite* the system.

Nor do we want to suggest that the mainstream is static. As the chapter by Sliwka and Klopsch (Chapter 16) indicated, what goes on in the alternative space can affect the mainstream. There is no doubt that some progressive practices have had an impact in the mainstream, as many conservative commentators are wont to articulate in their denouncements of 'modern schooling'. In what could possibly be interpreted as a backlash to such practices, there is a constant bemoaning of a supposed interrelationship between the state of discipline in schools, progressive teaching methods and poor performance on international rankings in many countries (see, for example, Donnelly, 2013; Gove, 2013). However, we are of the view that the mainstream still has much to learn from the alternative sector. Central to this view is the evidence provided by students who have been considered unteachable in mainstream settings, and who, when presented with an alternative, have become fully engaged in the learning process. This does indeed encourage those who are concerned for the well-being of students often excluded from school that there are ways of engaging such students.

Towards a socially just approach to schooling

Fielding and Moss (2011: 163) have noted that: 'When we actually encounter radical alternatives it is in large part their brute reality, their enacted denial of injustice and inhumanity and their capacity to live out a more fulfilling, more generous view of human flourishing that in turn moves us to think and act differently'. It is the possibility that alternative schools might offer a radical alternative to the many injustices we have observed being perpetrated through the mainstream education system that first attracted us to the alternative education field. We were interested in what the field might offer to understandings of social justice and schooling. In thinking through this, we have, in our previous work, been attracted to Nancy Fraser (1997, 2009; see also McCluskey *et al.*, 2016; Mills and McGregor 2014). For Fraser, the general meaning of justice is 'parity of participation' (2009: 16), whereby all are able to participate in social life as peers. A socially just education system then would work to ensure that barriers to such participation are removed, both within the practices of schooling and beyond. Removing these barriers means, in Fraser's terms, addressing economic, cultural and political injustices through acts of redistribution, recognition and representation.

Economic injustice refers to what Fraser calls a 'maldistribution' of resources. When such maldistribution occurs it becomes impossible for those who receive fewer resources to participate in society as peers. Poverty, for example, has negative consequences on housing, engagement with the welfare and justice systems and schooling. Cultural injustice refers to all circumstances that lead to what she calls 'status inequality', for example, homophobia, misogyny and racism. Such status inequality impacts upon one's standing in society and one's ability to participate fully in all its benefits. Political injustice occurs when 'misrepresentation' is present. Misrepresentation refers to the exclusion that some people experience from decision-making processes that impact upon their lives, and hence on their ability to make justice claims when treated unfairly. These injustices are of course all interrelated.

The vast majority of young people who attend flexi-style alternative schools experience all of these forms of injustice, as contributors to this book have demonstrated. They tend to come from high poverty backgrounds, be from marginalized cultural backgrounds and have very little voice in the decisions that impact upon their lives. The students who attend fee-paying schools often do not experience the same degrees of oppression faced by those students in the flexi-schools. However, such alternative schools are not necessarily wealthy, and also seek to support students who cannot afford to attend them. Furthermore, the voices of *all* young people are still rarely heard in the mainstream, especially not to the degree that they are in the alternative schools, and the discipline regimes in many schools work in ways that actively work against student voice. To this extent alternative schools of many kinds offer insights into what a socially just education system might look like.

The details and analyses of alternative schools and their policies and practices presented in this book would seem to suggest that alternative schools can both reproduce and disrupt some of these injustices. If the schools do not provide the students with an education that opens up opportunities for them and instead act as a 'dumping ground' for those unwanted by the mainstream (Mills *et al.*, 2013), then they are likely to perpetuate economic, cultural and political injustices. Without such opportunities the students may well have been better off staying in the mainstream.

However, those schools which act as 'radical alternatives'; that seek to disrupt processes which made it difficult for young people to reap the benefits of schooling, that seek to change the school into a place that students want to attend, and into a place that offers young people holistic support in addition to formal qualifications, do give some pointers towards a more socially just approach to schooling.

Addressing the economic injustices faced by students is a core feature of many of the alternative schools that seek to meet the needs of highly marginalized young people. For example, many of these schools seek to alleviate the financial stresses faced by their students through homelessness, parenthood, and/or escaping domestic violence in order that they can attend school. It is clear that many of the young people in these schools would not have been in education if not for the existence of strategies designed to alleviate the consequences of poverty. These strategies include, for example: organizing transport to schools, either through school buses that pick students up from their homes, or the provision of public transport season tickets; services that link the young people with emergency and crisis accommodation; youth workers who attend social services meetings with students to assist them obtaining welfare payments; showers, soaps and spare clothes on campus; and meals before, during and after school.

Alleviating the ways in which cultural injustices impact upon students' educational engagement is also a feature of many alternative schools. There are students in all types of alternative schools who have sought refuge there after having being bullied or having experienced some form of discrimination in a mainstream school. For these students, the high levels of acceptance by others of their sexuality, their race/ethnic backgrounds, physical and intellectual abilities, and/or their gendered way of being in the world was a major drawcard for enrolling in the school. There are several ways in which such 'status inequalities' can be addressed in the schools: through attention to the general climate in the school, for example in the approaches to building relationships and addressing conflicts; through the curriculum, for example building in marginalized communities' ways of seeing and knowing the world into everyday classes; the involvement of community members in the school, for example, in Australia having Indigenous elders contribute to the decision-making processes in the school; through material supports, for example, crèches for the children of young mothers; and through engagement with external agencies specializing in supporting young people, for example, LGBTIQ support organizations.

In multiple interviews we have conducted with young people who have been excluded from school or who have felt alienated in school, the issue of unfair treatment is raised. Similarly the issue of 'unfair' rules and practices is raised. Ensuring such political injustices are not reproduced is a concern of many alternative schools. For those operating within what could be called a democratic tradition, addressing 'misrepresentation', in Nancy Fraser's terms, is a central feature of their organization. For example, the centrality of the 'school meeting', which involves all students, teachers and other workers as the maker of rules, the arbiter of conflicts, the employment of teachers and sometimes enrolments of new students – as made famous through the writings of A.S. Neill (1968, 1970) on Summerhill – is the epitome of attempts to ensure all have a voice in the running of the school. These practices are not unique to fee-paying schools. There are also flexi-style schools that employ these strategies to ensure the engagement of the students in learning and to enhance their sense of belonging in the school. In such schools, negotiation, consultation and compromise are a key feature of all aspects of schooling, including curriculum.

We are not suggesting that all alternative provision of schooling or all alternative schools enhance social justice. In many ways the opposite is the case. The existence of the flexi-style school contributes to students being rejected by their original schools since there is an 'alternative' for them to attend. This ensures that mainstream schools are not compelled to change because they have a safety valve for ridding themselves of those who are perceived as having a negative impact upon school reputations and outcomes. That is, alternative schools operate to defend the current order, by providing an opportunity to remove students who are damaging the normal functioning of school, rather than as a means of challenging the inequities in the system. For this reason, Shay and Heck (2015) reject the term 'alternative', suggesting it implies a deficit construction of young people. We are sympathetic to this claim. We recognize that some alternatives can be seen as perpetuating current patterns of social division. Those who can afford to pay for an alternative school very often benefit from the creative pedagogies, opportunities to exercise voice and from the positive relationships with adults. Those who are 'sent' to alternative provision, flexi-schools or second-chance schools can find pathways shut down and opportunities for rich learning experiences restricted.

However, there are lessons that can be taken from some of these schools in relation to how they enhance parity of participation though their attention to economic, cultural and political injustices. Fraser speaks of the need for 'transformative remedies' for the problems of injustice. In education such remedies may render schooling unrecognizable. Schools as we know them seldom have crèches for the children of students, the teachers are rarely known to the students by their first names, students do not come to school to access support for housing, domestic violence and/ or legal problems, they do not regularly sit on interview panels for new teachers, they are not consulted about or involved in creating school rules. The curriculum is rarely negotiated in ways that take into account their backgrounds, knowledges and interests, while still ensuring that they are challenged academically. Making the principles that underpin these schools the model for all schools would truly be a transformative remedy.

Note
[1] See Sands School, for example: www.sands-school.co.uk

References
Abelmann, N., Choi, J. and Park, S.J. (eds) (2012) *No Alternative? Experiments in South Korean education*. Berkeley: University of California Press.

Bourdieu, P. (1984) *Distinction: A social critique of the judgement of taste*. Trans. Nice, R. Cambridge, MA: Harvard University Press.

Darling-Hammond, L. (1997) *The Right To Learn: A blueprint for creating schools that work*. San Francisco: Jossey-Bass.

Donnelly, K. (2013) The lost art of discipline, *The Australian*, October 9, www.theaustralian.com.au/national-affairs/opinion/the-lost-art-of-discipline/news-story/d00862b24efa37ecae303b75f2df77b3?sv=8316a2df9bf46fd0e0f053aaf964802a (accessed 25 June 2018).

Fielding, M. and Moss, P. (2011) *Radical Education and the Common School: A democratic alternative*. London: Routledge.

Foucault, M. (1977) *Discipline and Punish: The birth of the prison*. Trans. Sheridan, A. London: Penguin Books.

Francis, B. and Mills, M. (2012) 'Schools as damaging organisations: Instigating a dialogue concerning alternative models of schooling'. *Pedagogy, Culture and Society*, 20 (2), 251–71.

Fraser, N. (1997) *Justice Interruptus: Critical reflections on the "postsocialist" condition*. New York: Routledge.

Fraser, N. (2009) *Scales of Justice: Reimagining political space in a globalizing world*. New York: Columbia University Press.

Golden, N.A. (2018) 'Narrating neoliberalism: alternative education teachers' conceptions of their changing roles'. *Teaching Education*, 29 (1), 1–16.

Gove, M. (2013) Michael Gove speaks at the SMF: The Progressive Betrayal, www.smf.co.uk/michael-gove-speaks-at-the-smf/ (accessed 25 June 2018).

González, N., Moll, L.C. and Amanti, C. (eds) (2006) *Funds of Knowledge: Theorizing practices in households, communities, and classrooms*. New York: Routledge.

Hayes, D., Mills, M., Christie, P. and Lingard, B. (2006) *Teachers and Schooling Making a Difference: Productive pedagogies, assessment and performance.* Crows Nest, NSW: Allen and Unwin.

McCluskey, G., Riddell, S., Weedon, E. and Fordyce, M. (2016) 'Exclusion from school and recognition of difference'. *Discourse: Studies in the Cultural Politics of Education*, 37 (4), 529–39.

McGregor, G. and Mills, M. (2014) 'Teaching in the "margins": Rekindling a passion for teaching'. *British Journal of Sociology of Education,* 35 (1), 1–18.

McGregor, G., Mills, M., te Riele, K., Baroutsis, A. and Hayes, D. (2017) *Re-imagining Schooling for Education: Socially just alternatives.* London: Palgrave Macmillan.

Mills, M. (2001) *Challenging Violence in Schools: An issue of masculinities.* Buckingham: Open University Press.

Mills, M. and McGregor, G. (2014) *Re-engaging Young People in Education: Learning from alternative schools.* London: Routledge.

Mills, M., Renshaw, P. and Zipin, L. (2013) 'Alternative education provision: A dumping ground for "wasted lives" or a challenge to the mainstream?'. *Social Alternatives*, 32 (2), 13–18.

Neill, A.S. (1968) *Summerhill.* Harmondsworth: Penguin.

Neill, A.S. (1970) *Summerhill: For and against.* New York: Hart.

Raywid, M. (1990) 'Alternative education: The definition problem'. *Changing Schools*, 18 (4–5), 25–33.

Shay, M. and Heck, D. (2015) 'Alternative education engaging Indigenous young people: Flexi schooling in Queensland'. *Australian Journal of Indigenous Education*, 44 (1), 37–47.

Te Riele, K. (2007) 'Educational alternatives for marginalised youth'. *Australian Educational Researcher*, 34 (3), 53–68.

Te Riele, K. (ed.) (2009) *Making Schools Different: Alternative approaches to educating young people.* London: SAGE Publications.

Thomson, P. and Russell, L. (2007) *Mapping the Alternatives to Permanent Exclusion.* York: Joseph Rowntree Foundation.

Tyack, D. and Tobin, W. (1994) 'The "grammar" of schooling: Why has it been so hard to change?'. *American Educational Research Journal*, 31 (3), 453–79.

Woods, P.A. and Woods, G.J. (eds) (2009) *Alternative Education for the 21st century: Philosophies, approaches, visions.* New York: Palgrave Macmillan.

Young, M.F.D. (2008) *Bringing Knowledge Back In: From social constructivism to social realism in the sociology of education.* London: Routledge.

Zipin, L. (2015) 'Chasing curricular justice: How complex ethical vexations of redistributing cultural capital bring dialectics to the door of aporia'. *Southern African Review of Education*, 21 (2), 91–109.

Zipin, L., Sellar, S. and Hattam, R. (2012) 'Countering and exceeding "capital": A "funds of knowledge" approach to re-imagining community'. *Discourse: Studies in the Cultural Politics of Education*, 33 (2), 179–92.

Index

Index